Imperialism, Academe and Nationalism

IMPERIALISM, ACADEME AND NATIONALISM
Britain and University Education for Africans 1860–1960

APOLLOS O. NWAUWA
Rhode Island College, Providence, RI

LONDON AND NEW YORK

First Published in 1997 by
FRANK CASS & CO. LTD.

This edition published 2014 by Routledge
2 Park Square, Milton Park, Abingdon, Oxon, OX14 4RN
711 Third Avenue, New York, NY 10017

Routledge is an imprint of the Taylor & Francis Group, an informa business

First issued in paperback 2016

Copyright © Apollos O. Nwauwa 1996

British Library Cataloguing in Publication data
Nwauwa, Apollos O.
    Imperialism, academe and nationalism : Britain and
university education for Africans, 1860–1960
    1. Education, Higher - Africa - History - 19th century
    2. Education, Higher - Africa - History - 20th century
    3. Education - Great Britain - Colonies 4. Africans -
Education (Higher) - History
    I. Title
    378.6
    ISBN 0-7146-4668-7

Library of Congress Cataloging-in-Publication data
Nwauwa, Apollos O. (Apollos Okwuchi), 1960–
    Imperialism, academe, and nationalism : Britain and university
education for Africans, 1860–1960 / Apollos O. Nwauwa.
    p. cm.
    Includes bibliographical references and index.
    ISBN 0-7146-4668-7
    1. Education, Higher--Political aspects--Africa--History--19th
century. 2. Education, Higher--Political aspects--Africa-
-History--20th century. 3. Great Britain--Politics and
government--19th century. 4 Great Britain--Politics and
government--20th century. 5. Nationalism and education--History.
6. Educational anthropology--Africa--History. I. Title.
LA1533.N93 1996
378.6'09'034--dc20   96-2116
                                                                       CIP

All rights reserved. No part of this publication may be reproduced in any form, or by any means, electronic, mechanical, photocopying, recording or otherwise, without the prior permission of the publisher.

ISBN: 9780714646688 (hbk)
ISBN: 9781138972377 (pbk)

Table of Contents

Acknowledgements		vii
Abbreviations		ix
Introduction		xi
1	African Initiatives for a West African University and their Frustration, 1862–90	1
2	Indirect Rule, Education for Intermediaries, and the Impact of Criticism: The Beginnings of a Policy Framework for Education, 1900–34	34
3	The Ice Begins to Melt: Initiatives from London and the Plan for an East African University, 1932–39	68
4	Seizing the Initiative: The Academic Lobby and the Planning of Post-war Universities, 1939–43	105
5	The Asquith and Elliot Commissions, 1943–46: Laying the Foundations for University 'Imperialism'	134
6	Colonial Territorial 'Nationalism' and the Implementation of the Asquith and Elliot Schemes, 1945–48	170
Conclusion		201
Epilogue		210
Bibliography		221
Index		239

Acknowledgements

This book is a revised version of my doctoral dissertation at Dalhousie University, Halifax, Nova Scotia, Canada. For a study of this scope to come to fruition several individuals and institutions played major roles. First and foremost, I am grateful to Dalhousie University which offered me a Graduate Fellowship in 1988. I also thank the Board of Trustees of the Izaac Walton Killam Funds for awarding me a Killam doctoral scholarship for three consecutive years. Furthermore, I am thankful to the Faculty of Graduate Studies and the Department of History Turbay Trust Funds (African History) for providing me with the necessary research/travel grants which made possible the visits to England, Sierra Leone, Ghana and Nigeria.

Many individuals aided the successful completion of this study. I am particularly grateful to the staff of the Public Record Office, Kew Gardens, London; University of London Archives and Palaeography; National Archives of Ghana, Accra; National Archives of Nigeria, Ibadan; and Sierra Leone Archives at Fourah Bay College, Freetown, who helped me tremendously during the process of data collection. I would not fail to mention the invaluable assistance of the staff of the Killam Library, especially those in the Inter-Library Loan Department who combed libraries all over north America and Europe for materials relevant to this study. Similarly, I thank the staff of Balme Library, University of Ghana, Fourah Bay College Library and Dike Memorial Library, University of Ibadan for their patience while I consulted their reserve collections.

I remain indebted to my research supervisor, Professor John E. Flint who, apart from providing the inspiration for this study, also took pains to guide me in the art of historical scholarship. In spite of his retirement from active teaching in mid-1992, Professor Flint was determined to see this study through. Special thanks also go to Professor James B. Webster, whose perceptive comments and suggestions resulting from his personal experience, having taught at the University of Ibadan (Nigeria) and Makerere University (Uganda) for so many years, have greatly benefited this work. I

ACKNOWLEDGEMENTS

would like to thank Professor Jane Parpart whose comments and suggestions on the draft chapters proved useful.

I am grateful to those who accommodated me during my research trips. While in London, the International House run by the International Students Housing Society in Woolwich provided me with accommodation. I appreciate the support of Mr Solo Fofana of the Department of Languages and Literature, Fourah Bay College, in guiding and accommodating me in Freetown, Sierra Leone. While in Accra, Ghana, the late Mr Peter Nortey (Snr) was most helpful. In Nigeria, I remain grateful to the late Mr A. O. Adeoye, a doctoral student and colleague with whom I stayed at the University of Ibadan while consulting the University and National Archives. I thank all faculty and staff of the History Department at Dalhousie University who helped me in one way or another during the duration of this study. To my colleagues – Wilson, Tim and Julius – who completed the doctoral programme (African history) with me at Dalhousie in the same year, I say, 'Cheerio'! Without these cronies and other acquaintances in Halifax, studying at Dalhousie would not have been so exciting and eventful.

Lastly, but most importantly, I am indebted to my wife, Helen, who endured my irritating working habits and schedules conditioned by the nature of this research. Without her care and continuous encouragement, this work would have suffered greatly. To my parents-in-law, Joe and Christina Hagan, who encouraged me, and to my mother – Veronica – brothers, sisters, and relatives who patiently endured my long absence from home, I say, 'Thank you'. I remain very pleased that all our efforts and sacrifices were not in vain.

Providence, Rhode Island   A. O. Nwauwa
February 1996

Abbreviations

AC	Academic Council Files, University of London
ACCCAST	Advisory Committee on Colonial Colleges of Arts, Science and Technology
ACEC	Advisory Committee on Education in the Colonies
ACNETA	Advisory Committee on Native Education in Tropical Africa
CD&WA	Colonial Development and Welfare Act
CO	Colonial Office
Cmd.	Command Paper issued by the British Government
CMS	Church Missionary Society
CSO	Colonial Secretary's Office (Territorial)
CUGAC	Colonial University Grants Advisory Committee
EAJ	East Africa Journal
HMSO	His (Her) Majesty's Stationery Office
IUC	Inter-University Council for Higher Education in the Colonies
IUP	Ibadan University Press
JAS	Journal of African Studies
JHSN	Journal of the Historical Society of Nigeria
NAGA	National Archives of Ghana (Accra)

ABBREVIATIONS

NAI	National Archives of Nigeria, Ibadan
NCBWA	National Congress of British West Africa
NUT	Nigeria Union of Teachers
NYM	Nigerian Youth Movement
PC	Privy Council
PRO	Public Record Office
SLA	Sierra Leone Archives at Fourah Bay College, Freetown, Sierra Leone
SLC	Sierra Leone Collection, Fourah Bay Library
UCGC	University College of the Gold Coast
UCI	University College, Ibadan
UIA	University of Ibadan Archives
ULAP	University of London Archives and Palaeography

Introduction

The British establishment of universities in tropical Africa is a recent phenomenon, first occurring in 1948 soon after the Second World War and just before decolonization. For almost a century – 1860 to 1948 – the British had systematically ignored the demands of educated Africans for the provision of facilities for university education. The demands by James Horton and Edward Blyden for a West African university between 1860 and 1900 were frustrated by missionary opposition strongly supported by British officials in Sierra Leone. Even though their efforts ultimately resulted in the minimal degree work in Theology and Classics at Fourah Bay College, this fell short of what the African élite desired. During the heyday of indirect rule – 1900 to 1940 – efforts by the African-educated élite and 'nationalists' to obtain a university were utterly stifled by British officials on the spot. In both periods, the impetus for a university issued almost exclusively from Africans. The Colonial Office remained indifferent while colonial governors and administrators were generally opposed to the idea.

However, between 1940 and 1948 the Colonial Office plunged into action and was ready, even in the face of continued opposition from officials on the spot, to promote efforts towards the establishment of universities in tropical Africa. This time, the initiative came almost entirely from London and not from Africans. Why did the earlier period witness such stiff opposition while the 1940s recorded a major shift in British colonial policy in favour of African universities? Though there are a number of scholarly works devoted to the history and evolution of African universities, which will be discussed below, few have focused on the vitally political nature of the policy of university development in British Africa. This book argues that the university question is central to the understanding and analysis of colonial reform in British Africa in the 1930s and 1940s.

I do not wish to focus merely on the story of the origins of Africa's premier universities. This is a study of the impact of British imperial politics and policies on the foundation of colonial universities.

INTRODUCTION

Although this work concentrates on the former British West and East African colonies, it is necessary to define its scope further for purposes of clarity. In West Africa, the territorial focus will be on Nigeria, Sierra Leone, the Gold Coast and the Gambia; and in East Africa the spotlight will be on Uganda which for so long held the torch of higher education in the region. In essence, this analysis will relate British imperial policy to the emergence of the first university colleges in Ibadan, Nigeria; Legon, Gold Coast; Fourah Bay, Sierra Leone; and Makerere, Uganda. These represent the institutions founded in British colonial Africa under Colonial Office authority. The development of universities in Egypt and the Sudan, though in some ways parallel, was carried through in different circumstances by the Foreign Office and the Anglo-Egyptian Condominium, over which the Colonial Office had no control. Developments in South Africa, independent of Colonial Office control after 1911, were little influenced by British colonial parallels, and indeed, after 1948, diverged fundamentally from them with the introduction of apartheid and legal segregation of education there.

It is important to point out that while in theory British officials in both the colonies and London were expected to carry out Colonial Office guidelines on matters of high policy, in practice the onus remained with the officials on the spot as to whether or not to comply with orders from London. This was the case particularly in the pre-1940 era when each of the colonies was supposed to be financially self-supporting. British officials in the colonies could easily flout orders from London using the excuse that they had no resources to pursue instructions. Hence, it should not surprise the reader if sometimes, particularly on issues relating to huge costs such as the university question, the actions and attitudes of colonial administrators contradicted instructions from the Colonial Office. It was not until the arrival of Malcolm MacDonald as the Secretary of State for the Colonies and the passage of the Colonial Development and Welfare Act of 1940 (which provided funds for development schemes in the colonies) that the Colonial Office began to assert its claim to control both colonial policy and the means of its implementation.

Literature on the history of tropical Africa normally indicates the flourishing of 'the University of Sankore' at Timbuctu in the Kingdom of Mali by the twelfth century.[1] However, Spencer Trimingham believes that Sankore did not actually exist as a university in the strict sense but rather was a place where Muslim clerics lived.[2] In any case, whether it thrived as a university or not, what remains clear is that the Sankore tradition was purely religious in orientation, where Muslim clerics taught Islamic science. As Ashby noted, Sankore's curriculum aimed at transmitting 'truths' which 'rested on authority, and not on observation or enquiry'.[3] Thus it was hardly a university in the modern and Western sense.

In sub-Saharan Africa, indigenous education hardly went beyond the level of that conducted by members of the extended family. Nevertheless, the educational training adequately served the needs of society. The aim of the education revolved around character training, instruction in crafts and duties to the community. Girls were specially instructed in the duties of domestic life. In his *African Survey*, Lord Hailey noted that initiation ceremonies and 'regimental training' 'are usually the culminating point' of indigenous education, aimed at fitting the youth to his or her place in traditional life.[4] But with European contacts and the advent of colonial rule in Africa, Western education began to provide a new direction, and the missionaries provided the initiative. Since the African environment was transformed by foreign, particularly Western influences, the need arose to fit the peoples into these new conditions, and hence Western education took root. Nevertheless, whatever education the British provided at the early stage of contact was aimed at three objectives – converting the Africans to Christianity, making them intelligible to the Europeans, and 'civilizing' their ways of life. Since education served as a good tool for the conversion of Africans to Christianity, missionary societies sought to monopolize it.

However, with the establishment of colonial rule at the beginning of the twentieth century, and the British adoption, and consolidation of the indirect rule system as an ideal administrative mechanism in the 1920s, the direction and purpose of African education changed. Indirect rule depended largely upon African traditional chiefly rulers, chosen by the British for their ascribed status in 'traditional' societies, often though not always illiterate in English. There was no room in that system for educated Africans, often of low 'traditionally' ascribed status, whatever their Western-style 'class' position won through educational attainments. Thus, for the British the question arose not only as to what should constitute the content of education offered and how far and fast the process should go but also what positions the educated African should occupy in the colonial state. Under indirect

INTRODUCTION

rule, as Anthony Enahoro observed, 'The British didn't want to rush education. They built schools with reluctance'.⁵ Using Nigeria as a case study, Uduaroh Okeke has contended that:

> the British rulers did not want to educate Africans for positions which provided jobs for themselves. Many of them knew that if they intensified the education of Nigerians they would hasten the end of occupation. So they rationed education cautiously, hoping that it would be many centuries before the Nigerians would be able to govern themselves. They feared that educated Africans would agitate over many things.⁶

Significantly, Hailey noted that among the many problems of Africa 'there is none that has attracted more discussion, and indeed more controversy, than that of the type of education which should be given to the African'.⁷ While Africans wanted the type of education which would make them equal to their British overlords, the British desired the kind of training which would fit Africans into subordinate positions in the colonial administrative arrangement. Hence, to the British, the type of education provided should be strictly correlated to colonial administrative requirements – in which the perpetual duty of the educated African was 'to assist his imperial masters, not to supplant them'.⁸

Since indirect rule had no place for highly educated Africans, the question of the establishment of universities in Africa naturally faced opposition from British officials. Unless the place of educated Africans under colonial rule was ascertained, the question of education would continue to be determined by political considerations. Hailey also anticipated this problem when he stated that:

> what at times has been put forward by administrations as a policy of education has in truth been only the expression of a political determination, or an effort to implement the view held of the place which the African should occupy in the social economy [of the colonial state].⁹

It is therefore my aim to demonstrate how the principle and practice of indirect rule constituted a stumbling block to the British establishment of universities in tropical Africa.

It was not until the middle of the twentieth century that universities emerged in tropical Africa through a well-planned process laid out by Britain. By this time the British had become convinced that it was far more dangerous for Africans to continue to acquire advanced training overseas than to provide them with university facilities locally. During this period British colonial policy came under attack both in London and overseas. Indirect rule began to be seen as a system which needed modifying in order to bring educated Africans into the mainstream of governance. The social, political and economic conditions in the colonial empire resulting in the West Indian riots had convinced imperial statesmen that reforms were needed if the empire were not to disintegrate. Once the Colonial Office had shown some readiness to go ahead with the university question, the African educated élite quickly seized the initiative to determine the nature of progress. It was in this climate of opinion that the British decided to establish universities in tropical Africa.

The centrality of the role of universities in the development of the social, cultural, economic, and political conditions of a society in the contemporary world can hardly be over-emphasized. To this, a host of scholars agree. Ashby has observed that 'Universities have become absolutely essential to the economy and to the very survival of nations.... Under the patronage of modern governments, they are cultivated as intensive crops, heavily manured and expected to give a high yield to the nourishment of the state.'[10] For J. F. Ade Ajayi, himself the product of overseas university education in Britain and a pioneer historian at the Ibadan University, education constitutes 'a mechanism by which society generates the knowledge necessary for its own survival and sustenance, and transmits this to future generations through processes of instruction to the youth', and the university 'describes the apex of the pyramid where the most fundamental ideas about the society are explored, new knowledge and fresh insights into the old are generated, and the leaders and the élite are trained.'[11] Chinweizu agrees. For him, 'Universities serve as finishing schools for those who have to lead and develop the traditions of a society.'[12] Thus to deny any society the necessary facilities for university education is to frustrate its ordered and sustained development. Why then did the British oppose the idea of an African university despite awareness of the important role universities play in the development of a society?

This book will further examine how racism, the nature of British administration, and the place Africans were expected to fill in society

INTRODUCTION

informed British negative attitudes towards the idea of a university. I will also attempt to show how and why the establishment of universities in Africa became a matter of high policy in the Colonial Office calculations in the 1940s. Many factors influenced this shift in policy: the fear of American influence, and the growth of nationalism in the colonies; the activity of the British academic lobby in favour of colonial universities; the 'anticipatory factor' generated by the West Indian crisis; the Second World War and the reform process initiated by Malcolm MacDonald which created the need for the expansion of the African educated class, and the broadsides on British imperial policy by critics of empire within and outside Britain.

Specific literature on the origins of the various universities in tropical Africa is not entirely lacking. Much work has been done on the University College of Ibadan, Nigeria,[13] and Margaret Macpherson's study on Makerere University College, Uganda provides some glimpses into the origins of the institution.[14] However, for the Gold Coast University College and Fourah Bay College, there are no existing works of any significance except when treated under a general study on education.[15] Most of these regional works say little about the period before 1948 when the universities were founded and, in addition, their analysis tends to concentrate on the internal workings of the emergent institutions. A. M. Carr-Saunders' *New Universities Overseas*, and I. C. M. Maxwell's *Universities in Partnership* belong to this category since they focus on the activity of the Inter-University Council in the actual foundation of the colonial university colleges.[16] Where some of these works explore the period before 1948, they hardly attempt an explanation of why the idea of an African university was resisted by the British for nearly a century.

Except for Eric Ashby's classic work, *Universities: British, Indian, African*,[17] no one has attempted a unified study of the establishment of universities in tropical Africa. There has been no effort to correlate the emergence of these institutions to the exigency of the British colonial policy framework emanating from London. Despite the fact that Ashby's work is broad, encompassing the evolution of British and Indian universities, it gives a profound account of the history of universities in English-speaking tropical Africa. Viewing the emergent African universities as mere transplantations of the British model, Ashby insists that in a modern state a university 'cannot remain a facsimile of some foreign model'.[18] It was to this question of adaptation that Ashby devoted his earlier work *African Universities and Western Tradition,* published in 1964.[19] Using Ghana and Nigeria as models Ashby illuminated the interaction between higher education and African society, arguing that as Western education changed the patterns of thought all over Africa, the forces arising from African nationalism were also changing the patterns of Western education.

Ashby's *Universities: British, Indian, African* has been an important reference for this present study, not only because it provides a strong historical background but also because it reproduces some important primary sources (Channon's papers on colonial universities, and the correspondence on Fourah Bay between Blyden, the Sierra Leone government and the Colonial Office). Nevertheless, Ashby's work is weak on the political aspects of the university question. It lacks analysis of the important political considerations at the heart of the British policies in Africa between 1860 and 1939 on the one hand and between 1940 and 1948 on the other. Ashby also fails to place either the pre-1940 British negative attitudes to the idea of an African university within the larger imperial spectrum of the exigencies of indirect rule, or the positive action of the 1940s within the ambit of the reform process, which required the creation of a large body of educated Africans. This is not surprising. Since his study was extensive in scope and content, including both British and Indian material and was not entirely devoted to tropical African universities, it was bound to be much in the nature of a survey. Ashby appeared to be aware of this when he noted: 'Our task is unfinished.... We hope that other scholars, particularly in Africa, will continue the work we have begun'.[20] This present work is an attempt not only to respond to Ashby's appeal but also to try to suggest a broader and more analytical approach.

Since it is a study of British imperial policy and attitudes, this analysis relies heavily on Colonial Office (CO) materials from the Public Record Office, London (PRO). Furthermore, as the University of London played a dominant role not only in the external degree arrangements in the colonies but also in the actual foundation of colonial universities under the scheme of special relationship, it was necessary to consult the records of that university. Eureka! I discovered a large body of relevant documents preserved at the University's Archives and Palaeography (ULAP) which no scholar before me, including Ashby, seems to have consulted. These documents are valuable evidence of the motives and aspirations of

INTRODUCTION

the London University's own faculty, who had powerful vested interests as well as idealism and pride in their own institution, and illuminate the role of the university and the Colonial Office in the forging of the scheme of special relationship between the University of London and the new colonial university colleges.

Any study of the origins of universities in British Africa would be incomplete without careful exploration of archives and collections in Africa itself.[21] These are particularly important for locating the 'voice' of Africans in shaping university development, and for analysis of the crucial way in which African opinion, often reflected and pushed forward by colonial governments, succeeded in West Africa in revising decisions made in London. The use of these local archives was extremely rewarding. In fact, Chapter 6 relies almost entirely on such source materials. Sometimes, Colonial Office documents which could not be found even at the Public Record Office in London were procured from the African archives as well as the special sections of university libraries.

Unfortunately, I was unable to visit Makerere University as a result of the civil war which was raging in Uganda in the later part of 1990. Worse still, the news from the country confirmed that both the Ugandan National Archives and the Makerere Library had been so pillaged that there was little or nothing a researcher could procure from the war-ravaged country to augment the materials from London. In any case, this predicament and the seeming imbalance in the East African sources has been compensated for by the huge body of documents obtained from the PRO combined with other sources. Chapter 3, which deals with the establishment of Makerere as a higher college, draws heavily from the extensive Colonial Office materials from London which no scholar has yet utilized. Indeed, since this book revolves more on the politics of the establishment of African universities correlated to changing British attitudes towards colonial development, the Colonial Office sources must be central to what is, after all, a study of the 'imperialism of decolonization'.

NOTES

1. See Basil Davidson, *Old Africa Rediscovered*, Gollancz, London, 1961, pp. 90–91; Flora Shaw, *A Tropical Dependency* (first published in 1906), reprinted by Frank Cass, London, 1964, pp. 202–208; and Joseph E. Harris, *Africans and Their History*, Mentor Books, New York, Revised Edition, 1987, pp. 60–61.
2. J. Spencer Trimingham, *A History of Islam in West Africa*, Oxford University Press, London, 1962, p. 98.

3. Eric Ashby, *Universities: British, Indian, African*, Harvard University Press, Cambridge, Massachusetts, 1966, p. 147.
4. Lord Hailey, *An African Survey*, Oxford University Press, London, 1938, p. 1207.
5. Anthony Enahoro, *Nigerian Daily Times*, 5 March 1963.
6. P. Uduaroh Okeke, 'Background to the Problems of Nigerian Education', in Okechukwu Ikejiani (ed.), *Nigerian Education*, Longman, Ikeja, 1964, p. 4.
7. Hailey, *An African Survey*, p. 1208.
8. Okechukwu Ikejiani, 'Nigerian Universities' in Ikejiani (ed.), *Nigerian Education*, p. 130.
9. Hailey, *An African Survey*, p. 1208.
10. Eric Ashby, *Adapting Universities to a Technological Society*, Jose-Brass, San Francisco, 1974, p. 7.
11. J. F. Ade Ajayi, 'The American Factor in the Development of Higher Education in Africa', *James Smoot Coleman Memorial Papers Series*, African Studies Centre, University of California at Los Angeles, 1988, p. 3.
12. Chinweizu, *The West and the Rest of us*, Random House, New York, 1974, p. 322.
13. See Nduka Okafor, *The Development of Universities in Nigeria*, Longman, London, 1971; J. F. Ade Ajayi and Tekena N. Tamuno (eds), *The University of Ibadan 1948-1973*, Ibadan University Press, Ibadan, 1973; K. Mellanby, *The Birth of Nigeria's University*, Ibadan University Press, Ibadan, 1958; Pierre L. van den Berghe, *Power and Privilege at an African University*, Schenkman Publishing Company, Cambridge, Massachusetts, 1973; Chukwuemeka Ike, *University Development in Africa: The Nigerian Experience*, Oxford University Press, Ibadan, 1976; A. Babs Fafunwa, *A History of Nigerian Higher Education*, Macmillan, Yaba, 1971; and J. T. Saunders, *University College, Ibadan*, Cambridge University Press, Cambridge, 1960.
14. Margaret Macpherson, *They Built for the Future: A Chronicle of Makerere University College, 1922-1962*, Cambridge University Press, Cambridge, 1964. There is also a profound treatment of the Makerere University College history in O. W. Furley and T. Watson, *A History of Education in East Africa*, Nok Publishers, New York, 1978.
15. Refer to H. O. A. McWilliam and M. A. Kwamena-Poh, *The Development of Education in Ghana*, Longman, London, New Edition, 1978; R. J. Mason, *British Education in Africa*, Oxford University Press, London, 1959; and Colin G. Wise, *A History of Education in West Africa*, Longman, London, 1956.
16. A. M. Carr-Saunders, *New Universities Overseas*, George Allen and Unwin Ltd., London, 1961 and I. C. M. Maxwell, *Universities in Partnership: The Inter-University Council and the Growth of Higher Education in Developing Countries 1946-1970*, Scottish Academic Press, Edinburgh, 1980.
17. Eric Ashby, *Universities: British, Indian, African*, op. cit.
18. Ibid., p. 5.
19. Eric Ashby, *African Universities and Western Tradition*, Harvard University Press, Cambridge, 1964.
20. Ashby, *Universities: British, Indian, African*, p. xiii.
21. I consulted the National Archives of Nigeria at Ibadan (NAI), National Archives of Ghana, Accra (NAGA), and Sierra Leone Archives at Fourah Bay College (SLA). Materials located on the reserve sections of the University of Ibadan Library; Africana Collection, Balme Library of the University of Ghana; and Sierra Leone Collection (SLC) of Fourah Bay College Library, Freetown were also very useful.

1 African Initiatives for a West African University and their Frustration, 1862–90

The ideas which in the twentieth century led to the creation of the African universities were articulated, in their essentials, by Africans between 1865 and 1874. The desire of the emerging African educated class to enter the élite ranks of the bureaucracy and participate in central political institutions and the establishment of European-style 'self-governing' states remained fundamental in both the nineteenth- and twentieth-century concepts of an African university. The late-nineteenth-century ideas never came to fruition, except in the minimal shape of Durham University degrees in theology and classics at Fourah Bay College in Sierra Leone. This chapter seeks to examine why these earlier ideas of an African university were frustrated and crushed by British colonial officials and missionaries. The causes of this early failure can illuminate the enormous contrast with the situation and policies of the initiatives, feebly initiated in the 1920s but strengthened in the 1930s, which culminated in the successful foundation of universities in British tropical Africa in the 1940s.

African demand for the provision of university facilities, which began in the second half of the nineteenth century, consistently faced formidable opposition from British colonial officials and missionaries, particularly those of the Church Missionary Society (CMS), until the late 1930s. Sometimes Colonial Office officials seemed sympathetic to African aspirations, and sometimes, too, they turned their back entirely against such agitations. The posture of the Office usually depended upon the dispositions of the colonial officials on the spot, and missionary bodies upon whose budgets the execution of projects such as the university scheme depended.

Colonial governments opposed the idea of an African university not only because of the problem of funding but also to secure the positions of British officials against African competition; missionary agencies resisted it because university proponents called for a secular institution under government control. Missionaries cherished their controlling influence over education because it had become their most successful instrument of evangelization. Thus, any interference in education, whether by the government, interest groups, or individuals, constituted an invasion of their sphere of influence. They opposed it fiercely.

In West Africa, the demand for the provision of an indigenous university was initiated by the Creoles of Sierra Leone whose contact with Western civilization had imbued them with a literary consciousness as early as the 1840s.[1] In tropical Africa it was the Creoles who bore the torch of transplanted Western culture in the region, having come into contact with foreign influences during their sojourn overseas as victims of the slave trade. In East and Central Africa, however, the 'liberated Africans' only developed 'freed slave' settlements from the 1870s, hence the development of similar intellectual awareness was delayed until the effective establishment of colonial rule in the first quarter of the twentieth century. Thus it is hardly surprising that the early demands for an indigenous university in Africa emanated from West Africa, and almost entirely from Sierra Leone.

From 1865, when James Africanus Horton first pleaded for the establishment of a West African university, to 1872 when Edward Wilmot Blyden reiterated it, British official hostility, and CMS opposition towards such a demand were quite predictable. For one thing, this was well before the scramble for African territories which began in the 1880s and Britain had hardly established an effective administration anywhere in its tropical African possessions except, perhaps, in Sierra Leone, where British officials had governed since its settlement in 1787. This was also the period when Victorian England was reconsidering the wisdom of setting up permanent administrations, and was contemplating an ultimate withdrawal from Africa. Britain believed it could hold its own under free trade, without territorial acquisition in the emerging legitimate commerce of West Africa. Spending British taxpayers' money in founding a West African university under these circumstances appeared imprudent, despite the Creole arguments that a university would be viable.

The first recorded appeal for a university in tropical Africa was made by Horton in 1865. He was a Creole, born in Freetown, Sierra Leone in 1835. His father was a recaptive of Igbo descent.[2] Horton graduated from Fourah Bay College in 1855. Fourah Bay Institution was founded by the CMS in 1827, but partly funded by Sierra Leone under Charles Macarthy, for the purpose of training Africans as schoolmasters, catechists and clergymen. From the onset, liberated Africans had been impressed with the role of Western education in the material and mental development of Africans, and had sought such good training for their children.[3] It was in the light of this that a school had been founded at Leicester Mountain, Sierra Leone, in 1816. But increasingly the CMS found it difficult to recruit Europeans for its work in Sierra Leone and, two years later, the school was transformed into a seminary 'designed primarily for the training of ministers and catechists'.[4]

Shortly afterwards the school was moved to Regent, Freetown, where it remained in operation until 1823. However, it lay dormant from 1823 until the CMS reopened it at Fourah Bay in 1827.[5] In 1828 new and larger premises were acquired from the estate of the late Charles Turner for £320 11s 6d.[6] Henceforth the college, which would play a significant role in the higher education of Africans, took root. From its inception in 1827 the life of Fourah Bay College remained precarious. Ashby has suggested that the chequered history of the college was due to the difficulty of finding suitable staff.[7] This is true. What this reflected, however, was the problem of adequate funding, which overwhelmed every other consideration.

Horton was one of the brilliant and fortunate three Sierra Leoneans who were selected from Fourah Bay College in 1855 to be trained as medical officers at the University of London King's College at the insistence of the War Office.[8] It was decided to train some African students to replace British medical officers serving in West Africa, whose mortality and morbidity rates were high. The British had realized that the physical make-up and resilience of Africans in coping with the harsh climate (and particularly malaria), made them useful agents of interior penetration. Thus the British concern for the education of these Africans, as noted by Wyse, reflected no real commitment to higher education, but merely an assertion of self-interest.[9]

Horton completed his studies at the University of Edinburgh in 1859, having left King's College because the institution would not award an MD after four years of studies.[10] Edinburgh would do so, and since the War Office urgently needed African medical officers, Horton proceeded to Edinburgh after spending three years in London working for an MRCS (Membership of the Royal College of Surgeons). At Edinburgh, he completed the fourth year and was awarded an MD.[11] While in Edinburgh, Horton adopted the name 'Africanus' as he began to see himself as an epitome of African achievement. His doctoral thesis was later published as *The Medical Typography of the West African Coast*. Thereafter he returned to Sierra Leone and was appointed as assistant surgeon in the British army stationed in the Gold Coast. While in the Gold Coast, he 'participated in the Ashanti Wars and played a significant, though behind the scenes, role in the Fanti political revival of the period'.[12] Consequently, military duties took him to many parts of West Africa where he familiarized himself with the people, their institutions and their social conditions. As one of the first West Africans to earn a doctor's degree, Horton fully realized the necessity of education if Africans were to make any meaningful advance. He was determined to arouse intellectual consciousness among his people by advocating the provision of university facilities in Africa.

Horton's interest in education began in 1861 when he proposed a local preliminary medical education for British West Africans. Realizing the value of an indigenous institution, he appealed to the War Office for the establishment of a small medical school in Sierra Leone. His scheme for the school was that 'certain young men, and not above the age of twenty, be selected ... [and] be prepared in the preliminaries of Medicine ... for a certain period, from one year and a half to two years' before proceeding to England.[13] He argued that an African instead of a European should be appointed to oversee the affairs of the proposed institution because 'he will take a far greater interest in performing what will tend to elevate his country'.[14] Indeed, he suggested himself for the job. Horton wanted to put Africans in control of medical services since they were more likely to work in sympathetic harmony with the people than European doctors.

On receipt of Horton's request, the Secretary of State for War transmitted it to the Principal Medical Officer and the Officer Commanding on the Gold Coast for comments on whether the replacement of European medical officers by Africans 'is likely to be successful'. Predictably, British officials presented 'a combined and warm opposition' as they advised the War Office that Africans preferred European rather than African doctors.[15] Even though Governor Pine of the Gold Coast felt strongly that the medical profession should be cleansed of its 'mischievous prejudice against colour', the War Office remained apathetic.[16] Consequently the Secretary of State, George Lewis, acting through the Under-Secretary, rejected Horton's appeal stating that he 'does not consider it necessary to enter into the scheme'.[17] It would appear that the vested interest of European medical officers ultimately coalesced against Horton's scheme.

Nevertheless, while Horton's effort appears to have been guided by patriotism it also seems to have been influenced by self-interest. Being one of the few 'pure' Africans to secure a medical doctorate and be employed by the War Office, Horton certainly desired to be accorded equal respect with his European counterparts. Having trained in the most prestigious universities in Britain he could not tolerate subordinate positions in the medical services. Thus he craved for a medical school where he could build a reputation as well as self-employment for himself. No doubt the difficulties he experienced in Britain prompted his proposal for a preliminary course before students proceeded to England. For him, it was absurd for African students unacquainted with medical matters to compete with those who generally had obtained preliminary education on some of the subjects before they entered university. Yet his insistence that 'the Master of the establishment' must be an African[18] meant that while Horton was enamoured with European culture he vehemently pushed for Africanization of the medical profession.

Horton seems to have envisaged a private medical college controlled by Africans (with himself as the head), and funded by the British Government. He should have known better. The futility of such a proposal was predictable since the British Parliament was yet to be convinced of the economic value of colonial possessions in Africa. Worse still, the British Government remained convinced that West Africa was the 'white-man's grave', particularly after the disaster of the Niger Expedition of 1841. Forty-eight Europeans who had ascended the Niger River died from malaria. Led by humanitarians such as Fowell Buxton and fully backed by the British Government, the expedition had been intended to 'open up' Africa, to stop the slave trade at source, and to introduce model farms at Lokoja for the promotion of legitimate trade in the African interior. This tragedy resulted in the withdrawal of all white personnel from the interior.[19] On a different level, it is surprising that Horton would be unaware that his demands struck at the vested interests of European medical officers. By arguing indiscreetly that his project aimed at replacing European officials 'who are opposed to the African race and who would not in any way favour any plan that tend[ed] to better their condition', Horton's proposal was bound to be stillborn.[20] He appealed to the War Office over the heads of the local European doctors and, in fact, the War Office might have found his scheme much cheaper in the long run. However, although Horton's appeal for a medical school failed, his educational ideas soon began to grow more ambitious.

In the meantime, Britain was not comfortable with its presence on the west coast of Africa. British involvement in Lagos politics in 1851 and the subsequent annexation in 1861, the ferocious Ashanti–Fanti conflicts which were taking their toll in men and resources, and the high mortality and morbidity rate of British officials had compelled policy-makers in London to reconsider the political and economic prudence of retaining British possessions in West Africa. A withdrawal began to be contemplated. Thus in 1863 when the Ashanti army invaded the coast, demanding that Governor Pine surrender some refugees, Britain advised against a counter-offensive fearing that it might mean the extension of spheres of influence. The Ashanti invasion coupled with other difficulties convinced staunch imperialists that 'energies were better directed to colonies in Australia and New Zealand than to the "white-man's grave" of West Africa'.[21]

Such a withdrawal could have entailed the training of Africans who would have replaced European bureaucrats in the administration of the colonies on behalf of Britain. It is, therefore, not surprising that prior to the establishment of colonial rule, the British Government and officials were more willing to create an educated African middle class which, having been educated in England, would constitute an important link between Britain and Africa should the former choose to withdraw from the political administration of its settlements.[22] These Africans were thought to be more resistant to the deadly malaria, and it was felt that they would also 'civilize' their own people more easily. No doubt, the education of Horton and his colleagues was undertaken with the same considerations.

But as quinine became effective as an antidote against malaria, and as colonial subjugation later became inevitable, colonial officials began to feel that there was no need for the continued expansion of the educated class. The educated class of Africans was soon to be seen as undesirable. Furthermore, it would seem that French activities in Senegal and the Lower Niger still remained a problem even though Britain was confident that it would commercially outstrip France under free competition and given its naval preponderance. British colonial attitudes began to waver. Policy remained uncertain, and sometimes principles contradicted themselves. Robert July succinctly depicted the situation thus:

> During the early decades of the nineteenth century, British policy in West Africa was uncertain and contradictory, reflecting the diverse pressures upon it at home. Committed to a laissez-faire philosophy towards colonies in general, the English government sought to minimize its presence along the West African coast and to reduce the expenditures incurred on behalf of its settlements there.[23]

Horton's demand for a West African university in 1868 was as a result of the recommendation of the Select Committee of the House of Commons appointed in 1865 to review whether or not the four West African settlements should be retained. Deliberating on the issue some members of Parliament 'felt that the colonies were useless, [as they were] neither suppressing the slave trade nor encouraging legitimate trade and therefore should be abandoned'; others argued that they should be kept.[24] Those officials who pushed for withdrawal 'accused the mission-educated colonials [Creoles] of being "notorious rogues" and "dishonest trouble-makers"'.[25] Early British travellers had described the Creoles disparagingly: as 'immoral prating knaves whose malign influence tended to depress the rest of West Africa'.[26] British officials in Africa employed these narratives to dismiss missionary efforts as harmful and also useless since they seemed to have led the educated Africans to think themselves equal to Europeans.[27] Hence while the British Parliament was thinking about possible withdrawal and a hand-over of administration to the African educated élite, colonial officials were arguing that the educated Africans were not worthy of such responsibility. British officials were protecting their positions. Thus the seeds of discord were sown quite early between colonial officials and the African educated élite.

In any case, it would seem that the lure of legitimate commerce, the curiosity to explore the interior, as well as French activities in West Africa, discouraged an outright decision by the House of Commons for a withdrawal. Instead, Parliament resolved in favour of the retention of its settlements without further expansion. Accordingly,

> all further assumption of territory or assumption of Government, or new treaties, offering any protection to native tribes would be inexpedient; and that the object of our policy should be to encourage in the natives the exercise of those qualities which may render it possible more and more to transfer to them the administration of all the Governments, with a view to our ultimate withdrawal from all, except, probably Sierra Leone.[28]

Between 1865 and the 1870s there was renewed official support for British traders in response to the political backing given by the French government to its traders, and the establishment of French settlements at Assine, Grand Bassam, the Popos, Porto Novo and at Libreville.[29] Official British actions from the 1870s ignored the 1865 resolution of the House of Commons as the acquisition of more territories accelerated.

The decision for 'ultimate withdrawal' by the British Parliament suggested to Horton that Western education was necessary. But why was Western education vital for self-government since at that time sovereign African states (such as Asante, Dahomey, Benin and the Yoruba states) were not ruled by Western-educated Africans? As a member of the emerging educated class, Horton desired the creation of new Western-style states ruled by Western educated Africans and not the traditional rulers. Thus he felt that education in Western tradition and civilization was necessary to train the African political and bureaucratic élite. Horton's effort seems to reflect the early stages of conflict between an African educated élite and traditional authorities which climaxed in the 1920s. In a pamphlet issued in 1865[30] and expanded into a book in 1868,[31] Horton noted that 'education would form an essential element in the [self-]government of the coast', and called for the establishment of a West African university. According to him,

> We want a University for Western Africa, and the Church Missionary Society has long ago taken the initiative and built an

expensive college, [Fourah Bay College] which should now be made the focus of learning for all Western Africa.[32]

In Horton's time Fourah Bay College in Sierra Leone was the only higher educational institution of any significance in the whole of West Africa offering a diploma in theology and a few certificate courses. But most recaptives did not like the predominantly ecclesiastical education provided for their children by Fourah Bay. Thus in 1845 the CMS was persuaded to establish a grammar school encompassing education of a general and secular character 'open to all classes of the Public without regard to religious or other distinctions', founded in Freetown.[33] Fourah Bay's importance was reduced in the public's eyes as the grammar school 'was patronized by people all over West Africa who wished their children to choose careers other than the Church'.[34] Consequently, only those who wished to become clergymen continued at Fourah Bay College. It is not surprising that between 1845 and 1860 only ten students were educated at the college at a cost of nearly £800 a year to the CMS.[35] As a result, the college was closed down in 1859 but was reopened in 1863 by the CMS.

Nevertheless, the new Fourah Bay College awarded no formal qualifications. Rather it trained men almost exclusively for the ministry or as catechist schoolteachers. By and large, 'it functioned as a seminary and high school'.[36] During this period almost all the students admitted to the college were born in Sierra Leone with the exception of those brought to Freetown in childhood as slaves like Samuel Crowther.[37] Thus, to the CMS, the college well served its intended purpose as an institution where recaptive children could be trained in useful trades or farming, and the better ones as pastors and teachers.

By 1863 James Horton had returned home from Britain, and had begun to articulate his idea of a university. Horton wanted Fourah Bay College to serve a more practical and secular purpose for the intellectual and material advancement of the African people. He conceived of education as an indispensable part of development and 'the key to free Africans from the racists' prison of allegedly permanent inferiority ... [and] from the unenterprising ways that kept their countries economically stagnant'.[38] He therefore insisted that both his proposed university and education in general should be supported by local and British Government funds rather than the limited resources provided by the CMS. Thus Horton seems to have anticipated the concept of 'colonial development and welfare' which would dominate British colonial policy in the 1940s. He decried the refusal of the Sierra Leone Government to spend on education in the colony. He saw it as absurd that the Government should spend £400 on education while liberally committing the sum of £14,000 annually on police.[39] Hence Horton contended that the proposed West African University should be 'endowed by the Local Government, which should guarantee its privileges, and cherish the interests of literature and science in the Colony'.[40]

Horton seemed to have been strangely ignorant of the very basis and nature of British enterprise in Africa. From the beginning, educational efforts in British territories had been the work of missionary, and not government agencies – British or African. The British Government had thereby been relieved of any financial responsibilities for education. As missionary bodies scampered for converts the control of education became crucial, and the CMS jealously guarded it. The preponderance of the CMS had been so complete that education, as George observed,

> became inextricably blended with the history of that Society, so that it became impossible after this to treat of the education of the Colony without trenching on the history of the Church Missionary Society[41]

Clearly Horton's call for government involvement was a bold plea which would certainly face British official as well as missionary opposition.[42] The British Government regarded the policy of minimal spending for maximum profit as almost inviolate. Any schemes, such as a university or medical school, which implied additional expenditure were anathema. Thus when Governor Blackall of Sierra Leone suggested that more political functions should be exercised by Britain in its West African territories, officials of the Colonial Office disagreed. Such actions, as one official commented, 'must be costly' hence Britain should 'civilize' two or three stations on the West Coast 'at which merchants could place their goods in security and ship them in larger vessels for export to Europe..., costing us no money and involving us in no responsibility'.[43] Parsimony in spending was British doctrine. As Fyfe aptly pointed out,

> British colonial policy paid occasional lip-service to development. But a tradition of official parsimony restricted

public expenditure to the minimum necessary to keep administration going. If export-import trade brought in enough customs revenue to balance the budget the Colonial Office was contented.⁴⁴

Horton proposed a broad-based curriculum of instruction ranging from arts to science, and suggested that the educational tradition should be Western in style and content. According to him,

> Lectures should be given in the theory and practice of education, classics, mathematics, natural philosophy, mensuration, and book-keeping; English Language and literature; French, German, Hebrew, history in general, mineralogy, physiology, zoology, botany, chemistry, moral and political philosophy, civil and commercial law, drawing and music, besides the various subjects which might be included under the term of theology.⁴⁵

Although Horton desired the social, intellectual and economic development of his people through higher education, his approach was not racist. For him, foreign influence constituted the necessary catalyst for the advance of Africa. Horton did not allow the racial feelings of the time to diminish his admiration for the virtues of European civilization. As a product of European culture Horton was virtually indoctrinated. For him, therefore, Western standards became the unchallenged basis on which African achievement could be gauged. However, he emphasized the racial equality of humans on the basis that every race was capable of civilization by imitation and emulation. For Horton, there was nothing wrong with Britain influencing, through Christianity, the 'civilization' of Africa as Rome had inspired European civilization. He contended that 'the variations between human groups depended on nurture and environment ..., any race could be improved by education, and degraded by the lack of it'.⁴⁶ Furthermore, '[i]t is impossible for a nation to civilize itself; civilization must come from abroad'. He therefore enjoined Africans to respect and imitate 'the good and virtuous Europeans, whilst shunning those whose actions are a disgrace to civilization'.⁴⁷

Horton glorified European civilization, and saw nothing wrong in the transplantation of British virtues into Africa. But he acknowledged that there were some Europeans whose conception of Africans was totally objectionable. He was aware that 'those [Europeans] who come out are *opposed to anything that will raise the African* and therefore it will require time for them to conform themselves with any such plans...'[48] Thus he insisted that the improvement of West Africa, which the government expected, 'can never be properly accomplished, unless by the aid of the educated *native portion* of the *community*'.[49] Horton's contention that the 'Master' in the educational institution he proposed should be an African who 'will take a far greater interest in performing what will tend to elevate his country' remains an expression of doubt as to the sincerity of the British 'civilizing' mission in Africa. What Horton emphasized, therefore, was that while 'civilization must come from abroad', the civilizers must be indigenous if a nation were to make a meaningful advance. He was aware that Europeans normally came for reasons not far from those impelled by self-interest.

Horton was far ahead of his time. Not surprisingly, his pleas for a medical school, West African university, and government funding of education were stillborn. For one thing, the university facilities which he demanded would have elevated Africans to, or above, the level of British officials who had begun to cherish and protect their elevated positions. Already the educational advance attained by the Creoles of Sierra Leone had placed them in direct rivalry with the British officials, traders and missionaries alike. Higher training of Africans in the fields of medicine, law, engineering and administration would mean the displacement of British officials. It was not surprising that the Principal Medical Officer and the Commanding Officer on the Gold Coast recommended that the War Office turn down Horton's appeal for a medical school for the continued training of African medical officers to replace the British.[50]

Instead of the ultimate withdrawal from its West African possessions, as the Select Committee of 1865 had envisaged, from the 1870s Britain began to position herself on the West coast of Africa to meet the threat of French aggressive expansionist and protectionist activities in West Africa.[51] Thus, even though traders and missionaries supported the withdrawal because they preferred to trade and proselytize, respectively, beyond British jurisdiction where there were no officials to interfere with them, French protectionism troubled them.[52] However, colonial officials on the spot were not comfortable with the withdrawal argument because it entailed loss of jobs for them. Thus, whatever the case, the call for more British action by consuls far surpassed those of traders and missionaries.

Mainly for reasons of economics, and backed by the advice of the Colonial Office, Parliament resolved that the four British possessions be unified under one administration with a Governor-in-Chief to be resident in Sierra Leone, and paying occasional visits to the other territories.⁵³ This was effected in 1866. In each subordinate settlement – Lagos, the Gold Coast and the Gambia – administrators were to be appointed who would be responsible to the Governor-in-Chief, and who would correspond with the Colonial Office through him. This arrangement was intended to save costs. Instead of withdrawing, as Horton had presumably hoped, Britain set up a formal administration for its West African settlements with headquarters in Sierra Leone. As a result, the opposition of British colonial officials to the idea of a West African university began to harden. Although the British needed educated Africans to realize the process of Europeanization and civilization, the Sierra Leonean Government was perhaps conscious of its lean budgets upon which the university project would depend and hence the idea was ignored. Granted that Horton's demand produced no tangible and favourable response from Britain, there is no doubt that he was a great African patriot of his time. Clearly, his belief that education would be the chief agent of African development can hardly be written off as mere fantasy.

From the 1870s Edward Wilmot Blyden took on the mantle of Horton, in a more forceful manner, by appealing for the establishment of a university in West Africa. Blyden was born in 1832 in the Danish West Indian island of St. Thomas. Like Horton, he traced his descent to the Igbo ethnic group of modern Nigeria.⁵⁴ In his youth Blyden demonstrated a remarkable linguistic ability by mastering Spanish within two years. Encouraged by Reverend Knox of the Dutch Reformed Church, Blyden went to America in 1850 'in the hope that he might gain admission to appropriate American colleges and eventually enter the ministry'.⁵⁵ But he was denied admission on account of his race. According to him, a

> deep-seated prejudice against my race, exercised so controlling an influence in the institutions of learning, that admission to them was almost impossible. Discouraged by difficulties in my path, I proposed to return to St. Thomas and abandon the hope of an education....⁵⁶

The effects of this unhappy episode on young Blyden can be imagined but it would reshape and sharpen his future racial attitudes. He ultimately accepted an offer by the American Colonization

Society to relocate in Liberia in order to carry on with his education, arriving in Monrovia in January 1851.[57] Liberia was founded in 1822 as a haven for freed American slaves. Until 1847 when it became independent, Liberia was administered by the American Colonization Society on behalf of the United States Government. As with Sierra Leonean Creoles, literacy was high among Liberian settlers while the indigenous population remained predominantly illiterate. Thus agitation for university education was higher among Liberian settlers than the autochthones.

In Liberia, Blyden was admitted into the Alexander High School where he learned Latin, Greek, geography and mathematics, and later enrolled at Princeton Theological College where he trained for the clergy.[58] Between 1855–56 he served as the editor of Liberia's only newspaper, the *Liberian Herald*. When the Principal of Alexander High School, Reverend Wilson, retired in 1858, Blyden secured that position, and was ordained in the presbytery of West Africa. In 1861 Blyden was appointed professor of Latin and classics in the newly established Liberia College while retaining his post in the school. From then on, Blyden began to play a prominent role in the public life of his adopted country. In a sense, his relocation to Liberia afforded him the opportunity to become the leading African philosopher-statesman of his time. It is uncertain whether he would have attained such eminence had he not personally experienced open racism and resettled in Liberia.

Blyden became a scholar, clergyman, journalist, diplomat, administrator and pan-African theorist. His burning desire to elevate Liberia to a respected independent African country compelled him to accept a government post as Secretary of State. Strong racial feelings led to Blyden's campaign for the emigration en masse of American blacks to Liberia. Ardently convinced that no race could reach its full self-expression under alien control, he further stressed that 'no people can rise to an influential position among the nations without a distinct and efficient nationality'.[59] On behalf of the Liberian Government, he visited America in 1865 to recruit settlers, resulting in a settlement on the St. Paul's River.[60] Undoubtedly, Blyden's previous unhappy experience in the United States shaped his racial philosophy.

Indeed, he became very powerful in his position as Secretary of State. Increasingly the Liberian President, Edward Roye, developed high admiration for him. Together in 1870 they outlined a number of reforms which included a thorough financial reconstruction and the establishment of the national banking system, the general education of the masses, the introduction of railroads, and the improvement and incorporation of 'native tribes' contiguous to Liberia. But the reform process was opposed by Roye's political opponents, led by the powerful mulatto group.[61] In the political manoeuvres which ensued, Roye and Blyden lost control to the mulattos. Roye was deposed and ultimately murdered. To discredit Blyden his mulatto rivals accused him of seducing Roye's wife, and Blyden was forced to flee to Sierra Leone in 1871.[62]

Ultimately Blyden's effort to transform Liberia according to his vision failed. From then on, he no longer thought only in terms of Liberia but acted for the progress of the entire African continent. Arising out of his experience with the mulattos in Liberia, Blyden began to espouse the superiority of pure races over blood mixtures (or mongrelization). His ideas concided with the racial conclusion of many Europeans whose own interests in racial characteristics, race hierarchies and race superiority far surpassed Blyden's, and whose assumptions began to permeate the climate of opinion in the late-nineteenth century. Naturally, Blyden's racial theory catered to, and flattered, a wide audience among educated Africans as well.

It was while in Sierra Leone that Blyden's idea of a University of West Africa matured. Obviously aware of the earlier plea by Horton between 1860 and 1868, Blyden picked up the university question shortly after his resettlement in Freetown. In Sierra Leone, Blyden found an enthusiastic African collaborator in Reverend James Johnson with whom he edited *The Negro* newspaper. This newspaper, which they co-founded in 1871, was 'extremely distasteful to Europeans'.[63] Johnson was born to Yoruba recaptive parents between 1835 and 1840. He was ordained a minister in the Anglican Church in 1866 after his theological education at Fourah Bay College. As a priest of African descent, Johnson observed that there was some kind of discrimination in the state, as well as the church, targeted against Blacks. Thus he began to espouse the grievances of his countrymen against the racial policies 'pursued by the British rulers in Church and State'.[64] Not surprisingly, he was branded *persona non grata* in the Sierra Leonean CMS circle. Pointing out 'the denationalizing methods of the Christian Missions in West Africa', Johnson became a staunch advocate of cultural nationalism.[65] Johnson's philosophy on race was therefore parallel, if not exactly similar to Blyden's. Little wonder then that both men became perfect associates in the clamour for a West African university.

Unlike Horton, Blyden's demand for a West African university was more forceful, racial, and secular. Although he was subsequently overcome by the concerted opposition of British officials, championed by the CMS, Blyden took his argument to the highest level possible. His demand in relation to the provision of higher educational facilities for Africans began with a letter in April 1872 to Henry Venn, the Secretary-General of the parent committee of the CMS in London, about the establishment of a collegiate institution in Sierra Leone. Observing that 'there is no greater need in this Colony than a good Collegiate Institution both for preparing missionaries and men to act well their part in the ordinary pursuit of life', Blyden demanded that

> There should be located in Freetown, or its neighbourhood, some good Institution to which parents here and at other points of the coast, might send their children with the assurance that they would receive a training which would fit them for the practical purposes of life.[66]

From the onset Blyden frowned on the continued education of Africans in England where they imbibed foreign ideas and practices which disoriented them for leadership roles within Africa. He sought to preserve the essential virtues of black civilization, especially in an era when racial mythologies were disparagingly anti-black. Given his own experience in the United States, Blyden was determined to prove that the blackness of his skin had nothing to do with the sharpness of his intellect. He recognized that the continued training of Africans in England was a way of perpetuating in Africans a sense of racial inferiority. Worse still, Blyden felt that alienation was a concomitant of colonial education. In England, Africans were exposed to an educational curriculum which centred almost exclusively on Europe. Robert July has noted how this practice resulted in a thin stream of miseducated Africans who were 'untrained in self-respect, unqualified to deal with the problems of their own society, and lacking the necessary instructive, sympathetic response to the rhythmic pulse of Africa'.[67]

July seems to be almost rehashing Blyden who had stated that

> the strain which the mind of the African youth receives when he is sent to England ... often unfit him for usefulness when he

returns home. He either satisfies himself to remain in his artificial and stilted position – too elevated for practical purposes – or a reaction takes place and he sinks far below those who have never been on the coast. He has acquired tastes and practices which he cannot enjoy here and he therefore wastes his time pining after 'dear old England'.[68]

When William Grant proposed in the Legislative Council the establishment of a good educational institution in Sierra Leone, Blyden quickly sent him a powerful letter of support.[69] Grant's interest in the provision of a sound educational institution in Sierra Leone was understandable. As a successful Creole who had built a flourishing business in the early 1860s, and as a member of the Legislative Council, Grant desired suitable education for his children. Blyden wished to acquaint Grant with the kernel of his educational argument so that the latter could champion the cause further in the legislature. With the foundation of such an institution, Blyden told Grant,

> there would be a general diffusion of that higher intelligence which originates public measures, which stimulates the people, moderates their impulses, sustains and gives weight to noble enterprise, creates and expands a healthy public sentiment, and accelerates the moral and spiritual progress of the race.[70]

In his response Grant assured Blyden that he had a 'deep interest in the subject', and suggested that Blyden should publish his ideas on education as contained in his letter in *The Negro*. Grant suggested that 'the subject should be thoroughly ventilated and discerned, trusting that such discussion may lead to the adoption of such measures as will promote the educational interests of our people'.[71]

With Grant on his side and Johnson as a comrade, Blyden felt more confident to put forward his grand idea for the establishment of a West African university. While Grant was to lobby government, Johnson could push the case in missionary quarters, with Blyden as a sort of clearing house. The stage was thus set for what turned out to be one of the best articulated and promoted ideas of the period.

In December 1872 Blyden forwarded a letter calling upon Governor Pope Hennessy of Sierra Leone to establish a university in West Africa.[72] Stating that foreign influences, through education, had 'unduly biased their [African] development and hampered their progress', Blyden told Hennessy that able teachers of African descent could be recruited from all over the world, if necessary. These scholars, he argued, 'would have great influence in exposing and correcting the fallacies upon which our foreign teachers have proceeded in their utter misapprehension and, perhaps, contempt of African character'.[73] Blyden's statement seemed rather too harsh. Only a few white governors could tolerate such brazen criticism. Hennessy was one of those few.

Furthermore, Blyden insisted that the time had come for the education of Africans to be adapted 'to the exigencies of the country and race ... if the people are ever to become fit to be entrusted with the functions of self-government; if they are ever to become ripe for free and progressive institutions'. To press his point home Blyden concluded that

> to give the people the opportunity and power of a free and healthy development – to bring out that individuality and originality of character which is one of the sure results of advancing civilization and culture, the university is most important.[74]

The issue of adaptation of education to the African environment was one about which Blyden felt strongly. It was an issue which would later dominate the British attempt to evolve an education policy for their African territories from the 1920s. But while Blyden's call for adaptation was informed by a desire to preserve African cultural identity while still learning Western technologies, the adaptation of the inter-war years was an attempt to consolidate indirect rule as will be seen later. Thus Blyden sent a follow-up letter to Hennessy emphasizing that the university he envisaged should be 'in keeping with advancing the spirit of the age and adapted to the inherent necessities of the [African] race'.[75] Furthermore he subtly denounced the exploitative nature of British administration in Africa, which invariably ignored the mental and material development of the people. Accordingly,

> a Government which is more inert in developing the intellectual and moral character of these 'tribes' than in availing itself of the material resources of the country is of very questionable utility to the race.[76]

In his response Hennessy agreed with Blyden on the defective nature of education in British West African settlements. While recognizing the dangers of the formation of 'thoughtless, idle and ignorant character', Hennessy noted that Government and Missionary Societies had laboured seriously to promote education. However, he stressed that the failure of British education of Africans was 'mainly owing to the idea that the Negro should be Europeanized to be educated' pointing out that a similar mistake was made in the early days of British rule in 'Hindustan' with comparable results.[77] In any case, Hennessy contended that the foundation of a university 'must be the work of the Africans themselves'.

Evidently sympathetic to the issue of higher education for Africans, Hennessy recalled that there had been failures of so many benevolent projects in Sierra Leone that his government 'would shrink from undertaking the initiative of such an Institution, though a reasonable claim for some State support might be made, when the Promoters could show that their scheme possessed the real elements of success'.[78] Undoubtedly Hennessy was aware that Africans would not agree to bear the cost of Blyden's scheme even though they would benefit from it. In describing the attitudes of Africans towards such projects Ayandele aptly asserted that 'tax or self-help in any form was their bane', and to suggest that Africans should bear the initial costs of building the university was 'to touch them on their tenderest spot'.[79] In fact only a few Africans could afford the taxes. Thus by leaving the initiative to Africans it appears that Hennessy was either appealing to traditions in Britain where universities had been privately promoted or was tactfully putting the scheme off.

Consequently Blyden told the Governor that the mind of the educated African had been so enslaved as to disparage anything indigenously African. The liberated Africans had been so miseducated that they would prefer to pay any price to obtain their education from England rather than fund an indigenous university. In his own words: 'All educated Negroes suffer from a kind of slavery in many ways far more subversive of the real welfare of the race than the ancient physical fetters.' The slavery of the mind, Blyden further asserted, was far more destructive than that of the body. He regretted that those who fought to remove the shackles from the body of the 'Negro' transferred them to his mind 'with as little compunction as ever Hawkins or Da Souza prosecuted the slave trade'. Thus to leave the work of initiating the university project to this mentally enslaved class 'would be to put it off indefinitely'.[80] Nevertheless Blyden believed strongly that the Europeans had a responsibility to pay for the proper education of Africans. In other words, he considered British provision of educational facilities for Africans as a form of reparation for the atrocities committed against the black race in the era of the Atlantic Slave Trade. Affected by the obnoxious slave trade, Blyden's rage can be appreciated. Consequently,

> Europeans owe us a great debt, not only for the unrequited physical labors we have performed in all parts of the world, but for the unnumbered miseries and untold demoralization they brought upon Africa by the prosecution for centuries of the horrible traffic to promote their own selfish ends; and we feel that we do not simply ask it as a favor but claim it as a right when we entreat their aid as civilized and Christian Governments in the work of unfettering and enlightening the Negro mind, and placing him in a position to act well his part among the 'productive agencies' of time.[81]

Apparently knowing too well that the British Government would not agree to fund such a gigantic project – a university of West Africa – and granted that Sierra Leone resources could not bear the costs alone, Governor Hennessy assured Blyden that he would transmit the correspondence, including his own minutes upon them, to the British Secretary of State for the Colonies (the Earl of Kimberley) for necessary action.[82] It would appear that this was an attempt by Hennessy to put to an end the somewhat endless epistolary debate between himself and Blyden without provoking animosity between his government and the educated class of Africans.

Blyden also forwarded his correspondence to the Honourable William Grant. Grant expressed satisfaction that the governor was quite prepared to accept openly the failure of British African education policy. Acknowledging that this was the first time that public attention had been directed to this important matter, Grant concluded that 'the views brought out in the correspondence are of vital importance to the proper progress of the race', and he begged Blyden to publish the correspondence with the governor.[83]

In any case, Blyden was glad that Hennessy was willing to transmit the correspondence to London because at least that would make the 'effort assume an importance and gather to itself an element of speedy success'.[84] Furthermore, he asked Hennessy for permission to publish the correspondence to acquaint 'Negroes' all over the world about the steps being taken in Africa itself on the question of education 'to counteract the degeneracy which everywhere has marked our transit from barbarism to the complex forms of European civilization'.[85] Hennessy agreed.[86] Blyden did not realize that official and ecclesiastical opposition would soon crystallize against his scheme.

'As susceptible as ever to native pressure', according to Ashby,[87] Hennessy expressed his support for Blyden's university scheme. Rehashing Blyden's contention in his letter to the Secretary of State, he argued that 'the system of sending the Children of the wealthier Africans to Europe has been doubly injurious' because not only did it contaminate the character of those so trained, but also frustrated the policy approved by the Parliamentary Committee of 1865 which sought to make Africans capable of self-government.[88] Hennessy recommended that 'a West African University founded on a very humble basis ought to be established ...' and that the Wesleyan Training College on King Tom's peninsula should be the suitable site.[89]

Blyden's proposal, now with Hennessy's approval, 'met a cautious but not unfavourable reception at the Colonial Office'.[90] But before the Colonial Office considered the question the new Governor Keate had replaced Hennessy in Sierra Leone. In his response, addressed to Governor Keate, Kimberley stated that, although he was not prepared to express any opinion on the issue, the subject deserved the Governor's careful consideration.[91] It is important to consider why the Secretary of State was cautious about the scheme, but did not reject it outright. First, Blyden's argument in favour of the university was very powerful, and Hennessy's approval appeared to be equally forceful as he used the Indian situation to buttress the failure of missionary education. The Colonial Office presumably felt there was a consensus in West Africa in favour of the university. Caution, therefore, became necessary in order to avoid provoking trouble among educated Africans, especially the Creoles.

Earlier, Governor Hennessy and Reverend Johnson had 'condemned the excessive zeal of Christian Missionaries who were Europeanizing their converts and were ... robbing them of their racial virtues while making them helpless victims of European vices'.[92] It would seem that Hennessy's reason for supporting the university project was mainly to get at the CMS whose domineering influence in the territory had increasingly become disturbing to the governor. For one thing Hennessy was a Catholic and may have resented the

CMS, particularly in its absolute control of education in West Africa. However, this should not lead one to believe that Hennessy's condemnation of missionary education was entirely malicious since Johnson and Blyden, both members of the clergy, were also critical of the missionary enterprise. The CMS officials presumed that Hennessy's approval of Blyden's proposal was suspect. To them, the governor wanted to collaborate with Blyden to diminish their influence. Hence the Principal of Fourah Bay College (Metcalfe Sunter), himself a CMS man, expressed the hope that Mr Gladstone would 'not send out any more red hot Papists to this Colony'. Disparaging Hennessy in strong terms, Sunter alleged that

> [i]t has been his aim, ever since his first arrival here, to depreciate systematically, the European, especially the Protestant Missionary: and one thing is patent that whatever his intentions may have been, he has succeeded ... in doing more to excite a hostile feeling towards Englishmen in the minds of some Natives than any previous Governor....[93]

Clearly the CMS were anti-Catholic. Why else should Sunter pour such slanderous venom on Hennessy because the governor seemed to have sympathized with Blyden's proposal? After all, Blyden was a Protestant. In fact, the business had little to do with Hennessy's supposed Catholic bias. Rather, it demonstrated the CMS determination to keep a monopoly over all levels of colonial education. Hennessy appeared to be less anti-Protestant than he was against the near monopoly held by the CMS. Clearly, that Society must have been absolutely infuriated by the suggestion that a Methodist institution might form the nucleus of a university.

In any case, the CMS was horrified by Blyden's scheme. The fact that Blyden intended the university to be funded by government meant interference in the traditional role of the CMS. Furthermore, given that the range of subjects to be taught in the proposed university would be secular rather than ecclesiastical and that both Muslims and Christians would be admitted on an equal basis, the opposition from the CMS was almost inevitable. To the Anglican Bishop of Sierra Leone, what Blyden proposed 'is to be in our estimation a Godless University', and thus should be resisted strongly. He wrote to the Secretary of the Parent Committee of the CMS, Henry Wright, that he would open up Fourah Bay and expand its scope so 'as to cut to the ground the plea of necessity for another

College [or University]'.⁹⁴ The Society agreed with the Bishop that Fourah Bay should be made 'more of a University' offering higher and wider education, and that its doors should be 'thrown open to any well recommended Xtian Africans who may wish to enter it & are willing to pay'.⁹⁵ Shortly afterwards Fourah Bay was reconstituted as a college offering a wider range of courses but leading to the award of only diplomas and certificates.

It could be seen that while the CMS was willing to frustrate Blyden's plea for a 'godless' university, it was not prepared to make Fourah Bay a secular institution or a proper university. While the Society desired to maintain its dominant influence, the question of how to fund the university scheme in an era when the Society was consecrating African clergy to save cost 'both in salaries and capital outlay' was disturbing.⁹⁶ Faced with the problem of funding, the Principal of Fourah Bay, Metcalfe Sunter, proposed that it was necessary to begin to think about affiliation of the institution to a British university.⁹⁷ But what Blyden called for was a degree-granting university, and not a college which offered diplomas and certificates that were normally tinted with ecclesiasticism. Predictably, the CMS efforts to open up Fourah Bay did not satisfy him.

The Church and particularly the Anglicans had been instrumental in establishing universities in many colonies of the British Empire. Even in Britain itself, the Church had been significantly involved in education up to and including university. Hence there was little reason to argue that Sierra Leone should have been different. The combination of a governor and an educated African speaking for the élite had forced the CMS in the direction it should have moved without such pressure.

Nevertheless, as a first step the developments at Fourah Bay seemed satisfactory. As long as the colonial government remained amenable to the idea of a university, it could have supported the Western-educated élite's demands for the mission churches to move toward more full university status. Ultimately, as Hennessy argued, the government would be expected to assist financially. Thus by a normal, slow evolution Fourah Bay, and presumably other such institutions, would have developed and grown over the coming century. Such natural growth would have followed the path of similar institutions in the white colonies. Such a development was thwarted because colonial governments absolutely set their face against universities of any kind for another 75 years.

While the CMS was scheming to thwart Blyden's 'godless' university idea, the Government of Sierra Leone was also erecting a formidable opposition against it. Governor Keate, who had replaced Hennessy, died in March 1873 only a few weeks after assuming office and was succeeded by George Berkeley. Unlike Hennessy, Berkeley did not support Blyden's proposal. Hence he delayed action upon the Secretary of State's letter addressed to Keate. Perhaps he hoped that procrastination would force the matter to die quietly. Blyden would not give up so easily.

After waiting for ten months without any response from Governor Berkeley, Blyden wrote directly to Kimberley to restate his case, and to inform him that the university scheme was being opposed by those 'who seem to think that such [an] institution may conflict with their prerogatives and diminish their influence'.[98] Apparently referring to the Bishop of Sierra Leone and the CMS, he alerted the Secretary of State that those resisting the plan 'have, therefore, by various misrepresentations, raised a storm of persecution at Freetown against the propounders of the scheme'. Accordingly, he appealed to Kimberley to back his scheme, 'and thus weaken the opposition which may become so formidable as to crush out every aspiration to such facilities for progress among the Natives'.[99]

Wishing to sound out African opinion within the CMS, the Colonial Office invited Reverend James Johnson to London to discuss the university project. Although Johnson was concerned about the problem of funding, he expressed support for the university scheme as proposed by Blyden.[100] Consequently Kimberley reminded Berkeley of the university question and requested his opinion 'upon a subject which seems to me one of much importance'.[101] Still Berkeley did not respond until May of the following year, almost six months later. By this time he had weighed the pros and cons of the scheme, and learned of the Bishop of Sierra Leone's strong opposition to the project. Earlier, in April 1874, the bishop had advised the governor 'to pause to count the probable cost, the possible entire failure, the extent of beneficial result the most sanguine of reasonable men could expect'. Furthermore, he told the governor that

> The Church Missionary Society is willing to do very much what is now at the hands of the Government. The Society can do it at

very much less expense than the Government can, and on a much more reliable and less fluctuating basis, being subject, I mean, to none of the risks of external pressure and an annual vote.[102]

Realizing that the financial implications for government would be huge, and unwilling to take over the funding of education in Sierra Leone, it was only to be expected that Governor Berkeley would turn his back on Blyden's demand. In London, the liberal Kimberley had been replaced by the conservative Earl of Carnarvon as Secretary of State. In Sierra Leone, Hennessy had been succeeded as governor by Berkeley, and Reverend Johnson had been transferred to Lagos presumably to sever his alliance with Blyden. Thus Blyden was systematically subdued as his sympathizers were separated.

The way now seemed clear for Berkeley, 'with the bishop of Sierra Leone at his elbow', to advise the Colonial Office against Blyden's scheme.[103] In his despatch to the Earl of Carnarvon, therefore, Berkeley stated that the demand for a West African university had been met by the throwing open of Fourah Bay College to laymen.[104] In response to Berkeley the Secretary of State declared: 'I entertain ... grave doubts as to the expediency of attempting to establish a West African University', and thus concluded that he could not sanction such an undertaking 'which must of necessity be costly, and for which the natives are not yet sufficiently prepared'.[105] Blyden's hope for a positive response was dashed, and his demand was stifled. It is clear that the missionaries, led by the CMS, and supported by British officials, wrecked the efforts of Blyden and Johnson, Hennessy and Kimberley to establish a full-fledged university in West Africa.

But Blyden's scheme was not a total failure. It set in motion some sort of rethinking in CMS circles. Determined to forestall the possibility of any future haggling on the question of a 'godless university', the CMS parent committee met in London in July 1875 to discuss the university matter. The committee resolved to affiliate Fourah Bay with 'some English University' so that its students 'might have an advantage of a competitive examination and the opportunity of obtaining degrees'.[106] It was hoped that this decision would discourage any further agitation. The committee approved the suggestion of Sunter, the Principal of Fourah Bay, in favour of links with the University of Durham.

The choice of Durham may have been informed by two considerations. A precedent had already been set by Durham

University by its recent affiliation, early in 1875, with Codrington College, Barbados. The University of Durham had a very strong theological school which would consolidate the ecclesiastical programmes offered at Fourah Bay College.[107] Sunter had initially contemplated a link with the University of London, but the CMS did not favour that choice because the institution lacked two basic attractions. Within the CMS circle the University of London was considered a 'Godless University' because it did not demand that its staff and students be members of the Church of England (or any other church for that matter). Furthermore, it had no links with any other colonial college. In any case, after several months of negotiations the senate of the University of Durham finally recommended the affiliation which was unanimously carried by convocation on 16 May 1876.

The terms of affiliation allowed the students of Fourah Bay College to sit the same examinations as Durham students with the papers set and marked by that university. Once matriculated the names of Fourah Bay students were placed on the Register of the University of Durham.[108] The university programmes designed for Fourah Bay were those of BA pass, and the Licence in Theology (L.Th.). While a Licence in Theology was designed for those intending ordination in the Church of England, and also a step towards the BA pass, the latter 'stressed scriptural study and classics'.[109] Hence, although courses such as mathematics, English, history, geography and classics were added to Fourah Bay's curricula upon affiliation, the entire university education provided at the college remained fundamentally ecclesiastical. As Ashby aptly observed: 'In its emphasis on theology and the humanities, and its disregard of African environment, the character of instruction was simply the current type of missionary elementary education writ large.'[110]

Thus the CMS successfully hijacked the university scheme to cater to its own interests at the expense of the larger intellectual concern of Africans. Although degree courses were being provided at Fourah Bay, the content of the university education offered was hardly liberal or broad-based. In fact, it made a mockery of what Horton and Blyden had envisaged and 'it hovered uncertainly between a theological college and an incipient university'.[111] It was neither adapted to the African environment nor controlled by Africans. Caught between the opposition of the Colonial Office, the

Sierra Leone Government, and more seriously the CMS, Blyden despaired. Soon after, he returned to Liberia to accept an offer as the president of Liberia College.

Although Blyden's effort failed in its immediate purpose it did result in the establishment of the first university courses to be provided in British West Africa at Fourah Bay College. From its inception, however, Fourah Bay College suffered from financial starvation. The Colonial Office knew quite well that the British Treasury would not commit funds to the college and the Sierra Leonean Government did not wish to overstretch its lean budgets, and hence they both conveniently abstained from any serious involvement. Warily guarding its dominance, the CMS had bitten off more than it could chew. Consequently, the fortunes of the college faltered from lack of funds. In 1908, 30 years after affiliation, the funding crisis became so acute that the CMS considered discontinuing the university programme but it managed to continue until 1918 when the Wesleyans decided to co-operate with the CMS to maintain the college.

Lack of funds, the deficiency of courses provided, and also its strong theological bias, limited the number of enrolments at Fourah Bay. But despite its shortcomings, 'Fourah Bay enjoyed a great reputation with Africans as the only college in British West Africa at which degrees could be obtained ....'[112] The qualifications obtained from the college, even though mostly theological, carried the prestige of those obtained from Britain, a prestige which liberated Africans cherished dearly.

In the nineteenth century, therefore, there was a deep-rooted desire among educated Africans for a university. The efforts of Horton and Blyden in Sierra Leone were ahead of their time, and the initiatives came almost exclusively from educated Africans with the progression, via a sympathetic governor, to the Colonial Office. As will be shown later, this contrasts with the university campaigns of the 1930s and 1940s. The period between 1865 and 1890 was the era of the 'scramble and partition' when the talk of 'self-government', as mooted by the British Parliament in 1865, was evaporating and there was no longer a need for the creation of a well-educated African élite. Thus Horton's idea of the eventual transfer of power in the colonies to educated Africans could hardly get off the ground. Similarly, Blyden's more elaborate and sophisticated scheme, even with the sympathetic attention of Hennessy, failed to persuade the Colonial Office.

Perhaps the Colonial Office might have been interested had the plan for 'self-government' not dissipated before the 1870s. But by then the university scheme became impossible because it demanded British Treasury funds and ran totally counter to orthodox colonial financial policy. Furthermore, the CMS constituted a very powerful hostile lobby, determined to retain its monopoly in British African territories. Since the CMS in Sierra Leone provided what few social services (clinics and schools) there were, government was almost entirely dependent on them. This explains the final, very limited effect of the Horton/Blyden initiatives upon the Sierra Leone Government. Finally the CMS settled for linkages with Durham University to retain its monopoly, but this only led to a small degree granting institution, Fourah Bay College, which graduated laymen in Classics as well as clergy in Theology.

African desire for a fully fledged university persisted, but history began to move backward. The highly educated élite began to shrink in numbers, with leaders of less vision than Horton, Blyden, Grant and Johnson. This occurred because the 1865 idea of 'self-government' had been abandoned as the establishment of the empire became a matter of British policy; under the new policy, higher education for the continued expansion of a class of well-educated Africans was no longer encouraged and scholarships for Africans to pursue advanced training overseas were no longer emphasized. The increase in negative European racial attitudes as the era of scientific racism began to set in also contributed to the reduction in the highly educated class of Africans. European arrogance grew and the Western-educated Africans emerged as 'black Englishmen', while the era of the 'noble savage' was about to be ushered in by Frederick Lugard and his host of disciples. Consequently, the idea of a university, which received some attention in the mid-nineteenth century, was frowned upon by British colonial officials for almost the next 50 years.

NOTES

1. The term 'Creole' was first used in the sixteenth century to refer to people of Spanish ancestry born in the West Indies. In West Africa it was used in the nineteenth and early twentieth centuries to refer to the descendants of freed slaves and recaptives who were resettled in Sierra Leone.
2. The Igbo inhabit the south-eastern part of modern Nigeria. During the era of the slave trade they were known to have been victims in the human traffic which flowed down the Atlantic coast through the Aro middlemen, with the Efik and Ijaw in control. For details on the Aro-Igbo involvement see David Northrup, *Trade Without Rulers*, Clarendon Press, Oxford, 1978; A. E. Afigbo, 'The Eclipse of Aro Slaving Oligarchy of South-eastern Nigeria, 1901–21',

Journal of the Historical Society of Nigeria, Vol. 6, No. 1, 1971 and F. Ifeoma Ekejiuba, 'The Aro System of Trade in the Nineteenth Century', part 1&2, *Ikenga*, Vol. 1, No. 1&2, 1972.
3. John Peterson, *Province of Freedom: A History of Sierra Leone, 1787–1870*, Faber and Faber, London, 1969, pp. 284–286.
4. Ashby, *Universities: British, Indian, African*, p. 162, and Okafor, *The Development of Universities in Nigeria*, p. 11.
5. Peterson, *Province of Freedom*., pp. 284–286 and Ashby, *Universities: British, Indian, African*, p. 162. George gave the names of the first registered students in this new institution as Samuel Crowther, John Harvey, James Jones, John Pope, John Wright and William Samba in that order. See Claude George, *The Rise of British West Africa*, first published in 1904, and reprinted by Frank Cass, London, 1968, p. 424.
6. Refer to George, ibid., p. 423. Major-General Turner was the Governor of Sierra Leone between 1825 and 1826.
7. Ashby, *Universities: British, Indian, African*, p. 162.
8. Refer to Christopher Fyfe, *Africanus Horton: West African Scientist and Patriot*, Oxford University Press, New York, 1972, pp. 28–31. The other two were William Davies and Samuel Campbell. While Davies graduated with Horton, Campbell unfortunately died soon afterwards in Britain.
9. Akintola Wyse, *The Krio of Sierra Leone: An Interpretive History*, C. Hurst & Co., London, 1989, p. 34.
10. The period of study then prescribed for medical students in England varied from one institution to another. The University of London King's College insisted on six years of study before a student earned a medical doctorate. See Fyfe, *Africanus Horton*, pp. 30–31.
11. Edinburgh recognized King's three-year programme for an MRCS.
12. Arie J. Vanderploeg, 'Africanus Horton and the Idea of a University of Western Africa', *Journal of African Studies*, Vol.5, No.2, 1978, pp. 188–89. Refer also to Fyfe, *Africanus Horton*, pp. 91–118.
13. Horton to the Secretary of State for War, 13 July 1861 as reproduced in Davidson Nicol (ed.), *Black Nationalism in Africa: Extracts from the political, educational, scientific and medical writings of Africanus Horton*, Africana Publishing Corporation, New York, 1969, pp. 102–106.
14. Ibid., p. 105.
15. Ibid., p. 106. Refer also to Ashby, *Universities: British, Indian, African*, p. 170.
16. Ashby, ibid.
17. From Edward Lugard to Horton, 19 June 1862 as reproduced in Nicol, ibid., p. 108. General Edward Lugard was the Permanent Under-Secretary of State for War, 1861–71, and the uncle of Frederick (later, Lord) Lugard.
18. Horton to Secretary of State for War in Nicol (ed.), *Black Nationalism in Africa*, pp. 105–6.
19. See J.E. Flint, 'Economic Change in West Africa in the Nineteenth Century' in J.F. Ade Ajayi and Michael Crowder (eds), *History of West Africa*, Longman, London, 1974, pp. 395–396.
20. Horton to the President and members of the Educational Committee, War Office, 13 May 1862 as reproduced in Nicol, *Black Nationalism*, pp. 106–8.
21. John E. Flint, *Nigeria and Ghana*, Prentice-Hall, New Jersey, 1966, pp. 124–5.
22. See Robert July, *The Origins of Modern African Thought*, Frederick A. Praeger, New York, 1967, pp. 112–113. Britain looked forward to the eventual development of Westernized Christian societies in order to create the nucleus of an African middle class patterned on an English prototype.
23. Ibid., p. 110.
24. See as cited in Okafor, *The Development of Universities in Nigeria*, p. 19.
25. Christopher Fyfe, *A History of Sierra Leone*, Oxford University Press, Oxford, 1962, p. 337.
26. R. F. Burton, *Wanderings in West Africa*, Vol.1, pp. 266–268 as cited in July, *The Origins of Modern African Thought*, p. 118.
27. Okafor, *The Development of Universities in Nigeria*, p. 19. Most Creoles and liberated Africans in Sierra Leone were doing profitable business, and successfully competing with European merchants and traders.
28. Parliamentary Papers 1865, Vol.5, p. 2, *Report of the Select Committee on the State of British Settlements in West Africa*, House of Commons, 26 June 1865.
29. Flint, 'Economic Change in West Africa in the Nineteenth Century', p. 396.

30. J. A. B. Horton, *Political Economy of British Western Africa*, London, 1965.
31. James Africanus B. Horton, *West African Countries, British and Native. With the Requirements Necessary for Establishing that Self Government Recommended by the Committee of the House of Commons, 1865; and a Vindication of the African Race*, W. J. Johnson, London, 1868 and reprinted by Kraus Reprint, Nendeln, Switzerland, 1970.
32. Ibid., pp. 69 and 201. See also as reproduced in Nicol, *Black Nationalism in Africa*, pp. 97-102.
33. CMS Archives, CAI/0129(b) Papers on Education: The Grammar School Prospectus, as reproduced in Christopher Fyfe, *Sierra Leone Inheritance*, Oxford University Press, London, 1964, pp. 150-151.
34. E.A. Ayandele, *Holy Johnson: Pioneer of African Nationalism, 1836-1917*, Frank Cass, London, 1970, p. 71. The Grammar School was modelled on similar institutions in England with a curriculum which was largely classical and mathematical. Nevertheless, since it was founded and controlled by the CMS it is only predictable that it would have a strong religious bias.
35. Ibid.
36. P. E. Hair, 'An Analysis of the Register of Fourah Bay College, 1827-1950', *Sierra Leone Studies*, New Series, No.7, December 1956, p. 155.
37. Samuel Adjai Crowther was a recaptive from the Yoruba ethnic group of modern Nigeria. After his recapture by the British anti-slavery squadron he was taken to England for a few months by a missionary, and resettled in Sierra Leone where he began his missionary work after graduating from Fourah Bay in 1829. He later rose to prominence, and became the bishop of the Niger Mission in 1864. Refer to J. F. A. Ajayi *Christian Missions in Nigeria, 1841-1891: The Making of A New Elite*, Longmans, London, 1965, p. 26, and Fyfe, *Sierra Leone Inheritance*, p. 138.
38. Fyfe, *Africanus Horton*, p. 83.
39. Horton in Nicol, *Black Nationalism in Africa*, p. 97.
40. Horton, *West African Countries and Peoples*, p. 202.
41. George, *The Rise of British West Africa*, p. 415.
42. Vanderploeg, 'Africanus Horton...', p. 193.
43. CO 267/277 Minute by T. F. Elliott, Assistant Under-Secretary of State, on Governor Blackall's despatch No.18 of 16 February 1863, as cited in Fyfe, *Sierra Leone Inheritance*, pp. 189-190.
44. Fyfe, *Africanus Horton*, p. 83.
45. Horton, *West African Countries and Peoples*, p. 202.
46. Fyfe, *Africanus Horton*, p. 70.
47. Horton, *West African Countries and Peoples*, pp. 196, and 273-274. Horton asserted that the civilized continents of Europe and America were all involved in imitation and emulation, and hence Africa should not be an exception to that rule.
48. Horton to War Office, 13 May, 1862, as reproduced in Nicol, *Black Nationalism in Africa*, p. 107. Italics are as highlighted in the original correspondence.
49. Horton, *West African Countries and Peoples*, p. 48. Italics are Horton's.
50. Horton to War Office, 13 May 1862; and General Edward Lugard to Horton, 19 June 1862 as reproduced in Nicol, *Black Nationalism in Africa*. European resistance against African medical doctors seems to have involved quite deep questions of racism and racist psychology. The most common objection was that European women must not be examined by African doctors, however highly qualified, as this would break a sacred racial/sexual taboo. This eventually became the key argument for segregating the medical colonial service in the 1890s.
51. For details of French aggressive activity in West Africa which forced Britain to abandon its policy of abstention, see J. E. Flint, 'Britain and the Partition of West Africa', in John E. Flint and Glyndir Williams (eds), *Perspectives of Empire*, Longman, London, 1973; and 'The Growth of European Influence in West Africa in the Nineteenth Century' in J. F. Ade Ajayi and Ian Espie (eds), *A Thousand Years of West African History*, IUP, Ibadan, 1965, and G. N. Uzoigwe, 'European Partition and the Conquest of Africa: An Overview' in A. Adu Boahen (ed.), *UNESCO General History of Africa*, Vol.vii, University of California Press, Berkeley CA, 1985.
52. Evidence given to the Parliamentary Select Committee of 1865 confirmed that traders and missionaries would be content to operate beyond the area of British direct rule. See Fyfe,

Sierra Leone Inheritance, p. 189.
53. Fyfe, *Africanus Horton*, pp. 62 and 63.
54. P. O. Esedebe, 'Edward Wilmot Blyden (1832–1912): As Pan-African Theorist', *Sierra Leone Studies*, New Series, No. 25, July 1969, p. 14. Blyden was a contemporary of Horton. Since the Igbo, through the oracular devices of the Aro, were the most salient victims in the Atlantic Slave Trade, it is possible that Horton and Blyden's grandfathers were victims of the Aro slaving oligarchy.
55. Okafor, *The Development of Universities in Nigeria*, p. 26. Reverend Knox was an American in charge of the Dutch Reformed Church in St. Thomas, who guided Blyden in religious instruction.
56. E. W. Blyden, *Liberia's Offering*, J. A. Gray, New York, 1862, a biographical sketch, pp. i-iii. Refer also to V. Y. Mudimbe, *The Invention of Africa*, Indiana University Press, Indiana, 1988, p. 99; and Esedebe, 'Edward Wilmot Blyden...', p. 14.
57. Monrovia, capital of Liberia, was named in honour of President James Monroe of the United States.
58. See Hollis R. Lynch (ed.), 'Introduction', in *Black Spokesman: Selected Writings of Edward Wilmot Blyden*, Frank Cass, London, 1971, and Okafor, *The Development of Universities in Nigeria*, p. 26.
59. Refer to Blyden, *Liberia's Offering*, pp. iii-iv, and 27.
60. See July, *The Origins of Modern African Thought*, p. 211.
61. Lynch, 'Introduction', *Black Spokesman*, p. xiv. Roye and Blyden faced fierce political opposition because they were 'pure' blacks. The mulattos hated 'pure' blacks because they considered them 'uncivilized'. Even though these 'pure' blacks had no European blood, they controlled government. In reality, it was a struggle over power.
62. Refer to Henry S. Wilson, *Origins of West African Nationalism*, Macmillan, London, 1969, p. 229. Some literature on Blyden, for instance, Esedebe's 'Edward Wilmot Blyden (1832–1912): As Pan-African Theorist', left out the seduction story. Whether the story is false or not its deliberate exclusion from these writings tends to distort Blyden's biography. It would appear that European writers who seek to demonstrate that Blyden was not such a great man flaunt this story, while African scholars who seek to show that he was a distinguished patriot naturally expunge it. Either approach constitutes a distortion.
63. Ayandele, *Holy Johnson*, p. 36; see also his 'An Assessment of James Johnson and His Place in Nigerian History, 1878–1917', part 1, in *Journal of the Historical Society of Nigeria*, Vol. 2, No. 4, 1963, p. 498.
64. Ayandele, *Holy Johnson*, p. 36; refer also to James Bertin Webster, *The African Churches Among the Yoruba, 1888–1922*, Clarendon Press, Oxford, 1964. Webster regards the discrimination against African clergy as partly responsible for the formation of African churches.
65. Ayandele, *The Missionary Impact on Modern Nigeria, 1842–1914*, Longman, London, 1966.
66. Edward W. Blyden to Reverend Henry Venn dated 17 April 1872 as reproduced in Hollis R. Lynch (ed.), *Selected Letters of Edward Wilmot Blyden*, KTO Press, New York, 1878, pp. 112–113.
67. July, *The Origins of Modern African Thought*, p. 228.
68. Blyden to Venn in Lynch (ed.), *Selected Letters of Edward Wilmot Blyden*, p. 113. In other words, Blyden was more or less agreeing with Europeans who despised the educated Africans. In any case, he blamed the Europeans for the miseducation of Africans.
69. See Edward Blyden to William Grant, dated 22 May 1872, in Lynch, *Black Spokesman*, pp. 223–5. Grant was the son of Igbo receptive parents. Through personal efforts he became a successful trader in Sierra Leone attracting the attention of British officials. Although he did not use the term 'university' in the Council's debate, his plea certainly galvanized Blyden.
70. Blyden to Grant, p. 225.
71. William Grant to Edward Blyden, 23 May 1872, *The West African University*, Negro Printing Office, Freetown, 1872, p. 4.
72. Edward W. Blyden to Governor John Pope Hennessy, dated 6 December 1872, in *The West African University: Correspondence Between Edward W. Blyden and J. Pope Hennessy*, Negro Printing Office, Freetown, 1872, pp. 6–8; see also as reproduced in Eric Ashby, *Universities: British, Indian, African*, pp. 226–228.
73. Ibid.

IMPERIALISM, ACADEME AND NATIONALISM

74. Ibid., pp. 6–8. Blyden attempted to flatter Hennessy by asserting that 'it would be the crown and glory of all the beneficent acts' if the university which he proposed was organised under his administration.
75. Edward W. Blyden to Governor Hennessy, dated 9 December 1872 in *The West African University*, p. 11.
76. Ibid., p. 10. As a means of developing the intellectual and moral character of the people, Blyden insisted that the university was most desirable.
77. Governor Hennessy to Edward W. Blyden, dated 10 December 1872, in *The West African University*, p. 12.
78. Ibid., pp. 12–13.
79. Ayandele, *Holy Johnson*, p. 77.
80. Edward W. Blyden to Hennessy, dated 11 December 1872, in *The West African University*, p. 13.
81. Ibid., pp. 13–14.
82. Governor Hennessy to Edward W. Blyden, dated 11 December 1872, in ibid., p. 15.
83. William Grant to Edward Blyden, 13 December 1872, in ibid., p. 6.
84. Edward W. Blyden to Hennessy, dated 14 December 1872, in ibid., p. 16.
85. Ibid., p. 17.
86. Hennessy to Blyden, dated 14 December 1872, as reproduced in Ashby, *Universities: British, Indian, African*, p. 456.
87. Ibid., p. 163.
88. Hennessy to the Earl of Kimberley, dated 28 December 1872 as reproduced in Ashby, ibid., pp. 456–458.
89. Ashby, ibid.
90. Ashby, ibid., p. 164.
91. CO 267/317, Secretary of State to Governor Keate of Sierra Leone, dated 5 February 1873 as reproduced in Ashby, ibid., p. 459.
92. Ayandele, 'An Assessment of James Johnson ....', p. 500.
93. Metcalfe Sunter to E. Hutchinson (Secretary, Church Missionary Society, London), dated 7 June 1873 as reproduced in Ashby, ibid., pp. 465–466.
94. Henry Cheetham (Bishop of Sierra Leone) to Henry Wright (Honorary Secretary of CMS, London), dated 13 March 1873 as reproduced in Ashby, ibid., pp. 463–464.
95. Henry Wright to Henry Cheetham, 10 March 1873 as reproduced in Ashby, ibid., pp. 468–469.
96. On this cost-saving argument as put forward by Henry Venn, see James Bertin Webster, *The African Churches Among the Yoruba, 1888–1922*, pp. 4–6.
97. Metcalfe Sunter to E. Hutchinson, dated 20 June 1873 as reproduced in Ashby, ibid., pp. 466–67.
98. Edward W. Blyden to the Earl of Kimberley, dated 22 October 1873 as reproduced in Hollis R. Lynch (ed.), *Selected Letters of Edward Wilmot Blyden*, KTO Press, New York, 1978, pp. 144–146.
99. Ibid., p. 144.
100. Ashby, *Universities: British, Indian, Africa*, p. 459.
101. CO 267/324, Kimberley to Berkeley, dated 16 December 1873 as reproduced in ibid., p. 460.
102. The Bishop of Sierra Leone to Governor Berkeley, dated 17 April 1874 as reproduced in Ashby, ibid., pp. 460–461. What the Bishop had in mind was the opening up of Fourah Bay College and expanding its scope, and not necessarily establishing a university as Blyden demanded. The CMS dreaded Government intervention in education which would ultimately reduce its proselytizing influence in West Africa.
103. Ashby, *Universities: British, Indian, African*, p. 459.
104. CO 879/8, Governor Berkeley to the Earl of Carnarvon, dated 8 May 1874 as reproduced in Ashby, ibid., p. 460.
105. CO 879/8, Earl of Carnarvon to Governor Berkeley, dated 12 June 1874 as reproduced in Ashby, ibid., p. 462.
106. Minute of CMS Committee Meeting of 20 July 1875 as reproduced in Ashby, p. 470.
107. Ashby, ibid., p. 166.
108. See 'The Terms of Affiliation: Durham University Regulations' as reproduced in Ashby, ibid., pp. 471–473.

109. Ashby, ibid. Refer also to P. E. H. Hair, 'An Analysis of the Register of Fourah Bay College', *Sierra Leone Studies*, New Series, No.7, December 1956, p. 156.
110. Ashby, ibid., p. 167.
111. Ashby, ibid., p. 169.
112. Ashby, ibid., p. 169.

2 Indirect Rule, Education for Intermediaries, and the Impact of Criticism 1900–34

Between 1876 and 1900 there were virtually no serious demands for an African university comparable to those made earlier by Horton and Blyden. Although in the early 1890s Blyden attempted to instigate some agitation with Reverend James Johnson for the establishment of a university in Lagos, his efforts failed to yield positive results.[1] Like Hennessy of Sierra Leone, Governor Carter of Lagos pointed out that 'unless Africans took the initiative of founding such an institution, no aid could be expected from government'.[2] Similarly, like their Sierra Leone counterparts, educated Lagosians expected colonial government to bear the costs of the higher education of Africans. Blyden's effort to raise an initial sum of £2,000 from wealthy Lagosians in 1891 and 1896 failed woefully.[3] From then until 1920 no further realistic effort was made by Africans for a university. Blyden was worn out, having failed to achieve his lifetime ambition of a university in either Sierra Leone or Nigeria. The idea remained somewhat wishful thinking among educated Africans as African colonial governments stiffened their opposition to such schemes.

However, by 1900 the 'scramble and partition' of Africa was virtually over although some interior polities would not be brought under colonial administration until the late 1920s. The various colonial powers began to settle down to the business of governing their newly appropriated territories. The era of informal influence had come to a close, and Britain had to assume real political responsibility for governing her African territories. Dragged into territorial acquisition largely by the aggressive inroads of the French and their protectionist tariff policies in Africa, Britain faced difficult administrative choices, even though the new imperial scheme would definitely require huge spending. Because of the Treasury's reluctance to spend in the colonies, British colonial officials focused on how to maintain minimal government for the least cost. Indirect rule was designed fundamentally to cater to this financial parsimony.

First experimented with by Britain in India and Malaya, indirect rule was a system of administering the colonial peoples through their traditional political institutions. In Africa, Lord Lugard, who first introduced the system in the well-organized Buganda kingdom of Uganda, had no hesitation in extending it to northern Nigeria in the early 1900s, and later, supporting it in other British territories. Frederick Cooper, however, suggests that the British adopted this administrative system following the failure of the earlier 'interventionist imperial policy' of 'remaking rural African society' in the name of 'economic progress and social justice'.[4] One of the major features of the system was its reliance on African chiefs which was predicated upon the false assumption that 'all Africans were ruled by chiefs if not kings'.[5] Predictably, this assumption marred the success of the system in areas like south-eastern Nigeria and eastern Uganda where the British, still applying the Lugardian theory, ended up 'inventing' chiefs for societies whose political traditions were opposed to chiefly autocracy.[6]

Despite its shortcomings indirect rule met British objectives. It ensured minimum spending and 'met the need to rule broad areas with millions of subjects of diverse races and levels of development with the least possible outlay and a minimum of British personnel'.[7] Indirect rule was meant to prevent political conflicts between the British and African chiefs, and between officials and the African masses. In other words, it ensured followership, and diminished the frequency of civil disobedience since Africans had the erroneous impression that orders from the Native Administration issued from their chiefs. Ostensibly, the chiefs served as a buffer between the aggrieved masses and British colonial officials. This gave many Africans the false impression that since they were governed by their traditional rulers the old system (paramountcy of chiefs, kings, emperors and gerontocrats) continued with the British acting merely as overseers. So powerful was this myth that during decolonization in the 1960s the Baganda insisted that they were not subjects of the British but partners and allies.

Above the numerous Native Administrations of the chiefs and their resident supervisors, the central government of the colonial administration functioned under a governor with a senior service of all white officers (with high salaries, regular paid home leave, housing, paid education for children in Britain, clothing and other allowances, attractive pensions) and a junior service of Africans with none of the above. The vast majority of Europeans were thus clustered in the capital city of any colony, living together in garden-like suburbs often known as GRAs (Government Reserved Areas), and segregated from the African population usually by the military and police barracks. These pampered civil servants lived in housing and enjoyed a palatial life-style which no chief or even well-to-do African merchant could ever hope to emulate. Providing senior service amenities became the first and one of the heaviest charges upon the finance of the new colonies. This burden must always be kept in mind as the colonial cry of lack of finance continued to echo from one decade to another. At the very time when there was no money for a university, an all-white hospital with housing for its white directors and nurses might be under construction to provide free medical services to the Europeans. From an African perspective finance always seemed to flow effortlessly.

African personnel who spoke English began to be used, albeit in subordinate positions and at lower salaries, in order to save costs as well as to maintain stability. They were required to serve in junior and subordinate positions as clerks and assistants in government departments, and more were required following the depletion of the regular staff of the colonial service during the First World War. Highly educated Africans remained an aberration to the system. They would either seek to compete with Europeans for higher posts in the colonial service or destabilize the Native Administration system dominated by African chiefs. Hence the idea of establishing universities in Africa was vehemently opposed by colonial officials. African chiefs who benefited under the system naturally remained indifferent, if not hostile to the aspirations of the educated class. Alienated and relegated, African educated elements predictably began to oppose – or more often seek to reform – British rule, culminating in the emergence of the 'nationalist' movements from the 1920s onward.

However, the nature of indirect rule in East Africa, particularly in Uganda, presented a sharp contrast with West Africa. The dominant

Kingdom of Buganda, with its chiefly and royal élite, had negotiated its way into the British Empire on privileged terms as consolidated in the Buganda Agreement of 1900.[8] This agreement recognized the Baganda chiefs as British political agents, transformed them into a landed oligarchy, and granted them legislative powers and access to state-related employment. It further guaranteed that the Kabaka (King) and his chiefs 'would be the principal class mediating between the colonial power and the common people'.[9] Before the establishment of colonial rule, the Baganda had been receptive to alien ideas. As Sir Harry Johnston observed, there was a constant desire by the chiefs to bring their country into harmony with European ideas and development.[10] Unlike most African ruling groups, the dominant elements of the Baganda chiefly and royal classes had embraced Christianity, and its Protestant elements laid special stress on literacy in the period before colonial rule.[11]

Significantly, missionaries in Uganda, unlike their counterparts in West Africa, worked from the upper segment of society downwards. They had little choice because neither the common people nor the chiefly élite would tolerate any other method. Thus by 1920 the Baganda traditional élite had become the educated, economically secure, upper class who dominated the protectorate. So while indirect rule sought to stifle the expansion of the educated class in West Africa, it desired to cater to that group in Uganda. There was little distinction in Uganda between the traditional chiefly élite and Protestant educated élite. They were one and the same. However, the education provided for the East African chiefly élite did not go beyond primary and secondary training because university education still remained an anomaly to colonial officials.

Again, in contrast to West Africa, it became more prestigious to work for the Kabaka's government – a Native Administration according to West African terminology – than for the British colonial regime. An ambitious Muganda could rise higher, be paid more, work primarily in the vernacular, deal with a greater range of modern problems and find more dignity in the Kabaka's rather than the colonial administration. While the demand for a university in West Africa was spearheaded by the excluded educated élite, from the 1920s such agitation in Uganda was led by the Baganda privileged chiefs. Nevertheless, in both West Africa and East Africa the vested interest of the colonial officials remained the preservation of their tenure by keeping the educated African out of higher posts in the service.

The period between 1920 and 1930 marked a watershed in the history of the development of higher educational institutions in Africa. It witnessed the emergence of the National Congress of British West Africa (NCBWA), which turned itself increasingly into a political force with which West African colonial governments and the Colonial Office had to reckon. It was during the period that the American Education Commission on Africa, under the auspices of the Phelps-Stokes Fund, visited Africa to survey the education of the African peoples generally. This was followed by the appointment of an Advisory Committee on Native Education in Tropical Africa by the British Government, and the issuance of a White Paper marking the first education policy to be outlined by Britain on the education of its African subjects. The period also witnessed the foundation of Achimota and Makerere Colleges in the Gold Coast and Uganda respectively, and the preliminary arrangement to establish the Yaba Higher College in Nigeria.

From 1911, 'the torch of higher education in British West Africa' passed from Blyden to J. E. Casely Hayford and other West African politicians.[12] Casely Hayford was born on 3 September 1866 in the Anona clan on the Gold Coast, and was the fourth son of Reverend Joseph de Graft Hayford. He attended the Wesleyan Boys' High School at Cape Coast, and later went to Fourah Bay College in Sierra Leone where he secured his teacher's certificate. After teaching for a while at Cape Coast, Casely Hayford left for London for a legal education. On 17 November 1896 he was called to the bar and, soon after, returned to the Gold Coast to begin his remarkable career as a barrister, journalist and nationalist.

Hayford's plea for a West African university was first elaborated in his book, *Ethiopia Unbound*, published in 1911.[13] Arguing that 'you cannot educate a people unless you have a suitable training ground', Casely Hayford made a case for a West African university to be located in Kumasi, on the Gold Coast.[14] Conscious that Western educational methods had denationalized and enslaved Africans to foreign thought and ways of life, Casely Hayford envisioned the university of his dream 'to be the means of revising erroneous current ideas regarding the African, of raising him in self-respect; and of making him an efficient co-worker in the uplifting of man to nobler effort'.[15] Casely Hayford thus wished to preserve African identity and national consciousness while opening up the minds of Africans to Western education.

He proposed that the teachers in his envisaged institution be drawn from the ranks of locally trained university men. In an effort to preserve what was uniquely African, he also proposed a chair in history which should emphasize 'the part Ethiopia had played in the affairs of the world'. In addition, he envisaged separate chairs for the study of Fanti, Hausa and Yoruba languages as 'the safest and most natural way of national conservancy and evolution'. Deeply concerned about the corrupting influences of the European presence on the coastal peoples, Casely Hayford preferred to site the university in the interior of the Gold Coast.

> As a precautionary measure, I would take care to place the educational seminary in a region far beyond the reach of the influence of the coast.... It is not the spoilt educated African that may be expected to help in the regenerative work of the world. The unspoilt son of the tropics, nursed in the tropical atmosphere, favourable to the growth of national life, he it is who may show us the way.[16]

Clearly, Casely Hayford's argument for a West African university, and an education which would preserve African cultural identity and race instincts, seems to mirror Blyden's ideas. Ashby noted this when he concluded that 'it was Blyden's argument over again'.[17] This is not surprising because having attended Fourah Bay College after its affiliation to the University of Durham, Casely Hayford was undoubtedly aware of the controversy surrounding the institution of degree programmes there. Hence when Hayford suggested locating the West African university in the interior he was re-echoing Blyden who had contended that he preferred his proposed West African university to be situated away from the foreign influences of the seaboard and within the stimulus of the interior.[18]

Nevertheless, a world of difference existed between Blyden and Hayford. While Blyden was interested in arousing and consolidating African race consciousness especially among blacks in the diaspora, Hayford sought to develop an African national pride and to reclaim African political rights. Unlike Horton and Blyden, Hayford's call for a West African university was at first reserved to the pages of his book. He did not call for immediate action from the colonial government or the Colonial Office. It was not until the 1920s that he pushed the university idea through the platform of the NCBWA (which he helped to found, and which was composed exclusively of West

African educated elements). It is this that sets Hayford apart – he made the university question a political issue encompassing all the British West African territories and not merely a local affair of one colony.

It was not accidental that some educational advance was made during the 1920s. The period immediately following the First World War had stimulated the political and social consciousness of the colonial peoples. British colonial rule had by now been firmly established, and British determination to consolidate indirect rule, calm nationalist agitations, and convince the international community under the League of Nations that the welfare of the colonial peoples mattered in their considerations meant that something had to be done. Equally, there was a realization on the part of the British that if they did not face the question of the provision of higher educational facilities for Africans then the Americans might be eager to interfere. The consequence of such interference was weighed against the background of the rise of nationalism, which together might constitute a political danger to British rule in Africa.

It was at this point that Casely Hayford acted in 1920 when he convened the meeting of the leaders of the West African educated élite in Accra to form the NCBWA. Seeking the expansion of its class and continuing the tradition of agitation for higher training for Africans, the Congress resolved that 'the time has come to found a British West African University on such lines as would preserve in the student a sense of African Nationality'.[19] Obviously this resolution reflected Casely Hayford's belief in the importance of preserving African cultural identity in the educational process. It was an epoch-making conference because it was the first time the African educated élite, attracting delegates from Nigeria, Sierra Leone, the Gambia and the Gold Coast, had met to discuss the university question and other related issues.[20] Casely Hayford, therefore, ignited the flame of widespread nationalist agitation for the establishment of a West African university among this group, an issue which had hitherto been individualized. His contribution to the question of an African university lay in his ability to make the demand a pan-West African question. Furthermore, if finance was the British problem then surely sharing the burden among the four colonies was the logical path to follow.

Later that same year the NCBWA sent a delegation to London to present its resolutions to King George V through the Secretary of

State for the Colonies. The delegation failed to achieve its purpose; the Secretary of State refused to grant them audience. Many West African chiefs led by 'the important and influential' Gold Coast chief, Nana Ofori Atta, were opposed to the Congress.[21] They sought to protect their own interests and hence vilified the NCBWA group, and colonial governments were quick to denigrate the delegation as unrepresentative of the people. Despite the silence of chiefs in Nigeria, Governor Hugh Clifford, for instance, dismissed them as 'a self-selected and self-appointed congregation of educated African gentlemen'.[22] Thus the university question was not entertained by London. But the Colonial Office and colonial governments had been reminded that the issues of educational reform and the provision of university facilities could not be written off completely in British imperial considerations.

It is not surprising that some African chiefs and colonial governments presented such opposition to the Congress. The workings of the British indirect rule policy dictated such a response. Under that system, the chiefs revelled in their elevated positions to the exasperation and frustration of the African educated class. Indirect rule 'created a basic antagonism between the traditionalists and the emergent educated minority'.[23] The system of indirect rule offered no roles for educated Africans and it was only to be expected that the British would seek to suppress them. Likewise, since the educated élite (or more accurately its spokesmen in the NCBWA) were calling for the abolition of the Native Administration system, and the introduction of an embryonic parliamentary structure built upon the legislative councils, a clash between the educated élites and the chiefs was unavoidable.[24] Thus the opposition of African chiefs and colonial governments to the NCBWA delegation to London was quite fundamental. An African university was perceived as a means to expanding the educated élite class who would neither be accommodated under the Native Administration system nor employed in higher positions in the colonial service. Colonial governments thus continued to stifle proposals for such an establishment.

The Congress demonstrated considerable perception in seeing that a university and indirect rule were absolutely incompatible. However, the 1920s was a decade when indirect rule would reach the height of its popularity among the British. Lugard would publish his *Dual Mandate* and colonies which had never experimented with chiefly rule would be encouraged to establish it even where it appeared almost ridiculous: for instance, in Kenya where the Kikuyu had lost their lands and were being forced into migrant labour networks. Under the spell of indirect rule, British administrators lost their proud tradition of pragmatism and turned to a theory which they seemed determined to impose despite local circumstances. Any institution (such as a university) which could be shown as contrary to the theory had little hope of success. Little wonder the governors spoke so hotly against the idea. British opinion had also begun to swing against the academic bias of education which the missions had been providing. They toyed with ideas of vernacular education, proposing that secondary schools should emphasize crafts and manual training in order to create a new, basically educated class which would feed into the chiefly administrations. Leaders of the Congress became voices crying in a wilderness of hostility.

Meanwhile between 1920 and 1924 the Phelps-Stokes Foundation of the United States sent out a Commission to survey the nature and quality of education in Africa. The Commission visited West, South, and Equatorial Africa in 1920–21, and East Africa in 1923. Primarily concerned with 'Negro' education in the United States, the Phelps-Stokes Foundation had been persuaded by the Foreign Mission Conference of North America to sponsor the African enterprise.[25] The Commission, which was headed by Thomas Jesse Jones, had an African member – J. E. K. Aggrey of the Gold Coast.[26] Aggrey no doubt provided an inspiration to many Africans who listened to him. As the first African to be so elevated, Aggrey's status not only demonstrated that the British were suppressing African aspirations but also served as 'an embodiment of African accomplishments'.[27] The reports of the Commission[28] 'found much to criticise in the British possessions' in Africa.[29] The Commission observed that education in Africa had been largely a transplantation of the British system with no visible adaptation to the reality of the African environment. Furthermore,

> [i]t seems clear that the educational policies of the governments and the missions have hitherto been inadequate and to a considerable extent unreal so far as the vital needs of Africa are concerned.[30]

On the question of higher education, the Commission observed that there were only two institutions in the colonies visited – Fourah

Bay College in Sierra Leone and the South African Native College at Fort Hare – which offered a few courses of university level. However, they criticized the subjects taught in these colleges as too classical and ecclesiastical to the abject neglect of social science, agriculture, physical science, and even history. The Commission further regretted that while the educational goal of the missionaries was proselytization, that of the colonial governments was the production of clerical help for the administration.[31] The educational motives of missionaries and government were suspect. Pointing out that a number of Africans had distinguished themselves in the universities of Europe and America in the fields of medicine, law, theology and engineering, the Commission asserted that 'Africa should have its own colleges' if the development of Native leadership were to be achieved.[32]

Clearly the report of the Phelps-Stokes Commission marked a turning point in British education in Africa. Ashby stressed that for many the report of the Commission constituted 'a first introduction to the education-hunger of the African people and it had a profound effect on both sides of the Atlantic'.[33] C. K. Graham agrees, adding that it 'helped to give a fillip to educational expansion ... in Africa'.[34] Britain disliked any criticism suggesting official neglect of the welfare of the colonial peoples and, shortly before and after the publication of the report of the Commission in 1922, began somewhat feverish moves in search of a consistent educational policy for its African subjects.

Before the Commission's visits, the governments of Uganda and the Gold Coast had initiated some slow but progressive moves towards the higher training of Africans for colonial service. These efforts were accelerated in the 1920s by the visit of Phelps-Stokes Commission. Depleted by the drafting of many colonial officials into the army, and given the economic recession, after 1922 most African governments began to look to Africans to fill the intermediate positions in the colonial service. In describing the East African situation, as exemplified by Uganda, John Cameron notes that

> Just before World War I and especially just after it, government interest in education increased not so much because it had become more benign but because of its own needs for more educated and trained men and women – supervisors, clerks, storemen, hospital orderlies, nurses, dispensers, telegraphists, drivers, and artisans of many kinds.[35]

With the development of colonial economies and growing complexities of government, a need arose for what might be termed a middle civil service between the high salaried senior Europeans and the miserably paid African clerks, messengers and interpreters. This middle level required a type of training which the mission schools had not been offering and generally were not interested in providing.

Since most of the intermediate posts required some education beyond secondary level, it became necessary to train Africans for them. In September 1919, the Governor of Uganda, Robert Coryndon, set up an Education Committee to 'discuss without delay the part Government should play in education'.[36] In September 1920 the Governor obtained the approval of the Secretary of State, Winston Churchill, to open a 'Native' technical school in Kampala. A Board was appointed to find a suitable site. Out of the two sites considered – Bombo and Makerere – the latter was selected because of its proximity to Kampala, the centre of the dominant Baganda culture. Construction work began in March 1921, and in January 1922 classes started in the school with fourteen day boys who enrolled for courses in carpentry, building and mechanics.

In August 1922, the name of the school was changed to Makerere College since, according to the Principal, H. O. Saville, 'the term technical is not broad enough to include all the vocational training it is designed to give'.[37] The Principal did not act of his own volition. Initially the institution was to be of higher learning. But by the time colonial officials had mulled it over, it had become a technical college. The chiefly élite were outraged that their children were to be trained as 'technicians'. Thus Saville introduced the vague concept of vocational education which tended to mean one thing to the chiefs and quite another to the colonial officials. Thereafter, medical training began under Dr H. B. Owen who taught students in physics, chemistry, biology and pre-clinical subjects for two years before transferring them to Mulago hospital for clinical work.[38] Soon, courses in surveying, engineering and agriculture were added. The Ugandan Government was aware of the Phelps-Stokes' criticism of West African administrations over the narrow educational philosophy of the missions, which de-emphasized technical and vocational in favour of literary education.

Similarly, in March 1920, Governor Gordon Guggisberg of the Gold Coast appointed an Educationists' Committee.[39] This coincided with the visit to West Africa of the Phelps-Stokes Commission. The

Committee was given a mandate to investigate past educational efforts and the methods, principles and policy which should govern the progress of education in the colony.[40] The Committee recommended the establishment of a Secondary Boarding School at Achimota, near Accra. This signalled the beginning of an attempt to provide Africans with sound secondary education in the Gold Coast. Fired by the new concept of African education as laid out in the Phelps-Stokes report of 1922, Guggisberg appointed a new committee in May of the same year. With an African majority, this new committee was charged to report on how to make the Achimota plan a reality.[41] The new Gold Coast Educationists' Committee reported promptly in August 1923 and recommended the immediate development of higher educational facilities in Achimota.[42]

Clearly, government interest in higher education in both Uganda and the Gold Coast during this period was driven by the fundamental objective to supply the various government departments with intermediate African staff. The hiring of Europeans had become difficult as well as expensive to colonial governments.[43] For the Gold Coast, educated Africans were required to fill intermediate posts because the government 'could not afford to fill the increasing number of these posts with Europeans' considering the cost of their maintenance.[44]

In contrast to Nigeria, indirect rule was not strictly implemented in the Gold Coast during Guggisberg's time.[45] The Gold Coast operated a different system of chieftaincy, particularly among the Ga and Fante, whose chiefs were literate, elected, and could be unseated by electors. Hence conflicts between the chiefs and educated élite were more 'enlightened' and differed from those in Nigeria. The foundation of Achimota resulted from a combination of Guggisberg – a type of governor Nigeria had not yet had – and a more vociferous educated element.

In Uganda, similarly, Africans with technical training were required in the government departments to 'replace the more highly paid Asian artisans'.[46] Uganda had a well developed system of indirect rule with an expanded Native Authority, Native Courts, and Native Treasuries. But unlike the Gold Coast and Nigeria the educated Africans in Uganda did not develop as a separate class from the chiefly aristocracy, dominated by the Baganda. Since the chiefs constituted the larger proportion of the educated class, there was less fear about the disruptive influence of Western education and civilization. If anything, educated chiefs were seen as an added advantage to the Native Administration system and, normally, were preferred to the illiterate ones. In other words, education 'did not lead to the growth of an uprooted minority in an open hostility to the whole native administration system' as in West Africa.[47]

The real demand for educated men in Uganda was felt in the Native Administration of the Kabaka which controlled a whole host of modern functions which in West Africa were the exclusive preserve of the colonial administration. Most graduates of Makerere were likely to find jobs with the mission societies or within the Kabaka's government. Colonial officials rarely saw their own jobs threatened by them since most educated Baganda did not wish to work for the colonial administration which they felt was alien, uncomfortable and detached from their society. This attitude persisted even after decolonization had begun. By that time it was the other ethnic groups of Uganda, and not the Baganda, who began to stock the colonial civil service in the process of Africanization. Buganda became the example, *par excellence,* of indirect rule and the closest approximation to fulfilling the theory as Lugard had conceived of it. It is against this background that the Ugandan government's growing interest in education in the period, even if defective in scope and content, contrasted with that of West African colonial regimes.

However the exigency of the indirect rule system, the increasing need for a middle-level manpower, and the somewhat obsessive determination of colonial officials to guard their esteemed positions from African competitors should not cloud our judgement about the genuine intentions of some officials. Guggisberg, for instance, has often been portrayed as the most progressive of all the West African governors on educational matters.[48] Sammy Tenkorang would disagree. To him, Guggisberg's Achimota scheme was primarily undertaken 'in order not to turn moderate chiefs and other nationalists into extremists' over the university question as advocated by the NCBWA[49] Nevertheless, imperial and African commentators retained high regard for Guggisberg even if his Achimota plan was designed to make educated Africans accept indirect rule. Arthur Mayhew asserted that in Guggisberg, 'the Gold Coast found the right man, a man of vision, at the right time when there was a large revenue surplus'.[50]

In Nigeria, conversely, despite an increasing need for trained personnel in government services from the 1920s, colonial officials were not prepared to establish an institution of higher learning. For them, higher education 'was clearly a means of enabling Africans to compete for senior posts in the civil [colonial] service'.[51] In the Gold Coast, Governor Guggisberg was, at least, advocating the Achimota idea 'as a stepping stone to a University' irrespective of the hostility of other European officials who had 'a subconscious fear about their own declining influence and authority, even to the loss of jobs, if Achimota were ... to fulfil the governor's hopes'.[52]

Guggisberg did not allow the question of the possible friction between the African traditional and educated élites to affect his educational vision. Although, as a personal friend of Aggrey, he regarded the well-educated African as a 'crucial bridge' between European colonial rule and the African masses, he was not as liberal minded as he has often been depicted.[53] He was aware of the political effects on British rule of an unregulated African education, and he was basically preoccupied with how to fill the increasing openings in the intermediate cadres of the colonial service.

The same was true of Governor Coryndon of Uganda. Coryndon was a firm believer in practical as opposed to literary education. His Makerere scheme, according to Christopher Youé, was partly 'a response to the shortage of skilled artisans' as well as 'an attempt to accommodate growing African demands for education'.[54] In the case of Nigeria, the vested interests of the colonial officials, and their commitment to shield the chiefs (their indirect rulers) from the hostility of the educated élite, obliged them to oppose the idea of higher education vehemently. The Northern emirs particularly were not attracted to Western education even though the Southern chiefs remained indifferent. For the Nigerian Government, therefore,

> it was enlightened self-interest to prevent the emergence of a politically restive class that might result from the establishment of a University College. That would negate the very basis of colonial subordination, it would help to create a class of competitors to colonial authorities instead of producing political stewards.[55]

American involvement and the consequent critical reports of the Phelps-Stokes Commission together with the unguided educational efforts in the various colonies, prompted the Secretary of State for the Colonies to set up an Advisory Committee on Native Education in Tropical Africa (ACNETA) in November 1923, under the chairmanship of the Parliamentary Under-Secretary of State, W. G. A. Ormsby-Gore. Other members were Frederick Lugard, who implemented the system of indirect rule in northern Nigeria; James Currie, who had been a director of education in the Sudan; Hans Vischer who designed a school system in northern Nigeria; J. H. Oldham, who brought to the Committee a lifetime's experience from the mission; Michael Sadler, C. Strachey and A. J. Church of the Colonial Office; and Bishop M. Bidwell as well as the Bishop of Liverpool.[56] Given its composition, the Advisory Committee would naturally defend the principles of the indirect rule system as well as preserve missionary interests. The terms of reference of the Committee were:

> To advise the Secretary of State on any matters of Native Education in the British Colonies and Protectorates in Tropical Africa which he may from time to time refer to them; and to assist him in advancing the progress of education in those Colonies and Protectorates.[57]

Although the British response was quite unusual it was also predictable. Hitherto the education of Africans had been left to the discretion of the missionaries and colonial governments whose efforts depended on their respective group interest, both real and imagined. Many years of persistent African demands for government participation in mission-dominated education, as demonstrated in the efforts of Horton, Blyden and Hayford, had consistently yielded no positive British response. This was largely predicated on the British Government's insistence that colonial governments must be self-supporting. Abstention from educational matters, therefore, was preferred on the premise that much involvement would ultimately imply financial commitment.[58] It was convenient for Britain to leave the entire enterprise to voluntary agencies dominated by the missions, which bore the financial responsibility. But from the 1920s other considerations began to impinge on British educational arrangements in the colonies. These considerations, seemingly more political, made abstention from direct involvement not only undesirable but also harmful to Britain's imperial image.

By the end of the First World War, with its massive carnage and destruction, the colonizing powers of Europe were exhausted, and their confidence in the perfection of their civilization was greatly shaken. New concepts of national self-determination 'forced government to reconsider their colonial policies' resulting in the principle of trusteeship which was intended to be more humane.[59] Consequently a more critical attitude came to be adopted towards the quantitative and qualitative aspects of colonial education. To be accused of economic exploitation of the colonies in utter neglect of the social and economic well-being of the people was abhorred by the colonizing powers in the stimulating aftermath of the war. The Phelps-Stokes Commission visited Africa against this background. In reaction to the changing climate of opinion, Britain began to take more direct steps in the education of its African colonial subjects.

Although initiated by a missionary body it would appear that the Colonial Office was hardly comfortable with the American involvement under the auspices of the Phelps-Stokes Foundation. The naked criticism that the Commission levelled against British education in Africa represented a direct indictment of British colonial rule. It was partly to present British colonial policy as more humane as well as to avoid further American intervention that the Colonial Office quickly appointed the ACNETA which began to advise the British Government on the best approach to education in Africa.[60] Even if one agrees with Ashby that the appointment of the ACNETA was nothing more than a British 'conventional response',[61] there is no question that it was unprecedented in relation to education in Africa, which, hitherto, had been a 'no go' area for the Colonial Office in London.

As a result of the recommendations of the Phelps-Stokes Commission, the demands of the colonial service, and the consequent appointment of the ACNETA by the Secretary of State, African colonial governments began realistically to give attention to the question of higher education for Africans. In the Gold Coast, for instance, in March 1924 Guggisberg addressed the Legislative Council on his Achimota scheme. This address was significant in that it was the first time the governor outlined his vision for Achimota, and his intentions eventually to develop the institution into the University of the Gold Coast. The idea was a landmark. Guggisberg's speech represented the first such pronouncement in favour of the establishment of a university during the period by any governor in the British tropical African dependencies. Accordingly,

> As I see it, Achimota will be more of the nature of a university than a secondary school.... In planning the administration I have

therefore thought it advisable to consider the prospect of the College eventually becoming a University.[62]

As a demonstration of the sense of urgency and vigour with which he hoped to pursue the Achimota objective, Guggisberg set aside a capital endowment of half a million pounds and an annual endowment of £60,000 for the institution which he intended as 'an educational model and power-house for West Africa'.[63] Later in 1924 he laid the foundation of the college – A. G. Frazer and J. E. K. Aggrey were appointed Principal and Vice-Principal, respectively, of the proposed college. With the appointment of these two experienced men, it was clear that Guggisberg was committed to the Achimota project.[64]

In Uganda in 1924, Governor Archer (who succeeded Coryndon) appointed E. R. J. Hussey, an inspector of schools in the Sudan, to report on the educational needs of the protectorate and to make recommendations.[65] It had become clear to the governor that among the Baganda chiefly class 'there is a growing demand for a higher standard of education than that obtainable locally'.[66] The chiefs were already asking for a comfortable arrangement to send their children to England for higher training. Hence the governor began to formulate plans to build Makerere into a 'respectable' college for the education of those who would be capable of filling all the minor posts and working at crafts and trade. Furthermore, the Phelps-Stokes Commission visited Uganda in the same year, and the Commission's disapproval of educational efforts in West Africa convinced the Ugandan governor of the need for reorganization. As a result, the acting Principal of Makerere College, Douglas Tomblings, suggested that the technical unit be removed in order to concentrate on vocational training. But the chiefly élite had no intention of turning their children into 'technicians' and the commoners had not yet aspired to higher education.

While agreeing with the governor that government should play a more active part in education, Hussey emphasized the need for expansion 'geared to the needs of the colonial and native administration'.[67] It would appear that Hussey's proposals were designed to counteract and preempt Phelps-Stokes. He proposed a scheme which would raise the level of the intermediate schools to London University Matriculation by using Makerere as a model. For Makerere, he recommended the establishment of a department for the provision of preparatory courses in medicine, agriculture, surveying and veterinary science, 'with an advanced course for sons of chiefs, school masters, and high grade clerks'. The Ugandan Advisory Committee on Education favoured Hussey's recommendations. They added, however, that the university department of the College 'may be the germ out of which in future a university college can grow'.[68] These recommendations were forwarded to the Colonial Office which, in turn, referred them to the ACNETA. Although, as Ashby noted, some members of the ACNETA viewed the Hussey proposal as too ambitious and costly, the acting Committee finally gave its approval.[69]

The appointment of the ACNETA marked the beginning of the evolution of British policy on education in Africa. In less than two years the Committee produced a memorandum which constituted 'a brief and definitive statement of British policy',[70] and which was published as a White Paper in 1925.[71] In the ACNETA's view 'the time is opportune for some public statement of principles and policy which would prove a useful guide to all those engaged, directly or indirectly in the advancement of native education in Africa'. It was believed that African colonial governments had generated enough revenues to enable them to take on larger educational tasks. Hence members of ACNETA reasoned that 'a policy which aims at the improvement of the condition of the people must therefore be a primary concern of Government and one of the first charges on its revenues'. It is significant that such a 'colonial welfare' idea, which would dominate the 1940s, was expressed so early, despite the proviso that funding should come from colonial, rather than British revenues. Nevertheless, it was consistent with the principle of indirect rule and minimal government since the 'educational tasks' ACNETA envisaged never went beyond the training of intermediaries for government departments.

Furthermore, when the Mandates to control the exercise of power in the territories were taken from Germany in 1919, the British began to use League of Nations ideas about Mandates as a 'yardstick' for judging their own colonial possessions. In other words, Britain began to realign her imperial policy to the principle that 'the Controlling Power is responsible as trustee for the moral advancement of the native population'.[72] Although the British were under no obligation to adopt the League of Nations' ideas on trusteeship, it remained the most effective way to prove to the international community that their imperial role was indeed nothing but that of a trustee. Lugard was obviously a major influence, and he was also the British representative on the League of Nations' Mandate Commission. In his *Dual Mandate,* he tried to establish the British system of government in tropical Africa as a prototype for the League of Nations' Mandate proposition.[73] This, of course, was useful propaganda to demonstrate that British colonial rule in Africa and elsewhere was humane, concerned and paternal.

The educational philosophy outlined by the ACNETA in its memorandum acknowledged that the results of education in Africa had not been altogether satisfactory, either to Africans or colonial administrations. To British officials, colonial education dominated by the Missions had failed to create the type of Africans who could be reconciled to the indirect rule system. The memorandum emphasized the need for adaptation and character-training. As it stated,

> Education should be adapted to the mentality, aptitudes, occupation and traditions of the various peoples conserving as far as possible all sound and healthy elements in the fabric of their social life; adapting them where necessary to changed circumstances and progressive ideas, as an agent of natural growth and evolution.... Education thus defined will narrow the hiatus between the educated class and the rest of the community whether chiefs or peasantry.[74]

Colonial administrations recognized the disruptive effects of Western influence and education under indirect rule. According to the memorandum, the types of Western education imparted to Africans 'tend to weaken tribal authority and the sanctions of existing beliefs ...'.[75] Thus character training as emphasized by the Committee was meant to be a necessary safeguard against the 'disruptive influence antagonistic to constituted secular authority'. The aim of education was hence redefined to fit the principle and practice of the indirect rule system. The training of those who were required to fill junior positions in the colonial service, as well as chiefs who would be used as indirect rulers, was the imperative. Anything more than this seemed undesirable. Thus,

> The first task of education is to raise the standard alike of character and efficiency of the bulk of the people, but provision must be made for the training of those who are required to fill posts in the administrative and technical services, as well as of

those who as chiefs will occupy positions of exceptional trust and responsibility.[76]

The question of adaptation was brought by the British into harmony with the educational requirement of the policy of indirect rule.[77] Since the African educated élites, especially in West Africa, saw themselves as socially above their illiterate brethren – both chiefs and commoners – they felt slighted under indirect rule, which assigned them no roles under the colonial dispensation. They became increasingly disillusioned. Worse still, when employed at all, colonial officials would not offer the educated Africans positions commensurate with their educational qualifications. Consequently they became antagonistic to both the African traditional rulers and British officials, and as a class began to constitute a formidable destabilizing force against the colonial establishment.

It was to make the educated Africans politically less troublesome that the whole question of adaptation and character-training as an ideal educational policy was stressed in the ACNETA's memorandum. It is noteworthy that Blyden, the NCBWA and other Africans had called for an education adapted to the African environment and culture. But British adaptation was primarily aimed at creating suitable candidates for middle-level positions which colonialism might permit Africans to hold. The African élite quickly began to categorize British adaptation as a justification of African inferiority.

Furthermore, the stress on adaptation appears to have been a convenient way of convincing the Americans that Britain was formulating a policy in response to the findings of the Phelps-Stokes Report. Ajayi asserts that 'for all the continued rhetoric about the need for adaptation, the need to keep control of higher education in specifically British hands was the priority'.[78] The education offered was to lead to middle-level employment that would never threaten the upper-level European managers. It became anathema to colonial officials that any situation might arise where an African assistant held higher 'paper' qualifications than his European boss. If such a situation threatened it meant that a whole tier of the civil service would have to be Africanized since it was unthinkable that any Europeans would occupy the same civil service level, far less ever work under Africans. Consequently the entire European civil service felt compelled to unite against even one competent and qualified African.

In any case, whatever policy the ACNETA envisaged on

adaptation was woven around the consolidation of indirect rule, and the fact that Lugard was an ACNETA member made the contrary almost impossible.[79] Those who sought to benefit from Western education must, of necessity, learn to respect the traditional authorities represented by chiefs since that presupposed compliance with colonialism. The demands of indirect rule implied that only chiefs needed to run the Native Administrations, and Africans required to fill intermediate positions, should be trained. Western and highly educated Africans were not required under the system which relied upon traditional authorities and a few European officials.

The higher education of Africans was, if possible, to be avoided in order to prevent the expansion of the highly educated class who would clamour for higher posts in the colonial service, or become a burden to the chiefly rulers. Uganda presented a contrast to this mindset because there the educated class was not separate from the chiefly élite. They were one and the same. In order not to close the door to higher education completely and possibly to mollify chiefly opinion in Buganda, the ACNETA recommended that,

> As resources permit, the door of advancement, through higher education, in Africa must be increasingly opened for those who by character, ability and temperament show themselves fitted to profit by such education.[80]

However, the emphasis which both the Phelps-Stokes Commission and the ACNETA's memorandum placed on agricultural education, followed by technical, literary and vocational training was fraught with problems. To the Africans, adapting education to their 'mentality and aptitudes' was suggestive of racial inferiority. It is difficult to imagine how the aptitudes of Africans were decided without implying racial stereotypes. To the colonial officials, occupational adaptation to the aptitude of Africans meant that agricultural education would be emphasized. While seemingly progressive when compared with missionary education, such a proposal, as Foster had observed in *Education and Social Change in Ghana* (p.162), 'combined inferior economic opportunities with the notion of tying the bulk of educated Africans to the land'. Certainly, although colonial governments wanted intermediate professionals for government departments they seemed very comfortable with the emphasis on agriculture because it would serve to divert Africans from politics, nationalism, and bitter struggles with the chiefs. The Baganda chiefs might be persuaded to tolerate agricultural education for commoners but they could not imagine their own children as farmers. This kind of education was frowned upon by the West African educated élites who saw it as a policy which

> would have deprived all but a tiny minority of Africans of the opportunity for effective social advancement in the colonial milieu and the opportunity to achieve social and political parity with the colonial élite.[81]

Meanwhile events were moving rapidly in both Uganda and the Gold Coast. In 1925 Hussey was appointed the first Director of Education in Uganda presumably 'to put into effect his own recommendations and those of the Phelps-Stokes Commission'.[82] Cognizant of the educational standards envisaged for Makerere and the progress made by 1925, the Education Department described the institution as 'destined to become the University College of the Protectorate'.[83] When the Prince of Wales visited the Gold Coast in April 1925, the governor, who believed strongly in the future development of Achimota into a university college, persuaded him to authorize the use of his name for the college. This granted, the institution became known as the Prince of Wales College, Achimota.[84] Consequently both Achimota and Makerere began the long march towards their envisioned destiny under the guidance of their colonial governments. Whatever success each institution was to achieve largely depended on the dispositions of their respective governors and the nature and dictates of indirect rule.

However, when Achimota College opened for classes on 28 January 1927 it 'started life as a more capacious compendium of education than even Guggisberg had supposed'.[85] The final instructional arrangement comprised the Prince of Wales School and the Prince of Wales College. While the former was composed of a kindergarten, a lower primary school for boys and girls, and an upper primary school for girls, the latter housed an upper primary school for boys, a secondary school, and a university department. The university department was intended to offer courses leading to intermediate degrees work. This structure was almost entirely the work of the principal, A. G. Frazer, and J. E. K. Aggrey, to whom Guggisberg had allowed a free hand. Frazer believed that the school had to begin from the bottom and so he introduced the kindergarten idea and incorporated the Accra Training College into the Achimota scheme.[86] Achimota was therefore designed to remove children at the age of six from their cultural environment and keep them away from it until their late teens or early twenties. It was not surprising that Achimota produced a stream of 'black Englishmen' unparalleled by any other institution in West or East Africa before 1948. What ultimately emerged in Achimota was neither the West African University which Casely Hayford and the NCBWA had demanded nor the future university college which Guggisberg envisioned. In fact, the college was to produce a moderately trained class of Africans qualified for the increasing number of openings in the intermediate cadres of the colonial service.

Given the centuries-long exposure of coastal communities in the Gold Coast to Europeans and the 80 years of colonial experience – compared to 20 years in Nigeria – the educated élite more closely approached the ideal of the 'Black Englishman' than any other community in West Africa, with the possible exception of a few Creoles in Freetown. Designing Achimota to immerse Africans from kindergarten to university in an English cultural environment was intended and expected to perpetuate this tradition. No other institution in colonial Africa had been so perfectly designed to denationalize its students and to divorce them from their society and their environment both culturally and physically. Ironically, the Gold Coast élite rarely complained about this concept of total cultural immersion. Not surprisingly Achimota graduates were not outstanding among the nationalists.

In 1929, the Advisory Committee on Native Education in Tropical Africa (ACNETA) was reconstituted under a new name, the Advisory Committee on Education in the Colonies (ACEC).[87] Its functions were expanded to serve all the British colonies rather than tropical Africa alone. The membership of the Committee was also enlarged to include renowned British academics such as Professor Reginald Coupland, Dr Franklin Sibly, Dr W. H. Maclean, Dr Sara Burstall, Dr W. W. Vaughan, and Professor Julian Huxley, with Ormsby-Gore as the chairman, and Hanns Vischer and Arthur Mayhew as joint-secretaries.[88] Although missionary bodies were still represented, they were in the minority and could no longer wield much influence. Despite the fact that Lugard was still a member of the reconstituted body his influence soon diminished as indirect rule no longer took precedence over educational policies. The academic members of the Committee were ready to push educational matters, as the 1930s would show. In fact, the reorganization of the Committee marked an important milestone in the history of university development in Africa since immediately after its inauguration, it 'took an interest in higher education'.[89]

Meanwhile in 1927, the first Kenyan student enrolled at Makerere and the Governor of Uganda noted that the college would soon become a territorial higher educational institution serving the whole of East Africa, especially in the field of medical training. Courses of instruction had been expanded so appreciably that when Julian Huxley, the famous biologist and a member of the ACEC, visited Makerere in 1929 he was so impressed by the progress, especially in medical training, that he noted:

> In due time, I think there can be no shadow of doubt, Makerere will become a true university of East Africa. It is difficult to prophesy; but I would put this time about forty or fifty years hence, after two more generations of education.[90]

Although his timing seemed overstretched because of the pervading notion in those days that colonial change was going to be a very slow process, Huxley appeared more progressive than most African colonial officials. At least he suggested a time frame when the university dream might come true. Clearly, Huxley represented a new outlook among members of the reconstituted ACEC.

Unlike Achimota, Makerere had no department providing university-level courses. Despite the declaration of all the East African Directors of Education in Dar es Salaam in 1929 that 'higher education for the whole of East Africa should be centred at Makerere', the standard of education it provided hardly went beyond the school certificate level. Those who enrolled for the professional courses were awarded certificates which were only recognized within Uganda. Whatever qualifications students obtained, they were expected to fill subordinate posts in the colonial service or, as members of the élite class, be employed in the Native Administrations. However, members of the aristocracy continued to go to Europe for studies. Efforts at higher education, therefore, were determined by the demands of government departments, and not necessarily by the needs or desires of Africans.

In Nigeria, until 1929 efforts at higher education did not go beyond that provided at King's College, Lagos, which had been opened since 1909 and prepared students for the Cambridge School Certificate.[91] But in 1929 E. R. J. Hussey was transferred from Uganda to Nigeria as Director of Education. It would appear that this appointment was intended to create a definite and proper education policy for Nigeria in line with the Colonial Office White Paper of 1925. Hussey's appointment 'presented another opportunity for discussing the whole question of higher education'.[92]

Soon after taking office Hussey proposed a scheme for the establishment of a higher college at Yaba along the lines of Makerere College in Uganda. Like similar institutions in the other British territories, the aim of Yaba as outlined by Hussey during the Legislative Council debate was 'to provide well-trained assistants for various departments of government and private enterprise'. The standard of courses provided, he further stressed, would gradually rise although 'it may take a long time before it reaches the standard which must be its ultimate aim, that of a British University'.[93] Instruction at the proposed Higher College, which would be of 'university or professional character', was to commence in five vocational fields of medicine, civil engineering, agriculture, surveying and teacher training.

By 1930 Hussey had persuaded the Nigerian Government to start the Higher College 'as a special medical school at King's College'. In 1932, the medical school became a distinct institution housed in a temporary hut while the permanent buildings were being erected. Soon, other courses in engineering, agriculture, surveying and teacher-training were added. However, Fajana expresses some doubts as to whether Hussey's enthusiasm and determination alone would have ensured the achievement of his scheme in the face of the financial crisis which began in 1929. For him, the fruition of the Yaba efforts demonstrated nothing but 'a reflection of a general change of attitude in British official quarters towards African education'.[94] The ACEC had begun to push for educational progress in the colonies. In Uganda, official opinion had been shifting in favour of some sort of higher education for Africans, and the East African Directors of Education were even considering a scheme of London matriculation as the standard of admission into Makerere College. Likewise, in 1931 the Gold Coast Government had gone a step ahead by elevating the engineering programme at Achimota to the B.Sc. degree level of the University of London. Nigeria simply could not isolate itself from these new trends. Even in the face of the depression the

Nigerian Government began to show some signs of commitment to go ahead with the Yaba scheme.

Colonial officials in Nigeria had long had reservations about the future of highly educated Africans under indirect rule. Consistently, 'preference for the uneducated over the educated native' had been exhibited in the Native Administrative system,⁹⁵ because '[l]east inclined to be blindly obedient, [the educated African] was even likely to be critical of his foreign ruler'.⁹⁶ The Nigerian Government took extra care to avoid the expansion of a highly educated class which would clamour for higher posts in the colonial service and also 'for fear of creating a politically troublesome class'.⁹⁷ Above all, colonial officials did not wish to disrupt the system of indirect rule which was working very well. Official thinking about the well-educated African remained that,

> by virtue of his high level of education, he was apt to imbibe such notions of representative government, the party system, constitutionalism, self-government and the like – notions that struck at the basis of colonial rule itself.⁹⁸

Ugandan colonial officials rarely adopted this line because the educated élite supported the official position of the Baganda government that colonialism did not mean subordination but rather an alliance between Buganda and Britain. Advice might be given to the Kabaka's government by colonial officials, but by the rules of the agreement the Baganda did not believe it had to be taken and frequently it was not, to the chagrin of the governor. Nationalism, therefore, such a potential threat in West Africa, took the form in Buganda of defending the powers and sovereignty of the Kabaka according to their treaty of 'alliance' with the British. In fact, so serious did the Baganda élite take their position as partners of the British and chiefly agents of colonialism among the other ethnic groups of Uganda, that A. D. Roberts has referred to them as sub-imperialists rather than nationalists.⁹⁹ In the 1920s and 1930s Baganda nationalism took the form of protest against British efforts to remove them as chiefs over the other ethnic groups of the protectorate. To the Baganda such policies were distinctly hostile to the imperial partnership. However, this role of the Baganda had not been guaranteed by the Agreement of 1900 which halted any major intrusion of the British into the internal affairs of Buganda itself.

Meanwhile the Nigerian colonial administration continued to

drag its feet. When the government ultimately decided to establish the Higher College at Yaba it emphasized vocational and technical courses, rather than literary education at diploma and certificate levels. This was hardly surprising. Okafor believes that the decision to establish Yaba was largely a result of 'man-power needs coupled with reasons of economy'.[100] Hussey seemed to have hinted at this when he reasoned that with the establishment of such a vocational Higher College 'a considerable reduction in European personnel is possible ..., with a consequent savings of large sums of money on European salaries'.[101] This made sense in the face of the economic depression which had struck colonial territories in the inter-war years. Although colonial governments normally preferred to work with European officials, the colonies needed to make serious cutbacks in expenditure if they were to find the money for 'essential' government services. No matter how highly educated, it was logical that Africans working in the colonial service were cheaper to maintain than their European counterparts. They were paid lower salaries, and normally received no annually paid leave and passages to London. There is also no doubt that the Yaba scheme was a belated response to the Phelps-Stokes Commission's recommendations as well as the Colonial Office White Paper on education in Africa. Furthermore the ACEC recommendation of the provision of higher education for Africans was gradually becoming accepted.

The Yaba Higher College officially opened in January 1934. Instead of expressing gratitude to the colonial government for ultimately finding its way to establish an institution of higher learning, the establishment of Yaba was 'greeted with a heavy barrage of public criticism' by Nigerians.[102] The first volley came four days after the opening ceremony in the editorial of the *Nigerian Daily Times*, then the leading newspaper in the country. The paper viewed the Higher College as 'a grand idea, and imposing structure, resting on rather weak foundations'. It flayed the low standards of the Middle Schools which would be feeders to the Higher College, and concluded that

> As far as Nigeria is concerned nothing but the best is good enough for Nigeria. If we must have higher education we wish to declare emphatically that this country will not be satisfied with an inferior brand such as the present scheme seems to threaten.[103]

The views of the *Nigerian Daily Times* would have been heartily applauded by the Baganda élite in any similar reference to Makerere. Only full university status would satisfy.

Efforts by Hussey to pacify public opinion, arguing that the standards at Yaba would not be inferior, did not produce satisfactory results.[104] Instead the issue shifted to the Legislative Council where Henry Carr, who was also an African member of the Nigerian Board of Education, led the attacks.[105] Evidently enraged, the Lagos intelligentsia convened a public rally at Glover Memorial Hall on 17 March 1934 to protest against the Yaba scheme. The prominent Lagosians who attended the rally included Mojola Agbebi, O. Alakija, Kofo Abayomi, Ernest Ikoli, S. A. Adesanya and others who later formed the pivot of modern Nigerian nationalism. The rally, in fact, turned out to be 'the first meeting of what became first the Lagos Youth Movement and later the Nigerian Youth Movement'.[106] Stating that their opposition was not against the establishment of higher education, the Lagos intelligentsia contended that the Yaba scheme would entail 'the isolation of Nigerian youths from the outside world and set up a false standard of values in the country'. Furthermore,

> [w]hile it may be expedient and desirable that opportunity should be provided locally ..., it is considered inimical to the highest interest of Nigeria to flood the country with a class of mass-produced men whose standard of qualification must necessarily be deficient owing to the limited facilities available locally both as regards material and staff.[107]

Given its stature as the most populous of British colonies in Africa (double that of the Gold Coast and Uganda combined), Nigeria possessed the smallest and weakest educated class which was more concentrated in one city than elsewhere. In Lagos it could be a nuisance to the colonial officials but beyond, in the vast hinterland, the influence of the educated élite was virtually nil. Its leaders were primarily Creole, for despite the Nigerian-sounding names of protesters listed above the majority had adopted Yoruba names. Small as the educated group was, it had lost many activists to the unusual proliferation of independent churches in Nigeria whose major aim was to convert the people to Christianity and who largely ignored political protests. Agbebi became something of an exception. Nevertheless, they had little of significance to say about education. Their vision appeared very restrictive. What they hankered for was an overseas education for their children. In Lagos the educated élite were riven by factional fights. As the heartland of indirect rule, Nigerian colonial officials and chiefs could ignore the small number of Lagos agitators who questionably paraded themselves as nationalists. Besides hankering for British degrees, the élite appeared to fear flooding the colony with a class of 'mass-produced men' whose qualifications were of 'less' quality than their own, as much as colonial officials. The people of Lagos, far less Nigeria, hardly could have been impressed. Their 'leaders' were not the calibre of Horton or Blyden, James Johnson or Casely Hayford.

Fundamentally, what seems to have separated colonial officials and the Nigerian educated élite was the objective of higher education. While the Nigerian Government was more interested in the production of middle-level human resources for government departments, and favoured the slow development of Yaba to university college standard, the nationalists demanded 'a full-fledged university or overseas training ... [as] the only means of producing men of good quality who would become leaders of their people'.[108] Colonial officials objected to both ideas. A full-fledged university under indirect rule would result in the over-production of highly educated Africans who would be 'a potential opposition to which no place could be given in the ruling system'.[109] Overseas training, especially in America, had begun to be seen as politically and socially dangerous. Thus while Hussey was prepared to consider a scholarship scheme which would open opportunities for more students at Yaba and possibly overseas, the Governor, Sir Donald Cameron, firmly rejected the idea.[110]

Clearly, while African colonial governments were now prepared to establish institutions of higher learning for the purpose of training subordinate staff for the colonial service, they still consistently opposed the idea of the establishment of any full-fledged university. To them, a university would be a burden on their already ailing economies, and more importantly, it would enlarge the class of educated Africans who would be a destabilizing factor to the colonial *status quo* which hinged on indirect rule. It is against this background that the extremely slow pace of progress was recorded in the advance toward university standards both in East and West Africa between 1920 and 1934. In Sierra Leone, the growth of Fourah Bay College had been stultified by its ecclesiastical bias, while its affiliation to Durham University gave it the facade of a university college. Achimota ended up as a 'capacious compendium of education' with a university department which, although it offered courses up to B.Sc. level in engineering, ended up as a higher school. Makerere, on the other hand, could not proceed beyond the status of a territorial college offering courses of higher school standards.

Nowhere in tropical Africa was anything approximating a fully fledged university established before 1935. The vested interests of British colonial officials consolidated in defence of the principle and practice of the indirect rule system. However, the ACEC, whose membership consisted mostly of renowned British academics, from 1930 onwards became increasingly less sympathetic to the indirect rule policy, and began to take charge of educational planning. Since universities would have to await the disintegration of indirect rule as a guiding philosophy of British colonialism, the opposition of African colonial governments to the university idea remained strong until the eve of the Second World War.

NOTES

1. See E. A. Ayandele, 'An Assessment of James Johnson and his Place in Nigerian History, 1874–1917, Part 11, 1890–1917' in *Journal of the Historical Society of Nigeria*, Vol. 3, No. 1, 1964, p. 90, and Ade Fajana, 'Colonial Control and Education: The Development of Higher Education in Nigeria, 1900–1950', in *Journal of the Historical Society of Nigeria*, Vol. 6, No. 3, 1972, pp. 326–327. Blyden left Liberia for Lagos in 1890 to take up a civil service appointment.
2. Fajana, ibid., p. 327.
3. *The Lagos Times*, 31 January 1891 as cited in ibid., p. 326.
4. Frederick Cooper, 'From Free Labor to Family Allowances: Labor and African Society in Colonial Discourse', *American Ethnologist*, Vol. 16, No. 4, 1989, p. 760.
5. Elizabeth Isichei, *A History of the Igbo Peoples*, Macmillan, London, 1976, p. 143. The Igbo peoples of Nigeria were acephalous, that is, they did not evolve a centralized political system revolving around a chief, king or emir. Rather they were gerontocratic. Hence the British could not find anyone with 'chiefly' power who could be installed as their indirect ruler. Therefore, they ended up 'inventing' chiefs which distorted the entire foundation of the traditional system. It unleashed violent protests in south-eastern Nigeria.
6. See A. E. Afigbo, *The Warrant Chiefs; Indirect Rule in Southeastern Nigeria, 1891–1929*, Longman, London, 1972 and 'The Warrant Chief System in Eastern Nigeria: Direct or Indirect Rule?' in *Journal of the Historical Society of Nigeria*, Vol. 3, No. 4, 1967; Obaro Ikime, 'Reconsidering Indirect Rule: The Nigerian Example' in *JHSN*, Vol. 4, No. 3, 1968 and 'Chief Dogho: The Lugardian System in Warri 1917–1932' in *JHSN*, Vol. 3, No. 2, 1965; and also see Philip Igbafe, 'British Rule in Benin 1897–1920: Direct or Indirect?' in *JHSN*, Vol. 3, No. 4, 1967.
7. Rudolf von Albertini, *European Colonial Rule 1880–1940*, Greenwood Press, Connecticut, 1982, p. 309. It was cheaper to pay African chiefs and clerks than to pay British officials whose wage package included paid annual leave in London and other costs.
8. For detail of this Agreement, see D. Anthony Low and R. Cranford Pratt, *Buganda and British Overrule, 1900–1955*, Oxford University Press, London, 1960; E. S. Atieno-Odhiambo, 'Politics and Nationalism in East Africa, 1919–35' in A. Adu Boahen (ed.), *UNESCO General History of Africa*, Vol. 7, Heinemann, California, 1985, pp. 648–673; Andrew Roberts, 'East Africa' in A. D. Roberts (ed.), *The Cambridge History of Africa*, Vol.7, Cambridge University Press, Cambridge, 1986, pp. 647–689, and D. A. Low, *Buganda in Modern History*, University of California, Berkeley, 1971.

9. Marcia Wright, 'East Africa, 1870–1905' in Roland Oliver and G. N. Sanderson (eds), *The Cambridge History of Africa*, Vol. 6, Cambridge University Press, Cambridge, 1985, p. 580.
10. Sir Harry Johnston, as cited in D. A. Low, 'Uganda: The Establishment of the Protectorate, 1894–1919', Vincent Harlow and E. M. Chilver (ed.), *History of East Africa*, Vol. 11, Clarendon Press, Oxford, 1965, p. 119. Johnston was the British Commissioner for the Ugandan Protectorate who negotiated and signed the Buganda Agreement in 1900.
11. Roberts, ibid., p. 649.
12. Ashby, *Universities: British, Indian, African*, p. 177.
13. J. E. Casely Hayford, *Ethiopia Unbound: Studies in Race Emancipation*, first published in 1911, and reprinted by Frank Cass, London, 1969.
14. Ibid., p. 194. He conceived the institution as 'Mfantsipim National University' which would serve the Fanti and the Ashanti.
15. Ibid., p. 195.
16. Ibid., pp. 194–197.
17. Ashby, *Universities: British, Indian, African*, p. 177.
18. See E.W. Blyden, *The Aims and Methods of a Liberal Education*, Cambridge, Massachusetts, 1882.
19. Resolutions of the National Congress of British West Africa at its Conference held in Accra, Gold Coast from 11–29 March 1920, as reproduced in Ashby, *Universities: British, Indian, African*, pp. 474–475 and Okafor, *The Development of Universities in Nigeria*, p. 41.
20. Other resolutions passed by the Congress included an African veto over taxation, appointment and deposition of chiefs by their own people, and the introduction by each Legislative Council of a few elected members with a property and educational franchise. See J. S. Coleman, *Nigeria: Background to Nationalism*, University of California Press, Berkeley, 1958, pp. 191–92.
21. See Von Albertini, *European Colonial Rule, 1880–1940*, p. 331; Okafor, *The Development of Universities in Nigeria*, p. 40 and Ashby, *Universities: British, Indian, African*, p. 179.
22. Hugh Clifford, Address to the Nigerian Council, 29 December 1920, Macaulay Papers as cited in Coleman, *Nigeria: Background to Nationalism*, p. 309.
23. Philip Foster, *Education and Social Change in Ghana*, University of Chicago Press, Chicago, 1965, p. 94.
24. The educated élite pressed for the expansion of the colonial service in order to secure positions for themselves. This was exactly what they meant when they pushed for Africanization and legislative reforms. For details see Coleman, *Nigeria: Background to Nationalism*, pp. 113–196 and Okafor, *The Development of Universities in Nigeria*, p. 39.
25. The Phelps-Stokes Fund was established in 1911 by Miss Caroline Phelps-Stokes for the education of 'Negroes' both in Africa and the United States. This, therefore, was its first attempt to extend its educational work to Africa according to the wishes of its benefactor.
26. Jesse Jones was the educational director of the Phelps-Stokes Foundation. Aggrey was a Fanti from Anomabu in the Gold Coast who was teaching at Livingstone College, Salisbury, North Carolina, having studied and taught in the United States for over 20 years.
27. See Thomas C. Howard, 'West Africa and the American South: Notes on James E. K. Aggrey and the Idea of a University of West Africa', in *Journal of African Studies*, Vol. 2, No. 4, 1976/76, p. 448.
28. *Education in Africa*, New York, 1922 and *Education in East Africa*, New York, 1924.
29. Ashby, *Universities: British, Indian, African*, p. 161.
30. Phelps-Stokes, *Report on Education in Africa*, abridged with an introduction by L. J. Lewis, Oxford University Press, London, 1962, p. 20.
31. Ibid., p. 43–44.
32. Ibid., pp. 122–23 and 167–68.
33. Eric Ashby, *African Universities and Western Tradition*, Harvard University Press, Cambridge 1964, p. 16.
34. Graham, *The History of Education in Ghana*, p. 156.
35. John Cameron, *The Development of Education in East Africa*, Teachers College Press, New York, 1970, p. 28.
36. Margaret Macpherson, *They Built for the Future: A Chronicle of Makerere University College, 1922–1962*, Cambridge University Press, Cambridge, 1964, p. 2.
37. Makerere College, *Annual Report*, 1922 (typescript) as cited in Macpherson, ibid., p. 5. Mr

Saville was from the Ugandan Public Works Department.
38. Macpherson, ibid., pp. 7–8. Owen, who retired from the medical service in Uganda, was recalled to be the first medical tutor of the college. The demand for medical assistants was acute at the Mulago hospital in Kampala, and the CMS hospital at Mengo immediately after the war.
39. Guggisberg succeeded Hugh Clifford as the Governor of the Gold Coast in 1919. Guggisberg was a Jewish Canadian whose father died in 1873 while he was four years old. His mother then married an Englishman, hence they found themselves in England where he completed his education, and joined the Royal Navy. His links with the Gold Coast began when he was seconded in 1902 by the Royal Engineers to special employment under the Colonial Office to survey the Gold Coast and Ashanti. For a biography see R. E. Wraith, *Guggisberg*, Oxford University Press, Oxford, 1967.
40. See C. K. Graham, *The History of Education in Ghana*, Frank Cass, London, 1971, p. 156.
41. Refer to Wraith, *Guggisberg*, p. 134. There were four African members of the Committee, Nana Ofori Atta, Hutton-Mills, Dr Papafio and Spio Garbrah, while the Europeans were the Director of Education, and two missionaries – Wilkie and Fisher.
42. Additionally, the new Committee enquired into how general secondary teacher training, and technical education might be combined in the proposed Achimota college under a co-educational system. This question of co-education was a radical innovation by Guggisberg. Hitherto, missionary education had disallowed the system of co-education.
43. O. W. Furley and T. Watson, *A History of Education in East Africa*, Nok Publishers, New York, 1978, p. 188.
44. Ashby, *Universities: British, Indian, African*, p. 188.
45. See Wraith, *Guggisberg*, p. 90.
46. Furley and Watson, *A History of Education in East Africa*, p. 188.
47. R. C. Pratt, 'Administration and Politics in Uganda, 1919–1945' in Vincent Harlow and E. M. Chilver (eds), *History of East Africa*, Vol. 11, Clarendon Press, Oxford, 1965, p. 519. Most educated Ugandans thus had close and intimate connexions with the ruling hierarchy. Hence ambitious, educated men, rather than reacting in hostility to the government system, tended instead to aspire to it.
48. Refer to Ashby, *Universities: British, Indian, African*; Wraith, *Guggisberg*; and Graham, *The History of Education in Ghana*, passim.
49. Sammy Tenkorang, 'The Gold Coast Aborigines Rights' Protection Society, 1897–1935', Bound Typescript, 1975, p. 302.
50. Arthur Mayhew, *Education in the Colonial Empire*, Longman, London, 1938, p. 162.
51. Fajana, 'Colonial Control and Education', p. 327. The Nigerian Government often dismissed agitation for the establishment of institutions of university college standards 'on the ground that it would be difficult to find sufficient numbers to feed the institution', ibid., p. 328.
52. See Wraith, *Guggisberg*, p. 142. It was further feared that 'higher education would result in Africans becoming politically conscious'.
53. See Tenkorang, op. cit., pp. 307–308. Guggisberg was an indirect ruler. He 'bolstered the power of the chiefs and refused to extend elected representatives to the intelligentsia'. Tenkorang further observed that Governors Clifford of Nigeria and Wilkinson of Sierra Leone introduced reforms 'with less reluctance' than Guggisberg.
54. Christopher Youé, 'The African Career of Robert Thorne Coryndon: Personality and Policy in British Colonial Rule', Ph.D. Thesis, Dalhousie University, Halifax, 1978, pp. 280–281.
55. F. O. Ogunlade, 'Education and Politics in Colonial Nigeria: The Case of King's College, Lagos (1906–1911)' in *Journal of the Historical Society of Nigeria*, Vol. 7, No. 2, 1974, p. 340.
56. See Ashby, *African Universities and Western Tradition*, pp. 16–17.
57. CO 987/17 Advisory Committee on Education in the British Tropical African Dependencies, 24 November 1923. Major Hans Vischer was the secretary. Other members were Major Church, Sir James Currie, Bishop M. Bidwell, Sir Frederick Lugard, the Bishop of Liverpool, J. H. Oldham, Sir Michael Sadler and C. Strachey.
58. Hitherto the Colonial Office had consulted the British Board of Education in relation to education in the colonies. Undoubtedly, this Board had a limited knowledge of the varying local conditions in the colonial territories and was not very effective.
59. Phelps-Stokes report, p. 1.
60. Refer to Kenneth James King, *Pan-Africanism and Education*, Clarendon Press, Oxford,

1971, pp. 95–104.
61. Ashby, *African Universities and Western Tradition*, p. 16.
62. Governor Guggisberg's Speech to the Gold Coast Legislative Council, 6 March 1924, as cited in Wraith, *Guggisberg*, p. 147. See also Guggisberg's *The Keystone*, London, 1924, p. 31.
63. Mayhew, *Education in the Colonial Empire*, pp. 162–163.
64. While Frazer had been for many years the Principal of Trinity College, Kandy, Ceylon, Aggrey had taught for several years in the United States where he earned a reputation for establishing interracial understanding. See Colin G. Wise, *A History of Education in British West Africa*, Longman, London, 1956, pp. 104–105. Frazer also shunned racism. His insistence that Aggrey must be allowed to reside in the European Reservation in Accra instead of African quarters before he (Frazer) could disembark from the ship to assume his office demonstrated amply his racial tolerance; Wise, ibid.
65. See Ashby, *Universities: British, Indian, African*, p. 192 and Macpherson, *They Built For the Future*, p. 9. Hussey was seconded at the request of the Advisory Committee on Native Education in Tropical Africa.
66. Ashby, ibid.; Mayhew, *Education in the Colonial Empire*, p. 169. This 'certain class of natives' that Governor Archer was referring to were obviously the Baganda.
67. Furley and Watson, *A History of Education in East Africa*, p. 187.
68. CO 847/6/12 Memorandum by the Ugandan Advisory Committee on Education, 1924.
69. Ashby, *Universities: British, Indian, African*, p. 192–3.
70. Ibid.
71. CO 987/13 *Education Policy in British Tropical Africa: Memorandum by the Advisory Committee on Native Education in British Tropical African Dependencies*, Command Paper No. 2374 of 1925.
72. CO 987/13 Note by the Chairman of the Committee, Ormsby-Gore, to the Secretary of State, dated 13 March 1925.
73. Lord Lugard, *The Dual Mandate in British Tropical Africa*, first published in 1922, Fifth Edition, Frank Cass, London, 1956.
74. CO 987/13 *Education Policy in British Tropical Africa: Memorandum by the Advisory Committee on Native Education*.
75. Ibid.
76. Ibid.
77. Foster, *Education and Social Change in Ghana*, p. 164.
78. Ajayi, 'The American Factor in the Development of Higher Education in Africa', p. 10.
79. Lugard's 'Education in Tropical Africa' in CO 847/9/9 rehashed the content of the ACNETA's memorandum in relation to the disruptive influence of unadapted Western education. Lugard insisted that African education must have roots in African traditions, beliefs and environment, which was the meat in the Committee's memorandum.
80. CO 987/13 *Education Policy in British Tropical Africa: Memorandum*, op. cit.
81. Ibid., p. 162.
82. Furley and Watson, *A History of Education in East Africa*, p. 189.
83. Uganda Education Department, *Annual Report*, 1925 as cited in Macpherson, *They Built For the Future*, p. 9.
84. However, this change of name did not make any difference to most West Africans who continued to refer to the institution as Achimota College. The new name only had relevance among officials in the Colonial Office.
85. Wraith, *Guggisberg*, p. 153.
86. Ibid.
87. CO 987/17 Historical Notes on the Advisory Committee on Education in the Colonies, (undated).
88. Coupland was a Beit Professor of History of the British Empire at Oxford University; Sibly was a well-known Geologist and Principal of the University of London; Maclean was a lecturer in Economics and a specialist in colonial economic planning in the University of London; Burstall was the President, Association of Headmistresses, a member of the Institute of Education Delegacy, University of London, and a famous public speaker on educational issues; Vaughan was the Headmaster of Rugby College and President of the Incorporated Association of Headmasters; and Huxley, also of the University of London, was the world famous biologist.

89. CO 987/17 Historical Notes on the Advisory Committee on Education in the Colonies.
90. J. Huxley, *African View*, London, 1933, pp. 279–80 as quoted in Furley and Watson, *A History of Education in East Africa*, p. 194.
91. For the history of the King's College see Ogunlade, 'Education and Politics in Colonial Nigeria: The Case of King's College, Lagos (1906–1911)'.
92. Fajana, 'Colonial Control and Education', p. 328.
93. Speech by E. R. J. Hussey, Legislative Council Debates, 8th Session, 27 September 1930, Government Printer, Lagos, pp. 29–32.
94. Fajana, 'Colonial Control and Education', p. 328.
95. Hailey, *An African Survey*, p. 259.
96. O. Adewoye, 'The Antecedents' in J. F. Ade Ajayi and Tekena N. Tamuno (eds), *The University of Ibadan, 1948–73*, Ibadan University Press, Ibadan, 1973, p. 10.
97. See F. O. Ogunlade, 'Yaba Higher College and the Formation of an Intellectual Elite' (MA Thesis, University of Ibadan), 1970, p. 352.
98. Adewoye, 'Antecedents', p. 10–11.
99. A. D. Roberts, 'The Sub-Imperialism of the Baganda', *Journal of African History*, Vol. 3, No. 3, 1962, pp. 435–50.
100. Okafor, *The Development of Universities in Nigeria*, p. 70.
101. Sessional Paper, No.31 of 1930, Government Printer, Lagos as cited in Okafor, ibid. He equally realized that sound education would enable the masses to harness the immense economic possibilities, hence a demand for an increasing number of well-educated natives was a natural corollary of economic progress.
102. Adewoye, 'The Antecedents', p. 13. He contends that the Yaba scheme 'was the most controversial issue in the nationalist movement in Nigeria in the 1930s', see ibid.; also refer to Obafemi Awolowo, *Awo: The Autobiography of Chief Obafemi Awolowo*, Cambridge University Press, London, 1960, pp. 115–116; and Ogunlade, *Yaba Higher College*.
103. Editorial, 'The Yaba Higher College', *Nigerian Daily Times*, 23 January 1934; Awolowo, *Awo: The Autobiography*, pp. 115–116.
104. *Nigerian Daily Times*, 25 January 1934.
105. See Nigerian Legislative Council Debate, 12th Session, 1934, pp. 39–44.
106. Ogunlade, 'Education and Politics in Colonial Nigeria', p. 325; Okafor, *The Development of Universities in Nigeria*, p. 75; see also Von Albertini, *European Colonial Rule*, p. 334.
107. Resolutions passed at a Public Rally held at the Glover Memorial Hall, Lagos on 17 March 1934, and published in *Nigerian Daily Times*, 19 March 1934.
108. Fajana, 'Colonial Control and Education', p. 330.
109. John Flint, 'British Colonial Policy and the Development of African Universities, 1872–1943', seminar paper presented at the Centre for African Studies, Dalhousie University, Halifax, Nova Scotia, 15 February 1979, p. 3.
110. See Fajana, 'Colonial Control and Education', p. 330. For colonial officials, the most disturbing aspect of nationalist demands was that Nigerians were not going to be content merely with competing for jobs with the British officials but they were determined also to lead their people to self-government.

3 The Ice Begins To Melt: Initiatives from London and the Plan for an East African University, 1932–39

The period between 1932 and 1938 witnessed not only an unprecedented drive to formulate a consistent policy on the question of university education for Africans but also marked the first attempt by the British Government to use the 'sacred' taxpayers' money to fund a scheme of higher education in Africa. This time the campaign came from the ACEC and the Colonial Office, and not directly from the Africans as in the pre-1930 demands. The change of attitude occurred for several reasons. By 1932 the academic members of the ACEC had constituted themselves into a strong lobby group to press for the provision of university facilities in the colonies. Dexterously, they correlated their ambitions for the academic profession in general with the larger imperial goal, arguing that it was far more dangerous to British imperial prestige, politically and socially, to deny Africans access to university education than to satisfy that urge. Gradually the Colonial Office became persuaded by the ACEC argument. Furthermore, the unstable social, economic and political climate in the various colonies, as exemplified by the West Indian crisis (a series of riots and disturbances that erupted in the British Caribbean islands between 1935 and 1937 in which 39 people were killed and 175 were seriously injured), coupled with domestic and international criticisms of British colonial policies from the mid-1930s, became unsettling to the Colonial Office and imperial thinkers alike. By 1938, therefore, the Colonial Office had become convinced that British colonial policy should be overhauled to harmonize with imperial long-term objectives. In these circumstances, serious discussion on African higher education began.

After its reconstitution in 1929, the ACEC, which comprised 19 members including seven British academics and three educationists (with the rest representing various interest groups), began to adopt a different attitude towards African education, particularly university education. As for the university representatives, it was only natural for them to seek to cater to their profession (education) in the imperial policy-making process. They were convinced that no people could attain any meaningful advance without proper and uninhibited education at all levels. Thus they were not prepared to allow purely political considerations to override academic reasoning. They constituted themselves into a formidable lobby group to persuade the Colonial Office and imperial statesmen of the need for, and the larger benefits of, a well-informed colonial population. The resolutions of the conference of East African Directors of Education (held in Zanzibar in 1932) to raise the standards of Makerere College provided the academic lobby with a launching pad. The appointment of the De La Warr Commission for Makerere College in 1936 also constituted a response by the Colonial Office to the academic pressure from the ACEC.

From then on, using weighty political arguments which were manifestly unharmful to British imperial rule, the academic lobby began to make one recommendation after another in favour of the establishment of universities in tropical Africa. To this end, they highlighted the social and political consequences of Africans going to America for advanced studies. Although the Colonial Office favoured most of the ACEC's views on the necessity for universities in Africa, the Office remained like a 'toothless bulldog' because it had no budget for that purpose. Since the Treasury would not release money, the Colonial Office was left at the mercy of the budgets of colonial governments whose opposition to university schemes often remained formidable. The Treasury grant of £100,000 for the endowment of the Makerere Higher College in 1938 constituted a turning-point, and may be considered, at least in part, a triumph of the academic lobby.

Serious British discussions about the question of the establishment of universities in Africa began in 1932. They were provoked by an aspect of the report of the conference of the East African Directors of Education dealing with Makerere College. The following section of this report, known as 'Paragraph 19', agitated colonial officials in both Britain and Africa:

The Directors noted with satisfaction that it is intended to start at Makerere in January 1933 a course leading to Matriculation by means of the University of London's School Examination. It was suggested that a syllabus should be drawn up covering the last five years of this matriculation course, and that the first two years of this syllabus should be undertaken in Secondary Schools, and the last three years at Makerere. As soon as a sufficient number of students have reached the stage of entering for the intermediate Arts Examination of London University, the Secondary Schools should undertake the whole matriculation course, and matriculation should become the standard for entry to Makerere.[1]

Although the directors meant that Makerere College should begin to offer courses of a university type, though not necessarily entire degree programmes, their declaration triggered chain reactions in the Colonial Office and the ACEC. Within East Africa, many British officials were apprehensive of the declaration's effects because of the danger of turning out students with purely academic qualifications who might find great difficulty obtaining employment.[2] Among British officials generally, education 'beyond that which was needed to provide subordinate staff was suspect', and worse still, there was 'no appreciation of the worth of an highly educated African élite'.[3]

On receipt of the Directors' Report, the Colonial Office was disturbed about the implications of the paragraph on general education policy in Africa. Consequently, the Secretary of State, P. Cunliffe-Lister, referred it to the ACEC for consideration. In turn the ACEC appointed a sub-committee in January 1933 under the chairmanship of James Currie, who was formerly the Principal of Gordon College in Khartoum and Director of Education in the Sudan and whose impressive educational work in the colonies recommended him for the task.[4] Other members of the sub-committee were F. O. Mann, Dr W. W. Vaughan, Dr Philippa Esdaile, Dr W. H. Maclean, Major A. G. Church, Hans Vischer and A. I. Mayhew.[5] This sub-committee was mandated by the ACEC to 'consider the educational policy underlying the views expressed by the conference on the question of standard of admissions to Makerere College, and submit recommendations'.[6] Dominated by British academics and advocates of a realistic colonial educational policy rather than political officers, it was clear that this sub-committee would favour a more radical approach to the question of higher education in Africa.

The appointment of the Currie sub-committee clearly marked the dawn of a new era – the era of positive thinking – on higher education in Africa. Earlier in 1925, the plan to develop Achimota into an eventual university was not seriously considered by the then ACNETA. The committee insisted that the question of full university degrees in Africa 'would not arise for some time to come'.[7] But ACNETA was mistaken. Barely eight years later the Makerere question was raised and signalled the advent of a new epoch. ACNETA had now become ACEC, and it was no longer prepared to permit sheer political reasoning predicated upon the consolidation of the principle and practice of indirect rule, and the maintenance of the selfish interest of the local colonial officials solely to dictate imperial educational policies.

The appointment of the ACEC's sub-committee under Currie provided a ray of hope. It marked the beginning of a concrete effort by the ACEC to consider the age-old issue of African aspirations and yearnings for the provision of university facilities. The Currie sub-committee reported in 1933, and its recommendations agitated British colonial thinking as they required a reconsideration of educational policy in the colonies. Ashby aptly described the report as 'bold and imaginative'.[8]

The Currie Report decisively shifted from the ultra-conservative approach of ACNETA to the question of higher education for Africans.[9] Like the 1925 White Paper issued by ACNETA which stressed the importance of the adaptation of African education to the 'mentality, aptitudes, occupations and traditions' of the peoples, the Currie Report was also persuaded by a similar concept. However, the kind of adaptation advocated by the sub-committee differed from that of the ACNETA, whose emphasis had been solely on how the colonial education policy should consolidate the indirect rule system. The Currie Report acknowledged that the education given to Africans, certified by external tests, was out of touch with the local needs of Africans. Thus African secondary schools administered courses 'which have been designed primarily with reference not to African, but to English conditions'. To the sub-committee, therefore, Paragraph 19 of the Report of the Conference of East African Directors of Education was 'illuminating; it shows in the most striking way how local schemes of education may be abandoned at the lure of an extraneous course leading to a degree'.[10] Accordingly, the Report commenced with the observation that

> the education provided must be of such a character as to encourage the development of the natural aptitudes of the peoples concerned to the fullest possible extent, having regard to the specific background and needs of the African environment.[11]

Acknowledging that the number of African secondary schools had increased and that the standards of their attainment had improved, the Currie Report also observed that most of these pupils were 'not only desirous but actually capable of continuing their studies up to a final university standard'.[12] It noted that 'there is a grave danger, as we see it, of the Africans' zeal for education being neglected and ignored by the government to whom they ought to be able to look for its reasonable satisfaction'. Furthermore, it indicated that 'there appears no prospect – nor is it in any event a prospect that can in the least be wished or desired – that the present vehement demand for higher education will slacken off'. Accordingly,

> It follows then, that, if that demand is not adequately met by a natural development in Africa itself under the wise control, which only British Government and experience can afford, it will spend itself in all sorts of individual and group educational enterprises, which can hardly fail to be eccentric, often self-defeating and sterile, and attended by social and political phenomena harmful alike to the prestige of this country and the true well-being of the Africans.[13]

The Currie sub-committee concluded that

> the only right policy for the [British] Government is to think out ahead a scheme of developing selected institutions in Africa up to a real university standard, and that this policy, as soon as decided upon, should be publicly announced as officially adopted.[14]

Significantly, the Currie group noted that 'the claims of African women to University education ought to receive equal attention with those of men'. This was the first such emphatic and authoritative statement in London on the question. The sub-committee pointed out that women's education in Africa 'is retarded by the understandable reluctance of women to proceed overseas'. It therefore concluded that 'Until there is in Africa provision for University Education in some form or other, it will only be very rarely that a woman will proceed beyond the Secondary stage'. To the sub-committee, women's reluctance was 'understandable' because of 'considerable though varying local difficulty'. This difficulty may have varied from religious norms (particularly among Moslems) to cultural beliefs that travelling overseas unaccompanied would make a woman 'loose', and hence a misfit in her community when she returned. Although often involved in productive work, African women themselves cherished their traditional role as 'housewives' and were therefore averse to losing their respectable status if they travelled overseas for higher education. In any case, the reluctance of African men to allow their wives to travel overseas for higher education presumably remained overriding in women's considerations. Thus the Currie sub-committee cautioned that 'in dealing with this particular phase of the problem [university education for women], it is of the highest possible importance that no action be taken except with the closest possible co-operation and advice of the African communities concerned'.[15]

Highly committed to push for the educational advance of British colonial Africa, the Currie sub-committee put forward social, political and economic arguments to reinforce its plea. The American factor was one of these, aimed at the very heart of Britain's imperial ego. The Report observed that Africans from the West Coast were increasingly leaving their own countries for advanced education in America, and pointed out the social and intellectual undesirability of this procedure. Asserting that 'the African thirst for higher education remains unabated', the Report warned that 'if this is not satisfied at home it can only lead to an increasing efflux of African students towards the Universities of Europe and America'.[16] Furthermore,

> It seems indefensible, for example, that the Gordon College should, at all events till very recently, have had to rely substantially upon the American University at Beyrut [sic] for the advanced training of natives needed for its own staffing. From another, and slightly different point of view it appears equally indefensible that intelligent Africans from the Gold Coast should most easily obtain further training of university type by taking advantage of American bounty and American institutions. On the political difficulties and the economic disabilities inherent in such a position continuing, it is not necessary to enlarge.[17]

Whether the fear of the American influence was real or imaginary, the Currie sub-committee apparently highlighted it to whip up sentiment among imperial thinkers, as well as African colonial officials, in favour of the establishment of universities in Africa. Even though African colonial governments were aware of the American factor, they do not seem to have foreseen the magnitude of the social and political consequences as highlighted by the Currie sub-committee. In the mid-1920s Dr J. K. Aggrey of the Gold Coast, who trained in America, was already showing signs of frustration with British rule in Africa. As a member of the Phelps-Stokes Commission which visited Africa between 1920 and 1924 he made several public appearances and speeches to his people, debunking the racial theories based on the alleged supremacy of the white man and the inferiority of the black. In fact, the Gold Coast Government became worried about Aggrey when it was claimed that he had sympathy with the Marcus Garvey extremist faction.[18] Worse still, the personality of Aggrey provided inspiration to Africans such as Nnamdi Azikiwe, Eyo Ita and others to set sail for the United States.[19] To British officials and the ACEC, this American influence was unhealthy to imperial interests.

Since its war of independence with Britain in 1776, the United States had adopted a type of anti-imperial and anti-British stance. Britain knew this. If there had been any reasonable relations between the two countries within the period, it had largely been a 'marriage of convenience'. Thus the close association between America and Africans was something hardly to be desired by Britain. British fear remained that

> the African student might encounter political movements considerably more militant than in his own country, and he might realize that educational standards in his own country were very low by comparison.[20]

In other words, it was appreciated that the American influence would reveal open racism and create nationalism of a kind which would be harmful to British rule in Africa. Africans could draw great inspiration from the spirit of the American Revolution in their struggle for social, economic, educational and political freedom from Britain. As Okeke remarked, British officials were aware that the American system 'is pregnant with ideas that have, more often than not, become valuable tools in the hands of colonials struggling to obtain their freedom from alien rule'.[21]

Only by expanding the focus from Makerere to all of Africa could the Currie sub-committee employ their most potent weapon, fear of American influence, since the potential catchment area for Makerere had been almost untouched by the American 'bug'. The tendency for Africans to look to America was most prevalent in West Africa and to a lesser degree in the Sudan. Many West Africans had gained experience of America of which Blyden and Aggrey were only outstanding examples. It is significant that the demand for a university during this period had arisen in East Africa. The attachment to indirect rule by the colonial officials in West Africa and especially Nigeria had long been more emotional and proprietary than among those in the East. Colonial officials in Uganda had found a way of marrying the educated élite to an indirect rule system which maintained a high degree of integrity and popular support. In Kenya, no real indirect rule had ever been established. Kenyan officials had merely gone along with the Lugardian fad which had swept over the colonial establishment. Indirect rule had little integrity, chiefs being viewed by both the people and colonial officials as mere labour recruiting agents. The demand for university training ran into less opposition from those not emotionally and psychologically attached to indirect rule. From the academic viewpoint in Britain, the looming problems for imperialism lay in West Africa with its volatile élite and the influence of American ideas.

It should be noted that the terms of reference given to the ACEC by the Secretary of State were specifically to 'consider the educational policy underlying Paragraph 19' in relation to Makerere College. But the Currie Report, as fully endorsed by the ACEC, turned the problem from a local Makerere and East African problem into a pan-African question. The Report recommended that the African colleges – Achimota, Yaba, and possibly Gordon College – should be turned into university colleges. 'From the first beginnings', the Report stressed, 'the problem of university education in West Africa should be envisaged as a whole' and 'the Secretary of State should examine carefully all proposals for the extension of existing institutions'.[22] Clearly, by examining the West African university question, which was not covered by the terms of reference, the ACEC was, more or less, imposing its own agenda upon the Colonial Office. Given the strength of its argument for urgent attention to be given to the question of university education for Africans generally, the Colonial Office could hardly reject the report.

Some officials of the Colonial Office received the Currie Report with mixed feelings. This was natural since most officials of the Colonial Office believed the indirect rule policy to be the cheapest and the most efficient system of colonial administration. J. E. W. Flood, for instance, viewed the report as provocative, woolly and too generalized.[23] To Flood, 'what, at the present time is wanted is not anybody highly trained, but an ordinary individual with some training, not too removed from the daily round and the common task to be unable to take part in local life and local habits of thought'. As he further described it:

> We do not want the Divisional Commander nor even the Platoon Leader. What is wanted is not even the Sergeant but something – which we are more likely to get – on the level of the Lance Corporal, i.e., men just a little removed from the common ruck who will be able to spread a bit of the leaven among the unresponsive lump.[24]

If ever the historian required a simple, crude yet pithy statement of the core of the philosophy of indirect rule, Flood provided it in the above quotation. Lugard's idea of allowing Africans to develop at their own speed and by their own norms, had been criticized because the 'common ruck' appeared to be an 'unresponsive lump'. For Lugard, colonial officials should constantly urge the chiefs and 'unresponsive lump' toward 'progress' and 'modernization', terms not employed then but nevertheless conveying the idea of pushing forward evolution. But colonial officials had been a reluctant 'leaven'. The feeling was growing that possibly they required help from a few skilled Africans, educated sufficiently in English norms, who would mix with the 'lump', 'leaven' it and create the beginnings of an evolution in chiefly government. These Africans would become willing and obedient 'lance corporals' at the behest of their British sergeants, platoon leaders and divisional commanders. To be avoided at all costs would be a university-educated class which would segregate itself from the 'lump' and develop ambitions to become 'sergeants' or the unthinkable 'divisional commanders'. For Flood it might be three or four generations before 'the highly trained leader might find scope'. In his conclusion:

> In my view education among most, at any rate, of the East African tribes, will have to be a slow growing plant, and it will

have to grow in the open and not in a hot-house if it is to do any good to the country.[25]

Flood was evidently a champion of the indirect rule system. Like African colonial governors, he did not support the expansion of the class of African educated élite who would constitute a problem for the efficient working of the system. He argued that highly-educated Africans would want to occupy positions which 'would put them inevitably very high up in the local organization and might easily lead to friction and trouble with Chiefs and Leaders'.[26]

However, there were other officials of the Colonial Office who, even though they did not wish to see the collapse of indirect rule, felt that the Report of the Currie sub-committee was quite progressive. In response to Flood's note, for instance, Hans Vischer insisted that the Report contained 'a good deal of meat'.[27] The divergence of opinion was obvious. Despite the fact that opinion within the Colonial Office was crystallizing in favour of the Currie Report, one major concern of officials generally was the possible effect of the sub-committee's proposal on the 'Native administration' system in Africa.[28] None the less, by accepting the pan-African nature of the Report, the university question now became a matter of high policy for the Colonial Office. What remained uncertain was whether colonial governments in Africa would support this 'radical report' since it aimed at the expansion of an African educated class; a phenomenon colonial governments strove to avoid. The Secretary of State, P. Cunliffe-Lister, now decided to sound out the views of African governors by transmitting copies of the Report to the governments of the East and Central African Dependencies in August 1934. Since the university projects were to be funded by the various African governments, it was essential that the Secretary of State have the views of the governors.

In September 1934 similar despatches were sent to the governments of British West Africa informing them that their Directors of Education, while in London, had agreed to lay before the authorities of the University of London certain conclusions of the ACEC sub-committee (Currie's Committee) in respect of external examination and assistance which might be obtained from British universities. Furthermore, the Secretary of State stressed the importance he attached to a common policy in the matter being followed by the West African governments. The Makerere problem had become a larger African question. Clearly, the Colonial Office had begun to accept the views of the academic lobby of the social and political danger implicit in the continued neglect of the provision of university education in British African territories.

On receipt of the Report, the East African governors forwarded copies to their respective Directors of Education who met in Nairobi in January 1935 to discuss it. The conclusions of the directors were disappointing not only to the ACEC but also the Colonial Office. The Directors were quick to point out that the Currie Report's reaction to their 'Paragraph 19' went too far. However, the Directors' response was hardly surprising. Actually, what the East African Directors of Education intended in the now famous Paragraph 19 was for Makerere to begin to prepare students for intermediate degree programmes (Inter-BA or Inter-BSc). These were not full degree courses. Rather they were in the nature of Higher School Certificates (HSC) which enabled the recipients to be admitted into full degree courses in British universities without doing a preliminary or an entry qualifying year. What the Directors envisaged in Paragraph 19 was an arrangement whereby brighter students who passed out of Makerere could be selected to proceed to the University of London or other British institutions to pursue their studies. In any case, the need for African junior staff for government departments far surpassed any other considerations in the Directors' calculations when they proclaimed 'Paragraph 19'. Makerere could be reorganized to train middle-level manpower for the various East African Governments. Furthermore, the Ugandan Government may have felt that the elevation of Makerere to higher college standards providing first year university entry courses could assuage the demand among the Baganda for higher education. Clearly, what the East African Directors of Education envisioned in Paragraph 19 was not fully fledged university education at Makerere.

It is not surprising that while agreeing that the type of education provided must be adapted to encourage the development of the natural aptitudes of the peoples concerned, having regard to the specific background and needs of the African environment, the Directors disagreed with the Currie Report's conclusion that there was a vehement demand for higher education in East Africa. They insisted that it would be 'unwise to accelerate such a demand'.[29] Generally, the Directors presumed that the merit of the Currie Report lay more in 'bringing this matter to the notice of the Secretary of State for the Colonies, to assist in the formulation of a common policy' than in its argument in favour of the provision of full university courses in Africa.[30] The East African Directors of Education were alarmed that the ACEC had seized upon their Paragraph 19 to push for a major shift in colonial policy towards a general scheme for unprecedented and large-scale development of African universities. The ACEC, however, dismissed the Directors' response as rather reactionary, and opted to wait for the opinions of the governors after their conference scheduled for late 1935.[31]

In West Africa, an education conference was held in Lagos in May 1935 with the Directors of Education of Nigeria and the Gold Coast, the Vice-Principal of Achimota, and the Principals of Yaba and King's Colleges, Lagos, in attendance. The governments of the Gambia and Sierra Leone were not represented. The Gambian Government felt that the small size of the colony could support neither a higher nor university college, given the lack of both resources and students, and hence there was no plan to establish any higher institution. For Sierra Leone, it would appear that Fourah Bay College, which was the only West African institution offering full degree programmes (in theology and classics), satisfied the colony's higher educational needs. Neither the Gambia nor Sierra Leone was involved in the 'cold war' between Yaba and Achimota over the question of co-ordination of medical and engineering courses which began in 1935 when the Colonial Office requested the governments of Nigeria and the Gold Coast to co-ordinate their educational programmes to avoid duplication of effort – the Colonial Office felt that Achimota should concentrate on engineering and Yaba on medicine, but both institutions wished to offer full courses in both fields and the debate created some 'bad blood' between them. The Lagos conference failed to achieve any meaningful progress regarding territorial co-ordination and co-operation. The participants concluded that 'the time had not yet come for any definite steps to be taken, but in the meantime both Yaba and Achimota would welcome individual students from other West African Colonies'.[32]

In relation to the Currie Report, the various West African governments chose to respond on an individual basis. In its response, and considering the costs involved in the establishment of a university, the government of the Gambia asserted that 'Gambians will have to look either to England or to institutions in other West African territories for higher studies'.[33] As for the Sierra Leonean response, acknowledging that the provision of higher education should be regarded as a pan-West African problem, the government noted that while the idea that Sierra Leonean students should look towards Yaba and Achimota 'seemed commendable in theory', it 'required further examination as to ways and means'.[34] It stressed that although Fourah Bay College primarily awarded University of Durham degrees in theology and classics, it did other useful work relating to teacher training.

Although the Sierra Leone government admitted that it lacked the resources to continue the training of students overseas, or to extend the scope of Fourah Bay College, it claimed that 'local sentiments would be offended if the suggestion were made that such facilities [provided by the College] should be withdrawn'.[35] Here lie the early signs of territorial nationalism ironically propounded by expatriate officials which, as will be seen later, would subsequently dominate the university question. Even when it was clear that territorial co-operation would benefit Sierra Leone because the colony acutely lacked the resources to build a new college or expand Fourah Bay, the government was somewhat reluctant to send students to the Gold Coast or Nigeria.

However, the views of the governments of Nigeria and the Gold Coast represented the clearest indication of the trend of resistance against the idea of African universities during the period. To both governments, the overproduction of African graduates, who would clamour for higher posts in the colonial service, was to be avoided. In an agricultural country, according to the government of the Gold Coast, 'there are only limited opportunities for remunerative type of employment or occupation which a Gold Coast graduate desires'.[36] Thus in response to the Currie Report on the danger inherent in alienating African public opinion and creating political and social confusion by neglecting to provide university facilities, the Gold Coast government maintained that

> While on the one hand, failure to respond to the demand would undoubtedly have these unhappy results, yet the creation of machinery which would probably lead to overproduction, would on the other hand, result in much disappointment and unrest.[37]

Assenting to the Gold Coast point of view, the Nigerian government[38] noted that the West African educated élite were often disappointed that the qualifications they acquired did not lead to lucrative jobs, 'for they take these courses as a means to an end rather than with a view to self education'.³⁹ In response, Hussey, the Nigerian Director of Education, proposed a cautious three-stage scheme. In *Stage A* West African colleges would produce students who would be fitted to hold positions of responsibility in government or private sectors, presumably at the 'lance corporal' level. At this stage, he insisted that 'it is of prime importance that the pace should not be hurried'.⁴⁰ Possibly, he would have agreed with the three or four generations proposed by Flood. *Stage B* was that at which the standard reached at the first stage 'warrants affiliation with an English University for the purpose of external degrees, preferably at the University of London' while the final stage, *Stage C*, was that at which a college 'may become itself a local university'. Hussey stressed the need for a slow pace in the transition from one stage to another in order to safeguard standards. As he declared: 'We must at all cost avoid giving what we proclaim to be a University degree, unless we can safeguard the standard.'⁴¹

Under the indirect rule system, there was virtually no place for university-educated Africans. Hussey knew this and therefore his gradual plan made sense. His scheme did not attempt to rock the very basis of the principle of Native Administration which relied heavily upon the African chiefs, and hence the Nigerian Government endorsed it. It was an effective way of regulating the number of those who would obtain university qualifications. It is not surprising that Hussey further recommended that the initial intention was to 'replace by Africans the type of Europeans usually called "junior staff" by men who had passed stage A who will be better qualified technically than the men they replace'.⁴² Although Hussey did not favour the continued training of Africans overseas at government expense, he maintained that there should be no undue haste to establish a fully fledged West African university outright as the Currie Report seemed to portend. Clearly the expansion of the educated class remained an anathema. Accordingly,

> If we train at once the fully-fledged professional, it will be a matter of extreme difficulty to regulate the position as between him and the British foreman, or what corresponds to him in other professions, especially if we partially fail in our efforts to produce the type, because we have hastened unduly.⁴³

When civil service matters arose as they inevitably did when education was being discussed, officials such as Hussey came up against an ingrained racism in the colonial senior service. A British 'foreman' would not work with an African on any basis of equality and collegiality. It always had to be 'man' and 'boy' or, better still, a British superior and an African subordinate. Being placed in a situation where African advice or expertise might be consulted or even worse acted upon, became an intolerable nightmare for many Europeans in the colonial service. A generation would have to die (or be pensioned off, compensated or otherwise pushed out) before this could occur. Whatever the sophisticated arguments surrounding the issue of university education for Africans, the inability of whites to work with, rather than command blacks in the civil service was central to the debate.

Another concern raised by the Gold Coast government against the establishment of a university was the fear that educated Africans would feel that second-rate standards were being foisted on them. The government contended that any university scheme on a West African basis, 'at this stage', would be opposed by Gold Coast public opinion and especially by the educated class. It observed that the latter was 'acutely suspicious of any step that may have the appearance of an attempt to meet African demands for education with a second-rate article', and hence they preferred to obtain their degrees overseas.[44] Given the Yaba imbroglio of 1934, the Nigerian government agreed with the Gold Coast emphasizing that there was no need for local degrees unless standards could be preserved, and unless African enlightened opinion approved of the awarding institutions.[45]

Generally, Africans were suspicious of the motives behind colonial education. Yaba was particularly notorious among the Nigerian proto-nationalists and the educated class. The number of failures recorded in the college from its inception, the non-recognition of its graduates in England and even beyond Nigerian borders, and employment discrimination suffered by recipients of the local qualifications fanned the embers of hatred for the college. Similarly, the effort of the Gold Coast government to 'Africanize' the Achimota curriculum by focusing upon local languages and customs infuriated the African members of the Legislative Council as well as the intelligentsia. The general suspicion was that 'special courses for Africans constituted an attempt to keep them in a subordinate intellectual and social position indefinitely'.[46] Nana Ofori Attah, for instance, asserted that 'it would be an unwise move to restrict studies to the African scene'. Casely Hayford also viewed as a 'dangerous policy' any attempt to lay down that one class and type of education was necessary for the African as against any other type'.[47] In Uganda, also, articulate African opinion pressed for changes which would increase rather than lessen the Western character of African education. Thus the government suggestion that 'school curricula should be revised to increase their African or their practical content invariably met with strong African opposition'.[48] Caught between the fear of second-rate education and over-deification of British standards, the ideas of the African nationalist élites at this time almost appeared to cater to 'imperialism'.

It made sense for both the Nigerian and the Gold Coast governments to employ the argument of African élite opposition to local education standards in order to demonstrate to the ACEC and the Colonial Office why any scheme of university development should not be pushed. It was a shrewd move. Both governments informed the Secretary of State that the only wise policy for the present was to concentrate on strengthening the intermediate courses while arranging for selected students to complete these courses in 'carefully chosen universities in Great Britain or elsewhere'.[49] The importance of arranging for 'selected students' to study in 'carefully chosen universities' seems quite clear. It meant that colonial governments were contemplating scholarships for Africans to study in Britain or 'elsewhere' so as to control the number of graduates and monitor the kind of courses students studied. However, there was hardly an acceptable way to keep Africans who had their own funds from studying wherever they could gain admission.

The question of Africans' preference for overseas training and qualifications has often been misunderstood. It seems ironical for Africans to be demanding the provision of higher education locally and at the same time preferring to obtain their education in England. The contradiction lies in the nature of colonial rule and its 'divide and rule' tactic. It was the attitude of British colonial officials toward locally obtained qualifications which engendered the African predilection for English training. Colonial officials deliberately debased local African diplomas and certificates to keep Africans in inferior positions in the service, and to ensure that their qualifications never equated to those held by their British 'superiors'. When employed for the same duty, Africans found that they were paid lower wages than their British counterparts who possessed the same diplomas or certificates obtained from England. This was racism, pure and simple.

Ashby gave a clear example of the discrimination in employment and wages between locally trained Africans and their British-trained counterparts. According to him a Yaba trained doctor was a 'medical assistant on salary scale of £120 rising to £400 after fifteen years' service whereas a doctor trained in the United Kingdom was a "medical officer" on a salary scale of £400–£720, though both might be performing similar duties'.[50] The only explanation openly paraded by colonial officials was that the standards of British education were higher than the local (African) ones. Africans therefore preferred to go to England for higher education which could place them on a par with their British colleagues in the colonial service. Thus British education became the hallmark of academic qualification. Given this framework, it is hardly surprising that educated Africans would view with suspicion any British attempt to establish half-baked institutions which were almost always intended to supply the various government departments with underpaid and undervalued African middle-level manpower.

Another fundamental reason for the African élite's drive for 'British standards' was connected with their resistance to racialist ideas of the time predicated upon social Darwinism and scientific racism. Africans were considered racially inferior to Europeans. Such a stereotype was firmly embedded in the American system and ideology of education. It also constituted a guiding principle of European imperial rule in Africa. As Philip Curtin noted, 'virtually every European concerned with imperial theory or imperial administration believed that physical racial appearance was an outward sign of inborn propensities, inclinations and abilities'.[51] The reasoning was that if Africans were by race inferior to Europeans, then it was imprudent to educate them as one would Europeans. African education should be suited to African 'racial characteristics'. Naturally, the African élite resented such ideas. To disprove them it became necessary to demonstrate that Africans could compete with Europeans in educational attainment. This could only be established by objective and irrefutable evidence that Africans could achieve the same or better grades and classes of degree in British universities in competition with white students. Only in this way could the élite prove that Africans were in no way intellectually inferior to the white 'race'. Significantly, this explains why Africans clamoured for British standards, British qualifications and British universities, and viewed African colleges almost with disdain.

British opposition to a university in Africa, however, had little to do with concern about second-rate standards. After all, it was mostly British academics who would constitute the bulk of the teaching staff of the proposed African university. African colonial governments resisted the university idea as proposed by the Currie sub-committee in order to keep at a minimum the number of Africans who would clamour for lucrative jobs in the colonial service, to preserve the Native Administration system from the onslaught of the educated class of Africans who would seek prominent roles in the colonial dispensation, and to maintain stability, low costs and minimal government. If African qualifications were of a lower standard than British qualifications, they were deliberately kept so by the colonial officials who, naturally racist, wanted educated Africans to remain in subordinate positions.

Furthermore, the issue of higher education adapted to the African environment, even if not racially motivated, was linked to preparing individuals as 'leaven' within the indirect rule system. It was designed to divert Africans from seeking or being qualified for, a civil service largely operating on English principles. Since the Nigerian élite in particular had been implacably and habitually opposed to the indirect rule system, any idea of educational adaptation was received with hostility. Moreover, it would seem that the longer colonialism persisted, the more the collective mind of the Western educated élite became 'Whitened'. By the 1930s a generation had come to maturity which had known no other form of administration than colonialism, living their lives totally outside of the local government system of indirect rule. They worked in schools, hospitals or other institutions under the colonial, not chiefly governments. They took their judicial cases to Magistrates Courts not Native Administration Courts. When seeking government permission for any activity they might wish to engage in, they normally dealt with an arrogant British official or his equally arrogant African 'boy'. They encountered racism and lived in an environment which had become totally different to that of previous generations with their Blydens, Johnsons and Hortons who had given serious thought to the Africanization of education.

However, the reactions of African colonial governments did not impress the Colonial Office and the ACEC. While the Colonial Office viewed their reactions as backward looking, the ACEC barely concealed its contempt. Consequently, the Director of Education of Uganda was invited to London in November 1935 to meet with the Currie sub-committee in order to explain what guided the negative attitude of East African directors to the university question. In his response, he told the sub-committee that the East African directors 'are neither apathetic nor opposed to the development of university education for Africans'.[52] Their main concern, he contended, was that 'a vicious circle might result – Makerere waiting on secondary schools and secondary schools waiting on Makerere'.[53] By choosing to listen to a Ugandan official, London had selected the most likely candidate to support its views. As noted previously, the chasm between indirect rule and the colonial civil service was far less deep in Uganda because the demand for a university arose within the personnel of the indirect rule system. Primarily the Baganda chiefs desired personnel for the Buganda government, seeking the 'leaven' which in theory the British appeared to desire. Ugandan colonial officials therefore felt less threatened than their compatriots elsewhere. Furthermore, middle-level positions whether in government or commerce, hospital or schools were frequently filled by Asians and British sympathy for Africans sometimes, at least, arose from anti-Asian sentiments. In any case the British felt less threatened in Uganda than elsewhere.

It was partly as a result of this discussion that the ACEC, at its sixty-third meeting, recommended to the Secretary of State the appointment of a commission on the development of Makerere College in Uganda. The Secretary of State promptly endorsed this recommendation and quickly referred it to the governor of Uganda for his consent. The approval of Uganda was important in many ways. It was in Uganda, especially among the Baganda, that the demand for higher education was most prominent, and Makerere College was located in the territory. Uganda was the richest of all the British East African possessions with a budget surplus of about £1.5 million.[54] It would also appear that the Colonial Office had noticed that Philip Mitchell, who became the governor of Uganda in October 1935, was particularly enthusiastic about the immediate development of higher education in Uganda. He did not share pervading apprehensions among British colonial officials about 'how educated Africans would be employed or how they might behave politically'.[55] After assuming office, he threw his weight behind the Currie Report and the Colonial Office scheme of developing

Makerere into a higher college. Interestingly, Mitchell was not persuaded by the idea common among colonial officials that primary and secondary institutions must necessarily precede universities.

The university, Mitchell insisted, could grow concurrently with the lower strata of educational institutions, and any country which created the latter without the former, 'will long have to expiate this fault by their intellectual mediocrity, their vulgarity of manners, their superficial spirit, their lack of general intelligence'.[56] There seems to be little doubt that a university by its admission standards alone would act as a major spur to the mission schools. Constantly aware of public opinion since their schools relied upon fees paid by parents, missionaries would strive to raise standards to prepare graduates for university entrance. Any school which did not was likely to find its enrolment falling. In Uganda such endeavour would be fuelled by the fiercest competition anywhere in British Africa between Protestants and Catholics. By supporting the idea of a university, Mitchell knew what he was doing. Not surprisingly, he accepted the proposal for the appointment of the Makerere Commission after consulting with the governors of the other East African territories.

Mitchell informed the Secretary of State that although 'the demand for higher education in Uganda is probably limited to a small minority, ... it is a minority which includes almost every influential African, especially in the Kingdom of Buganda'.[57] The Ugandan colonial situation had been unique. Although an indirect rule enclave, the chiefly class dominated by the Baganda had been very keen on education and Western 'civilization' since the protectorate negotiated its way into colonial rule after the Buganda Agreement of 1900. Ugandan Indians were also enthusiastic and probably better placed financially to take advantage of a university than were the Africans, with the exception of the sons of the Baganda chiefs who owned landed estates. However, the government was most concerned with the Baganda chiefly aristocrats who were British agents of indirect rule and Native Administration. Thus Mitchell admitted that

> There can be no doubt, therefore, concerning the political importance of the question, and little that early action is necessary to prevent the formation of suspicions which, once formed, it might be difficult to allay.[58]

The political implications of the question led Mitchell to declare that Uganda could bear the entire costs of the development of Makerere if other East African governments were unwilling to co-operate. Accordingly, 'the matter is so important, and for Uganda so urgent, that the Protectorate Government is willing to bear the whole expense'.[59] Persuaded by the strength of Mitchell's reasoning, and the views of the governments of Kenya, Tanganyika and Zanzibar that 'in time and method to be decided, Makerere College should be developed to a university standard',[60] the Secretary of State appointed a commission late in 1936 under the chairmanship of Earl De La Warr, who was the Parliamentary Under-Secretary of State as well as *ex officio* chairman of the ACEC. This was the first time that such an authoritative commission would look into the question of higher education in British African dependencies.

The membership of the De La Warr Commission was informative. De La Warr, himself, was well connected within the academic lobby and three members of the commission – Hans Vischer, Dr Philippa Esdaile and Dr W. Maclean – had served on the Currie sub-committee. It would not have been surprising if the recommendations of the De La Warr Commission rehashed the proposals of the Currie Report. The fact that Lugard and other colonial political officers who religiously defended the indirect rule policy were excluded from the membership of the commission signalled that radical conclusions, at least similar to those of the Currie group, were likely. And so it turned out when the De La Warr Commission reported in September 1937.[61]

Meanwhile in West Africa what persistently worried the Colonial Office and the ACEC was how to get a definite common policy working in all the four territories – Sierra Leone, Nigeria, the Gold Coast, and the Gambia. The Nigerian Director of Education, Hussey, who visited London in March 1936, was invited to the ACEC meeting to discuss the lack of co-operation among West African territories and also to throw some light on his three-stage scheme. Hussey told the Committee that as far as co-operation went, little progress was possible 'on account of inter-territorial jealousy'.[62] He therefore advised caution should be exercised 'in the matter of combining colleges, situated in different Colonies, into one University'.[63] Hussey's advice was ignored and the result, as will be seen later, was to cause serious problems for the Colonial Office when territorial nationalism became a potent factor in shaping the post-war effort for the establishment of a university college in West Africa.

Hans Vischer, who strongly believed that 'only a will to co-operate and co-ordinate is lacking' among colonial administrations,[64] visited West Africa to lobby influential persons in favour of regional co-operation in educational matters. No substantial success was recorded. From the establishment of colonial rule, however, British officials had fostered and maintained the idea of separate development among the various colonies. Even within territories, as the case of northern and southern Nigeria demonstrated, the British had isolated groups from their neighbours to sustain what was considered stable and efficient administrations under indirect rule.[65] Each of the regions had been made conscious of its separateness from, rather than its similarity to, the others. As a result, inter-territorial jealousy and rivalry were engendered and then ingrained in the developmental philosophy of these colonies as they began to view themselves as disparate entities.

It is clear that the Colonial Office now desired territorial co-operation because rigid financial parsimony dictated the exigency of colonial policies. The British feared the possible cost of establishing higher educational institutions in each of their colonies. Hence it became imperative to co-ordinate and lump colonies together under a unitary arrangement – as the British hoped would be the case in East Africa if Makerere College could be developed as the sole university institution. While in West Africa there could be competing claims between Fourah Bay, Achimota and Yaba, no competition to Makerere existed in East Africa. While educators in Kenya and Tanganyika were not greatly enamoured of university education, they could tolerate it in Uganda especially if that colony bore the main financial burden. Given the white-dominated economies of Kenya and Tanganyika, few Africans could afford Makerere unless on government scholarships. Consequently East African colonial governments could control, to a large extent, who was educated and what disciplines or professions they followed.

West African colonial governments were not prepared to accept the necessity of a large-scale university education for Africans. They considered the idea of facilities for university education as impracticable and inadvisable.

Thus the pressure from the ACEC and the Colonial Office in favour of the university scheme yielded no positive results. Colonial governments, particularly those of West Africa, were conscious that the burden of financing the university project would weigh upon them given that no funds were envisaged from the British Treasury. Hence at a time when a Commission was being set up for Makerere College in Uganda, Hussey was still insisting that 'the time for a University of West Africa was not on the horizon'.[66] It is difficult to assess how much territorial particularism was really the issue or whether it was a mask to prevent any further development of the university idea in West Africa as a whole. At best, what the Lagos education conference achieved was its recommendation that the University of London should adapt the matriculation regulations to West African needs, which was readily endorsed by the Colonial Office. In the absence of a West African governors' conference which made it difficult to secure unanimity on the question of the development of higher education, the Colonial Office began to consider the option of dealing with Fourah Bay, Yaba and Achimota colleges independently.

Although the Colonial Office and the ACEC were eager to push policies upon the colonial governments, they still basically remained at the mercy of the colonial officials on the spot, who dictated how their various local budgets should be disbursed. It is surprising to note that neither the ACEC nor the Colonial Office thought through the financial implications of founding the proposed new universities. 'In making this Report', as the Currie sub-committee asserted, 'we have abstained from any considerations of the financial issues involved'.[67] This was strange. If the proposed African universities were to be serious institutions, it was quite beyond the financial capacities of these colonies to find the capital to build them, or even the revenue to run them – especially in the middle of a world depression in 1935–36. Both the ACEC and the Colonial Office knew this. The Ugandan situation was very different. The protectorate was exporting cotton on a wide scale to the newly emerging textile industries of Japan and India; this was an export trade on a scale almost completely lacking in the other British colonies.

When it reported in 1937, the De La Warr Commission, like the Currie sub-committee, advanced a 'radical' proposal for the provision of university facilities in East Africa. Although the commission recognized the risks involved in the enterprise they were convinced that such hazards could be brooked for the interest of East Africans. According to them,

> [w]e are proposing the establishment of a University College in the near future, and of a University at no distant date. We are

aware of the present flimsy foundations of primary and secondary education upon which such institutions will need to be based, and realize the possible risks of too rapid advance and of a top-heavy structure. Nevertheless we are convinced that the material needs of the country and the intellectual needs of its people require that such risks as there may be, should be taken.[68]

Thus for a start, the commission proposed that Makerere College 'should be known at first as the Higher College of East Africa', doing post-secondary work in Arts, Science, Agriculture, Medicine, Education, Veterinary Medicine and engineering, and that as soon as the name was appropriate should be called 'the University College of East Africa'. The ultimate aim of Makerere Higher College, the commission concluded 'will be to secure from the Privy Council a charter empowering the College to confer its own degrees'.[69] Hence for the first time a British-sponsored authoritative commission recommended the necessity of the provision of a university for Africans.

Furthermore, the commission advised that, as a stepping stone, candidates should be entered for the external degree of the University of London, Durham University or the University of South Africa. In other words, the Report was the first authoritative document to suggest the need for a special relationship scheme, which dominated the post-war planning of universities in Africa. Although first suggested by the Currie sub-committee, the De La Warr Report was the first British official body to recommend that steps should be taken to build an African educational institution – Makerere – into a University College. Significantly, the De La Warr Report called for endowment funds for Makerere College to which not only Uganda and other East African governments were expected to contribute but also the British Government; a particularly bold plea in view of the British Treasury's financial parsimony. Such an argument which sought to commit the British Treasury to the funding of colonial colleges would have been derided had it been made a few years earlier when the ACNETA, unlike the ACEC, catered to the indirect rule philosophy and when domestic and international criticism of British colonial policy was hardly felt.

The De La Warr Report constituted a landmark not only in the history of the development of Makerere as a Higher College of East Africa, and later, as a University College, but also in providing the impetus for the foundation of university colleges in other parts of

Africa in the post-war period. It blazed a trail and was a precursor to the two wartime British commissions on higher education in the colonial empire. It also signalled the first major triumph of the academic lobby in its influence on British colonial policy on education. The Currie Report was never published, so De La Warr's Report became 'a seminal document' because 'it is the first published exposition of British policy for university education in tropical Africa'.[70]

When the ACEC met in November 1937 to consider the Report of the De La Warr Commission, the Committee wasted no time in resolving that 'the recommendation be put into force without delay'. Now, however, the ACEC introduced an idea which represented a fundamental departure in British colonial financial policy. Despite Mitchell's assertion that Uganda might foot the bill if other East African colonies refused to come on board, the ACEC members for the first time appear to have understood that local colonial financing for university development might be inadequate. To make sure that a university would emerge at Makerere, the ACEC endorsed the De La Warr proposal and asked the Colonial Office to seek 'financial assistance for the endowment of the Higher College ... from the Imperial Government and other sources outside East Africa which it may be decided to approach'.[71]

The recommendation for imperial funding was a watershed in the history of higher education in Africa. The Colonial Office gave full support to the ACEC's request, and quickly set in motion efforts toward its implementation. This is very significant because the change of attitude occurred before Malcolm MacDonald came to the Colonial Office and developed the idea of British funds for colonial development and welfare. Furthermore, it demonstrates that by 1937 the academic lobby had succeeded in enlisting the backing of the Colonial Office. From then on, the opposition of the local officials began to be undermined as the Colonial Office slowly sought to centralize and control colonial policies hitherto left to the discretion of the men on the spot.

In November 1937 the Secretary of State for the Colonies, Ormsby-Gore, made an official request to the Treasury for £100,000 towards the Makerere endowment funds.[72] The Colonial Office employed every conceivable argument to persuade the Treasury that financial assistance was essential. The Office knew full well that it was almost asking for the impossible. Given the poor finances of the East African territories, especially Tanganyika and Kenya, the

Colonial Office argued that 'quite apart from the sum contributed', a British financial subsidy would be 'invaluable from a propaganda point of view, and would provide a striking answer to the charge of neglect, a charge made not only by native races themselves but by foreign observers'. Furthermore,

> [i]t is continually urged that the British Government fails to show sufficient interest in the education of the native populations entrusted to its care, and it cannot be denied that where educational facilities are available they are mainly of an elementary nature and contain no provision for higher education for the professions. It may fairly be contended if the claim that Imperial policy is based upon the Principle of Trusteeship for native races that there is a definite obligation upon the British Government to contribute, wherever possible, towards the education of the native races of Africa.[73]

The Colonial Office's argument is very illuminating. Although it was conveniently employed to convince the Treasury of the need for a financial contribution, the latter's response still exhibited the traditional hostility toward any suggestion of committing British taxpayers' money in the colonies. 'If we contribute to this service', the Treasury responded, 'where will it lead us?' The Treasury saw the Colonial Office request as 'alarmingly indefinite, and one that might lead to almost unlimited commitments'.[74] It disagreed with the Colonial Office definition of the workings of the principle of trusteeship, and insisted that colonies must be financially self-supporting. Accordingly,

> [y]ou appeal to the analogy of trustee; but in private life the trustee does not have to supplement from his own pocket the funds he administers, and if our position were really comparable with that of the trustee we should have to do no more than the best we could with the Colonial revenues available.[75]

The Treasury was not convinced about the prudence of making such a contribution and felt that it was 'being launched upon an almost uncharted sea'.[76] Moreover, Britain's overall budgetary position was 'one of exceptional difficulty as long as armament expenditure continues at the present level'. The Treasury maintained that 'strong justification would be required if we were to ask the taxpayer to find a capital sum for a purpose which could be met equally well by voting annually the equivalent income'.[77] Further discussion was suggested to clarify the Makerere scheme. The Colonial Office was disappointed that the Treasury assessed its request so parochially. The Office's despondency was aptly depicted in a minute by Flood on 23 December:

> Surely an Imperial nation which is busy spending £1,500,000,000 on armaments and spends about £350,000,000 a year on 'social services' in this country, could afford to make a grant of £100,000 as a sign of interest in its childish wards in East Africa.[78]

Hence another letter was despatched to Treasury to drive the points home further. It was emphasized that the East African territories, apart from Uganda whose finances were fairly satisfactory, were generally too poor to embark upon any serious project of higher education compared to British West African possessions. The Colonial Office contended that it was wrong to view trusteeship from the 'purely financial point of view, which is altogether too narrow in this connection' and that 'when the phrase about trusteeship was first used in regard to our relation to the native population of Africa, finance was the last thing that was in the minds of those who used it'.[79] As guardian to a ward or an adopted child, which the 'backward' peoples of the colonies represented, 'it is the duty of the guardian (especially when he has taken on the duty on his own account) to provide him the necessary means to face the battle of life'.[80] Racism remained. 'Childish wards' or 'ward or an adopted child' and 'backward peoples' still permeated the official memos. However, by 1937 it had become paternal racism, which was some kind of improvement.

There was almost a deadlock. Nevertheless, the Colonial Office was seriously concerned about getting the Makerere project off the ground, and the Treasury made it clear that it was open to further persuasion and was eager to see stronger reasons why the grant should be made, and why its long-standing tradition should be set aside. The Colonial Office could not simply give up on a matter of such high policy. On 27 December 1937 a meeting was arranged by the Colonial Office between Sir Charles Bottomley (Colonial Office) and Sir E. Hale (Treasury), in which the modalities of the endowment and the amount to be contributed by the various British East African territories were discussed. Tentatively the amounts were fixed at Uganda (£250,000), Kenya £50,000) and Tanganyika

(£100,000), subject to the Treasury agreeing to give the requested sum of £100,000.[81]

The question transcended that of Makerere Higher College. In reality, it constituted a serious question of British imperial policy. Thus when the request was considered by the Lords Commissioners of Treasury, it was agreed that Treasury should contribute the sum of £100,000 for the Makerere College endowment 'as a wholly exceptional measure'.[82] Stressing that 'the financial obligation of the British Government have not been extended beyond affording assistance, commonly by loan, in cases where a territory cannot produce sufficient revenue to meet the necessary expenses of Administration', the Lords Commissioners insisted that the grant should not set a precedent. Finally, the Commissioners told the Colonial Office that they concurred with its request on the understanding that 'the capital of the Endowment Fund will be maintained intact, and will not be drawn upon for expenditure, at any rate without their prior concurrence'.[83]

Why the Treasury should take this 'wholly exceptional measure' was not outlined by the Lords Commissioners. It would appear that the decision was informed by the volatile situation in the colonies, and the increasing complaints from within and without Britain about the worsening social conditions in the empire. In Britain, critics of empire such as Leonard Barnes, insisted that the British system of imperial rule, particularly indirect rule, was evil and hence should be reformed with the purpose of training colonial populations for eventual self-government.[84] The desired change would include social, economic and educational reforms designed to create populations who had enough economic independence as individuals to operate a democratic system. Some MPs such as Lloyd George and Aneurin Bevan had also begun to feel that Britain was running a 'slummy' empire in Africa and the Caribbean. These critics constituted a powerful influence on imperial statesmen. As a result, British colonial complacency was greatly shaken.

Throughout British colonial territories there were constant problems of unemployment and low wages, largely as a result of the economic depression of the 1930s which resulted in complaints from governors about 'the debilitating effects of declining trade'.[85] In the Colonial Office, the fear had begun to grow that unless something was done urgently, the West Indian riots might be replicated in Africa where there were already signs of unrest in West Africa and among government workers in East Africa. To the Colonial Office, therefore, the West Indian revolts 'presented a timely warning of what might happen elsewhere', and hence efforts became focused upon how to reorder colonial rule 'before social unrest provoked greater violence'.[86]

Outside Britain, the United States was becoming increasingly concerned about the British West Indian situation. Although no major dispute occurred between Britain and the USA on the colonial question until the outbreak of the Second World War, the British certainly had become uneasy with their imperial policies. Germany's increasing influence in Europe by 1935, and its imperial interests became an inevitable concern to Britain. By 1937, Hitler had begun to demand the return of former German colonies in Africa, including Tanganyika. If Britain accused Germany of racism and of unworthiness to rule over subject peoples, the Germans retorted by accusing Britain of naked exploitation of her colonies. Thus the propaganda argument brandished by the Colonial Office revolved around the basis of the British Empire, and the Office felt strongly that it would sway the Treasury. Significantly, the Colonial Office request came exactly at the moment when the West Indies riots, over the worsening social, economic and political conditions under British rule, were destroying the old complacency. Although seemingly a coincidence, the timing of the request for financial aid was excellent from a political point of view.

Treasury's approval marked a departure from its parsimonious tradition, and constituted a real breakthrough in Colonial Office policy. Notably, this occurred before Malcolm MacDonald came to office and before the Colonial Development and Welfare Act had even been contemplated. The Colonial Office request would have been dismissed outright a few years before 1938. The idea of such a large sum going to a single educational institution out of the sacred British taxpayer's pocket was something which hitherto would have been anathema to the Treasury. But times had changed. Political events in the colonies had begun to influence British imperial actions, even among Treasury officials. 'Internationally', as Pearce observed, 'world opinion put the imperialist on the defensive and exploitative imperialism became the hate-word of world struggle against Anglo-Saxon domination.'[87] In the face of this international and imperial political climate the Treasury's fixed attitude was breached. Treasury's departure from convention, no doubt, was a kind of secondary spin-off from the bigger West Indian crisis, in order to show that Britain was becoming interested in investing money in 'social development and welfare' in the colonies. Clearly, the Colonial Office won on high political grounds.

Meanwhile, the East African governments, especially Uganda were ecstatic about the contribution to be made by the British Government towards the Makerere endowment. What now worried Governor Mitchell of Uganda was the question of the name and the site of the proposed Higher College, as well as whether the secondary school should co-exist with the Higher College. The De La Warr Commission had recommended that the site should be moved from Makerere to the area between Mulago and Kololo because 'the present site is not suitable to the Makerere of to-day and will be even less suited to the University of to-morrow'.[88] Mitchell disagreed with the Commission. He insisted that the name, Makerere, and the site at Kampala should be retained.[89] Mitchell knew that a new site and a change of name could provoke the opposition of the Buganda élite and delay his effort to ensure that the new higher college got off the ground at once. As he put it:

> If we have to wait until we can build a complete new College it will probably be three years before we could do anything, whereas ... in the meantime utilizing what we have got, we can make a start almost at once, as soon as points of principle have been settled.[90]

However, the Colonial Office seemed to favour the recommendation of the De La Warr Report for a new name and site as well as the separation of the secondary classes from the higher college because the Commission's view represented expert opinion. Mitchell's view ultimately prevailed, since the success of the higher college scheme depended largely upon his personal guidance, avowed interest, and Uganda's financial commitment in an era when colonial governments still determined policy initiative and implementation.[91] Thus the Colonial Office could not push Mitchell too far, granted that the other East African governments were interested only nominally in the Makerere College plan. But given the complex nature of the issues, both the Colonial Office and Mitchell were united about sounding out the views of all the participating East African governments to avoid possible trouble.

Consequently the Secretary of State asked Mitchell to convene an inter-territorial conference of East African governors in Kampala, on a convenient date, to consider the recommendations of the De La Warr Report, its financial implications, and the Secretary of State's proposals regarding the steps which should be taken to implement them.[92] Although, like Yaba Higher College in Nigeria, Makerere had been an object of local criticism since its establishment,[93] East African opinion had swung round to acknowledge the value of the college as soon as an outside commission suggested that it be superseded by a higher college, and then a university. The rumour that the British Government had agreed to contribute financially certainly rallied stronger support for the college. Seizing the opportunity presented by the renewed interest, Mitchell thus convened a governors' conference in Kampala in May 1938.

In his inaugural remarks at the conference, Mitchell expressed the desire that the higher college should be 'a centre of learning and culture enjoying the security, the liberty of thought and teaching which are essential and indeed implied in the word university'.[94] Mitchell's attitude represented a departure among African colonial governors of his time. Although his drive for the provision of a university for Africans was obviously a response to the pressure exerted by the Baganda, there is little doubt that he was genuinely devoted to the higher educational question. Uppermost on the agenda of the conference was the question of funding of the new college. Taking the lead, the Ugandan Government agreed to contribute towards the endowment the sum of £250,000. Additionally, Mitchell announced that his government would provide the sum of £170,000 to meet the building needs. The Ugandan local governments gave the sum of £7,550 while the Empire Cotton Growing Corporation provided £10,000 for a biological laboratory. The Makerere endowment thus appeared to be a Ugandan affair.

Encouraged by the generous grants by Uganda which totalled £437,550, Tanganyika and Kenya agreed to contribute their share of £100,000 and £50,000 respectively. Kenya's contribution was particularly small because while Uganda had a surplus of £1.5 million, 'Kenya had no money at all'.[95] It would also appear that Kenya's white settler-dominated administration was not particularly keen about the technical and vocational courses offered by Makerere College. Presuming that the proposed higher college at Makerere could hardly achieve the standards of British colleges, Kenyan settlers preferred to go overseas for their studies. No question had yet arisen in Kenya about Africans occupying intermediate posts in government. African participation in the Kenyan civil service barely reached beyond the level of messengers. However, with the sum of £100,000 forthcoming from the British Treasury, the De La Warr Commission's targeted figure of £500,000 for the endowment had been realized.[96]

On the issue of site, the conference recommended that the site and name of the college should be retained, and that 'powers should be taken without delay to secure possession of any building which may prevent future development and to obtain any additional land which may be necessary'. It also accepted the Commission's proposal for a university structure for the higher college, namely, the institution of the Assembly, Council, Principal, and Academic Boards of Studies. Furthermore the conference stressed the need for Council to have complete autonomy from the beginning. Resolving that both the Council and Assembly should be as broadly representative of the interests of all territories as possible, it was conceded that there should be a measure of external control to be exercised on behalf of the East African governments by the governor of Uganda 'until such time as the college attains university status'.[97] Thus, the proposal gave the Governor of Uganda wide powers over the affairs of Makerere Higher College. It could not have been otherwise given the huge amount of money Uganda had committed towards the proposed development of the college. Additionally, the College was located in Kampala and the majority of the students would naturally be drawn from the Baganda.

Concurrently with this conference, there was a cabinet reshuffle in London in May 1938. Malcolm MacDonald had briefly served as the Secretary of State for the Colonies in 1935 and he now came back to replace Ormsby-Gore.[98] Given his liberal and reformist perspective, MacDonald appeared to be more predisposed to the Makerere Higher College project, and the question of the provision of university facilities in the colonies. The Colonial Office's traditional policy of abstention from colonial schemes pursued by the different territories entered a period of revision. It began to move towards the centralization and control of colonial policies.[99] African administrations would now either realign their policies to the changing posture of the Colonial Office or be compelled to do so. In November 1938 the first sod of the higher college was cut by the

Duke of Gloucester, and in January 1939 MacDonald appointed George Turner and Dr W. H. Kauntze principal and chairman of Council respectively.[100] With the financial support of the British Government, Turner and Kauntze 'began the task of turning Makerere College into something more nearly approximating to a University College'.[101]

Nevertheless, what finally emerged in Makerere College was neither a university nor a university college as envisaged by either the Currie sub-committee or the De La Warr Commission. Rather, it was a higher college which awarded diplomas and certificates, and satisfied government's need for the supply of African middle-level manpower. Neither the demands of the Baganda traditional élite nor the desire of the academic lobby was realized. Africans wanted fully fledged university institutions. Anything less remained unsatisfactory. It took several years, as will be seen later, before Makerere Higher College ultimately attained a university college status awarding external degrees of the University of London.

What makes the history of Makerere College between 1932 and 1939 significant is the way in which the ACEC seized the opportunity provided by 'Paragraph 19' of the recommendation of the conference of East African Directors of Education to spur the Colonial Office's interest in the provision of university facilities for Africans generally. The Treasury grant of £100,000 towards the Makerere Higher College endowment was contrary to its traditional financial parsimony. It illuminates the gradual shifting of initiatives from African demands to an impetus emanating from the Colonial Office to break the opposition of colonial governors and their European civil services.

NOTES

1. CO 847/5/7 Report of the Conference of the East African Directors of Education held in Zanzibar in 1932.
2. Uganda Education Department, *Annual Report*, 1932, Chapter 6, p. 11 as cited in Macpherson, *They Built for the Future: A Chronicle of Makerere University College, 1922–1962*, p. 18.
3. R. C. Pratt, 'Administration and Politics in Uganda, 1919–1945', p. 526.
4. See Ashby, *African Universities and Western Traditions*, pp. 16–17. James Currie had been a pioneer member of the Advisory Committee since 1923.
5. Apart from Vischer and Mayhew (who were officials of the Colonial Office) and Mann (who was an MP) the members of the Currie Committee were British academics. Even then, with his experience as a Director of Education in northern Nigeria, Vischer had been a keen advocate of a realistic educational policy in the colonies.
6. CO 847/3/2 Minutes of the ACEC Meeting, January 1933.

7. Ibid.
8. Ashby, *Universities: British, Indian, African*, p. 193.
9. CO 847/3/2 Report of the ACEC sub-committee appointed to consider the policy underlying Paragraph 19 of the Report of the Conference of East African Directors of Education, 1933.
10. Ibid., pp. 2–3.
11. CO 847/3/2 Report of the ACEC sub-committee, p. 1.
12. Ibid.
13. Ibid., p. 5.
14. Ibid., p. 5. The report noted that at present 'while the Colleges at Achimota, Makerere, Yaba and Khartoum do not yet as a whole approach a real university standard, inevitably and at their own momentum they tend towards this final point', p. 3.
15. Ibid., pp. 2 and 8.
16. Ibid., p. 3.
17. Ibid., pp. 4–5.
18. See William Macartney, *Dr. Aggrey: A Biography*, SCM Press, London, 1949 as footnoted in Coleman, *Nigeria: Background to Nationalism*, p. 455. Marcus Garvey, a Jamaican who had emigrated to the USA, built up populist movement among black people which stressed racial purity, 'Africa for the Africans' and the expulsion of whites from Africa. Colonial authorities in Africa and Caribbean regarded Garvey as particularly dangerous and demagogic.
19. Refer to Nnamdi Azikiwe, *My Odyssey: An Autobiography*, C. Hurst and Company, London, 1970, pp. 36–40. Aggrey's remark which tremendously influenced Azikiwe was his insistence that 'Nothing but the best is good enough for Africa', p. 36.
20. Furley and Watson, *A History of Education in East Africa*, p. 297.
21. Uduaroh Okeke, 'Educational Reconstruction in an Independent Nigeria', Ph.D. Thesis, University of New York, New York, 1955 (in Microfilm), p. 69.
22. CO 847/3/2 Report of the ACEC sub-committee, 1933.
23. CO 847/3/2 J. E. W. Flood to Hans Vischer, Colonial Office Notes, 2 October 1933.
24. Ibid.
25. Ibid. Flood insisted that university education for Africans would be a mistake 'of trying to run before we are even able to crawl and I do not want to see it'.
26. Ibid.
27. CO 847/3/15 Hans Vischer to J. E. W. Flood, 12 October 1933.
28. CO 847/3/15 Charles Bottomley to Flood, 12 October 1933.
29. CO 847/5/7 Recommendations of the East African Directors of Education on the Currie sub-committee's Report, at their conference held in Nairobi, January 1935.
30. Ibid.
31. CO 847/5/7 Minutes of the ACEC Meeting, March 1935.
32. CO 847/5/7 Minutes of the Meeting of the West African Education Conference held in Lagos, 25–31 May 1935.
33. CO 847/5/7 From the Government of the Gambia to the Secretary of State for the Colonies, October 1935.
34. CO 847/5/7 Colonial Office Notes on Responses from East, Central and West African Governments on the ACEC sub-committee's Report, 1935.
35. Ibid.
36. CO 847/5/7 From the Acting Governor of the Gold Coast to the Secretary of State, Malcolm MacDonald, 12 October 1935.
37. Ibid.
38. CO 847/5/7 From the Officer Administering the Government of Nigeria to the Secretary of State, 25 October 1935.
39. CO 847/5/7 Response by the Nigerian Government on the Currie sub-committee's Report, October 1935.
40. CO 847/5/7 Note by E. R. J. Hussey on the Report of the Currie's sub-committee, October 1935.
41. Ibid.
42. Ibid.

43. Ibid.
44. CO 847/5/7 From the Acting Governor of the Gold Coast to the Secretary of State, 12 October 1935.
45. For the Yaba story, see F. O. Ogunlade, 'Yaba Higher College and the Formation of an Intellectual Elite', MA Thesis, University of Ibadan, Nigeria, 1970, and O. Adewoye, 'The Antecedents', in J. F. Ade Ajayi and Tekena Tamuno (eds), *The University of Ibadan, 1948–1973.*
46. Foster, *Education and Social Change in Ghana*, p. 167.
47. See Gold Coast Government, Legislative Council Debates, 1928–1929, p. 286 as cited in Foster, ibid.
48. Pratt, 'Administration and Politics in Uganda, 1919–1945', p. 524.
49. CO 847/5/7 From the Acting Governor of the Gold Coast to the Secretary of State, 12 October 1935.
50. Ashby, *Universities: British, Indian, African*, p. 196.
51. Philip D. Curtin, 'The "Scientific" Roots: Nineteenth Century Racism' in Curtin (ed.), *Imperialism*, Walker and Company, New York, 1971, p. 1. See also Christopher Fyfe, 'Race, Empire and the Historian', *Race and Class*, Vol. 33, No. 4, April–June 1992, p. 19.
52. CO 847/5/7 Colonial Office Notes on Responses from East, Central and West African Governments, November 1935.
53. Ibid.
54. CO 822/83/1 Minute by J. E. W. Flood (Colonial Office), 23 December 1937.
55. Furley and Watson, *A History of Education in East Africa*, p. 20 and Pratt, 'Administration and Politics in Uganda, 1919–1945', p. 533.
56. Sir Philip Mitchell, *African Afterthoughts*, Hutchinson and Co., London, 1954, p. 180–81.
57. CO 847/6/12 Minute by the Government of Uganda on Makerere College in relation to Higher Education for Africans in East Africa, 10 February 1936.
58. Ibid. On the educational reason for the Commission, Mitchell stressed that the anomalous intermediate position of Makerere at the time had caused an impression, certainly among Africans and perhaps among others, that standards had already been achieved which were in fact barely in sight; and the most certain and powerful corrective which could be applied would be the report of the proposed commission. Furthermore, he pointed out that Africans, in particular, could hardly be induced to accept a statement of the facts by any means other than the Commission.
59. Ibid.
60. See the views of the various East African governments as cited in CO 847/6/12 Minute by the Government of Uganda on Makerere College, 10 February 1936.
61. CO 822/83/11 Report of the Commission on Higher Education in East Africa, 1937.
62. CO 847/6/12 Minutes of the Sixty-Seventh Meeting of the Advisory Committee on Education in the Colonies, 26 March 1936.
63. Ibid.
64. CO 847/5/7 Colonial Office Minute by Hans Vischer, March 1936.
65. See Coleman, *Nigeria: Background to Nationalism*, pp. 45–47 and G. O. Olusanya, 'Political Awakening in the North: A Re-Interpretation' in *Journal of the Historical Society of Nigeria*, Vol. 4, No. 1, 1967, pp. 130–131. Separate development as pursued by indirect rule fostered inter- and intra-group disunity. The disunity resulting from the Lugardian system which developed the Hausa/Fulani peoples as separate from the Southerners has continued to constitute the crux of the problem of disunity in Nigeria today.
66. CO 847/6/12 Minutes of the Sixty-Seventh Meeting of the ACEC, 26 March 1936.
67. CO 847/3/2 Report of the ACEC sub-committee
68. CO 822/83/11 Report of the Commission on Higher Education in East Africa, 1937, pp. 118–19.
69. Ibid., pp. 79 and 87.
70. Ashby, *Universities: British, Indian, African*, p. 197.
71. CO 822/83/11 Extract from the Draft Minutes of the ACEC's discussion on the Report of the De La Warr Commission, November 1937.

72. CO 822/83/11 J. E. W. Flood (Colonial Office) to E. Hale (Treasury), November 1937.
73. Ibid. Additionally, it was stressed that a contribution 'would have an outstanding value, quite apart from the sum contributed, as a definite indication that Parliament is not unmindful of its responsibility towards the backward races of the Empire'.
74. CO 822/83/11 Hale to Flood, 18 December 1937.
75. Ibid.
76. Ibid.
77. Ibid.
78. CO 822/83/11 Minute by Flood, Colonial Office, 23 December 1937. It is most interesting that Flood, who in 1933 had written about a university, 'I do not want to see it', had come around by 1937 to complaining about the parsimony of the Treasury in financing a college.
79. CO 822/83/11 Flood to Hale, 27 December 1937.
80. Ibid.
81. CO 822/83/11 Bottomley's Discussion with Hale, 27 December 1937.
82. CO 822/83/11 Treasury's response to the Colonial Office request through the Under-Secretary of State, 5 January 1938.
83. Ibid.
84. Refer to R. D. Pearce, *The Turning Point in Africa: British Colonial Policy, 1938–1949*, Frank Cass, London, 1982, pp. 12–16. To these critics, the preparation for eventual self-government constituted the only possible justification for one country ruling over another.
85. J. M. Lee and Martin Petter, *The Colonial Office, War, and Development Policy*, Maurice Temple Smith, London, 1982, p. 29.
86. Lee and Petter, p. 30; Charles Peter Emudong, 'The Evolution of a New British Colonial Policy in the Gold Coast, 1938–1948: Origins of "Planned Decolonization" or of "Neo-Colonialism"', Ph.D. Thesis, Department of History, Dalhousie University, 1981, p. 37 and W. M. Macmillan, *Warnings from the West Indies*, Faber and Faber, London, 1936. Macmillan's book, which argued that without major reforms Africa would witness the same violence, became a reference work for the Colonial Office.
87. Pearce, *The Turning Point in Africa*, p. 12.
88. CO 822/83/11 *Report of the Commission on Higher Education in East Africa*, 1937, p. 85. Twice in later years proposals put forward to change the name of Makerere were abandoned following the unanimous outcry of the Baganda and alumni.
89. CO 822/83/11 Governor Philip Mitchell to Sir Bottomley of the Colonial Office, 12 January 1938.
90. Ibid.
91. Refer to Pearce, *The Turning Point in Africa*, p. 6.
92. CO 822/83/11 Colonial Office Notes on the proposed Makerere Higher College, February 1938. Refer also to CO 822/90/1 Memorandum for Circulation in Connection with the Kampala Conference..., undated.
93. See Pratt, 'Administration and Politics in Uganda, 1919–1945', pp. 523–525. Ugandan missionaries, backed by strong African support, led the criticism of the curriculum. While the Ugandan Government insisted that the courses provided in Makerere should be technical and vocational because it needed the recipients of such education for government departments, Africans and missionaries clamoured for academic education because they desired graduates of such a system to be equal to their European counterparts.
94. Opening Speech of the Governor of Uganda at the Inter-Territorial Conference held in Kampala, May 1938 as cited in Margaret Macpherson, *They Built for the Future: A Chronicle of Makerere College*, p. 26.
95. CO 822/83/11 Flood to Hale, November 1937.
96. Macpherson, *They Built for the Future*, p. 26. It was hoped that the endowment funds would yield about £16,000 annually which would be applied to the recurrent expenditure of the proposed Higher College, CO 822/83/11 Colonial Office Notes on Hale's Letter, December 1937. Interest rates at that time were about 2.5 to 3 per cent on British and colonial government securities and bonds.
97. Report of the Inter-Territorial Conference of East African Governments to examine the

practical steps necessary to implement the recommendations of the De La Warr Commission on Higher Education in East Africa in relation to the establishment of Makerere Higher College, May 1938, as cited in Macpherson, p. 26.
98. See A. H. M. Kirk-Greene, *A Biographical Dictionary of the British Colonial Service, 1939-1966*, Hans Zell Publishers, London, 1991, p. 231.
99. See Lee and Petter, *Colonial Office, War, and Development Policy, passim*.
100. While Turner was a notable Master of Marlborough College, Kauntze was the Head of Ugandan Medical Services Department.
101. Macpherson, *They Built for the Future*, p. 33.

4 Seizing the Initiative: The Academic Lobby and the Planning of Post-war Universities, 1939–43

As late as 1939, when the ACEC, the Colonial Office and East African governments had begun to move solidly in favour of schemes for the establishment of universities in Africa, West African governors continued to oppose the idea. A meeting of the governors to consider Currie's Report, and the problem of co-ordination and co-operation among the various West African colleges – Yaba, Achimota and Fourah Bay – as directed by the Colonial Office, was postponed until 1939. Even when they finally met their views remained reactionary compared to those emanating from London. However, Malcolm MacDonald's arrival as Secretary of State for the Colonies in 1938, with his determination to make policy, pay for it, and impose it upon colonial regimes, undermined opposition from the West African colonial governments to the university idea. The outbreak of the Second World War in September 1939 frustrated progress, particularly between May 1940 and November 1942 when the fortunes of war turned against Britain, and colonial reform was put aside. However, this chapter will demonstrate that from late November 1942, when Allied victory became more likely, colonial development and welfare programmes were revived along with the university question. The training of colonial leaders for post-war social, economic and political transformation once more came to the forefront and two authoritative Commissions on higher education came to fruition in mid-1943.

From 1933, when Currie's sub-committee reported, to 1937, when De La Warr's proposals were published, the importance of a conference of West African governors on the question of higher education had been stressed by the Colonial Office. Yet while East African governments were laying the foundations for a University College of East Africa at Makerere, West African administrations remained uninterested. The nature of indirect rule in West Africa which in effect set the educated and traditional élites into bipolar and antagonistic classes continued to determine the attitudes of officials towards the university idea.

During that period of deliberate delays, the Colonial Office could not make the governors comply. Colonial policies issued from the men on the spot (that is, governors) rather than from the Colonial Office, and the funds for their implementation were also provided by the various colonial governments. In this circumstance, the Colonial Office was more or less a 'toothless bulldog'. But MacDonald's stress on colonial reforms following the West Indian revolts had begun to make sense to the governors. It was also clear that what Emudong referred to as 'the anticipatory factor' to forestall similar riots in West Africa made an impression upon colonial administrations.[1] After many years of feet-dragging the West African governors finally decided to convene in Lagos in August 1939 to discuss the higher education problem.

Before they convened, however, the internal memoranda which the governors circulated among themselves did not make any decisive shift from their age-old opposition. Even though they agreed that a West African university was an ideal to be aimed at, the governors still believed this would happen only in the remote future.[2] The Nigerian Government, particularly, did 'not consider that West Africa is yet ready for the forward policy recommended by the Makerere Commission'.[3] While the governors seemed ready to provide courses leading to the award of diplomas, which would prepare African graduates for intermediate and subordinate government posts, they could not foresee the possibility of, or even the need for, fully fledged degree programmes.

One factor which encouraged the governors' 'remote future' posture towards the university idea was the attitude of Africans themselves. Ashby has noted that by 1939 'some of the enthusiasm for an indigenous African university had evaporated since the days of Casely Hayford and the West African Congress of 1920'.[4] However, Ashby does not explain the reasons for this attitude. The question of employment discrimination lay at the heart of the matter. This was an era when scientific racism, under the cloak of indirect rule and colonialism, questioned both the intellectual, cultural and political propensities of Africans. Many colonial officials believed that blacks were intellectually inferior and hence should do selective jobs. Africans sought to repudiate this claim by competing with Europeans in their own universities and countries. In this circumstance, any attempt at establishing an exclusively African university with peculiarly 'adapted' syllabuses became suspect to ambitious Africans.

Furthermore, on the issue of employment, it had become increasingly clear to Africans that locally obtained certificates and diplomas such as those from Yaba and Achimota received little respect from colonial officials in Africa and London. This accounted for the attacks on Yaba by the Nigerian intelligentsia from 1934. Since qualifications obtained from Britain were given more recognition than the local ones in employment and salary terms, it is little wonder that overseas education became the hallmark of academic achievement for African élites.

Clearly, the question of employment and the destabilizing influence of a highly educated class of Africans continued to trouble West African governments. Given the nature of indirect rule, which promoted the training of middle-level human resources rather than university-educated graduates, the latter had virtually no place in the colonial administration. Given the hierarchical nature of the senior civil service, together with the racial sensitivities of its exclusively English office-holders, incorporating Africans into it became almost impossible. The unwillingness of European civil servants to serve under Africans or even in an equal capacity with them meant that colonial governors faced an almost intractable problem should African graduates become available. Colonial governments were almost always short of staff, but qualified Africans could not be used because of this underlying but rarely discussed racism. Little wonder that the Gold Coast Government, for instance, insisted in carefully coded language that

> As far as this Colony is concerned, the time is by no means ripe for the provision of facilities for higher education on anything but a carefully limited scale ... the institution of an ambitious series of degree courses would merely lead to the creation of a class of university graduates who would clamour for lucrative posts in the Government Service and would become discontented and disaffected if this material reward for their labours were not, in each and every case, automatically forthcoming.[5]

Until the employment problem was clarified it would appear that any scheme for university education in the colonies would continue to be opposed by the men on the spot. Since discrimination in, or lack of, employment would naturally breed discontent, West African governments conveniently avoided higher education projects. Lord Hailey characterized the situation precisely when he observed:

> The considerations which decide the character of higher education are largely political, for the type of instruction given depends on the view held of the place in society which the educated African may be expected to fill.[6]

Thus the stance of the governors, as evidenced in their recommendations, was hardly surprising. Following an earlier report on Achimota College very closely,[7] the West African governors accepted the ideal of a university, but 'it would be some time before this ideal could be achieved'.[8] Dr A. W. Pickard-Cambridge's committee had been appointed by the governor of the Gold Coast in 1938 to inspect Achimota College. It considered proposals for developing the university work of the college, particularly the introduction of courses for the BA Pass degree. In its report, the inspection team advised the administration against the idea due to insufficient supply of students from the secondary schools and the lack of demand for 'native' graduates in government and industry.[9] This counsel coincided with the reactionary views of the West African governments and was re-echoed at the governors' conference.

The governors ultimately acceded to the ACEC and Colonial Office view that there was an urgent need for co-operation and co-ordination among the three existing West African institutions – Yaba, Fourah Bay and Achimota. This was with the object of 'avoiding wasteful duplication and establishing the various courses of study upon a common basis'. While they saw no problem with the duplication of courses up to the intermediate Arts and Science stages, 'duplication of higher or degree work should be avoided at all cost'.[10] With regard to the Yaba engineering programme, the governors recommended that the courses should be retained but not extended and that provision for training in electrical engineering should be confined to Achimota. Similarly, while theological training was left to Fourah Bay College which, traditionally, had performed that role, courses in medicine (including veterinary studies) and agriculture were left to Yaba. In addition, it was agreed that other governments 'should consider the acceptance of the Yaba Medical Diploma as valid for practice in any of the territories'.[11]

As for courses in Law, the governors unanimously agreed that 'the creation of a Law School in West Africa was undesirable'. Although they did not elaborate, this decision seems to have been informed by the fear that legal education might encourage African nationalism and consciousness of individual and collective rights. Thus, following Hussey's 'gradual stages' closely, the governors stressed the need for a slow pyramidal growth of the colonial educational structure. This entailed a gradual building up, layer upon layer, of the various stages of education – from bush schools, through primary and secondary schools, to the university. Finally, however, the governors recommended that a local Commission, headed by Hans Vischer and consisting of the Directors of Education of the four British West African territories, should be established to consider some of their suggestions and to examine the details of a co-ordinated scheme of higher educational development in West Africa.[12]

Before the views of the West African governors reached the Colonial Office, the Second World War broke out in September 1939. However, driven by the desire for reforms in British colonial policy, the Secretary of State, MacDonald, quickly referred the matter to the ACEC for consideration. By 1940 the ACEC membership had largely changed: Currie was dead; Sadler, Lugard, Vischer and Mayhew had all retired from the Committee; and a system of rotation of members with a three-year limit was introduced.[13] This brought in a wave of new members such as B. Mouat Jones, G. Anderson, H. J. Channon, H. M. Grace, W. M. Macmillan, Margery Perham, and Christopher Cox.[14] Soon after, Christopher Cox was appointed as the educational adviser to the Secretary of State for the Colonies, and his position in the ACEC was filled by R. A. M. Davidson[15] from the Colonial Office. Cox, however, remained in the ACEC in a different capacity as an adviser and *ex-officio* member.

These changes in membership and the dislocations caused by the war meant that issues relating to higher education, which the ACEC had almost elevated to high policy since 1933, had to be considered all over again since they were unfamiliar to the new members.[16] Since members of the reconstituted ACEC needed some time to familiarize themselves with the task thrust upon them, they could not act promptly on the recommendations of the West African governors. Furthermore, between December 1939 and February 1940, Malcolm MacDonald was preoccupied with the Colonial Development and Welfare Bill, which he intended to introduce in Parliament. Since the Bill aimed at asking Parliament to approve funds for programmes of social and economic development, including higher education, in the colonies, it would appear that the ACEC awaited the outcome.

The Colonial Development and Welfare Bill was presented to Parliament for its first reading in February 1940. It proposed a maximum expenditure of £5 million a year for ten years on schemes of development and welfare, as well as £500,000 a year for promoting research and enquiry in the colonies subject to review from time to time.[17] Introducing the Bill for its second reading in May 1940, MacDonald stressed the contribution of the colonial peoples towards the Allied war effort 'by gifts of treasure, by production of essential foodstuffs and raw materials, and by the eager raising of Colonial military units far in excess of anything that they did at a similar period in the last war'. However, the Secretary of State further added that the proposals for assistance towards colonial development 'are not a bribe or reward for the colonies' support in this supreme crisis' since 'they were conceived long before the war' and 'are part of the normal peace-time development of our colonial policy'.[18]

While it is true that the main points of colonial reform policy had been laid down just before the war, there is no doubt that the crisis in the West Indies, and the outbreak of the European War pushed matters further forward than British policy-makers would have allowed in peacetime. Supporting the Bill in the Commons, for instance, Jocelyn Lucas (Portsmouth South) affirmed: 'it gives us another opportunity of refuting the accusations of our enemies that we won the Empire by rape and that we play the part of the dog-in-the-manger'.[19] Thus Padmore insisted that the Bill was 'a sop to the colored races of the Empire, whose support was essential to Britain's war effort'.[20] Naanen has also argued that the Bill was 'a political and propaganda initiative designed to mollify rising political tempers in the colonies'.[21] Certainly the pre-war socio-economic conditions in the colonies coupled with the exigencies of the war allowed the Colonial Development & Welfare Act (CD&WA) an easy passage in Parliament.

The Act empowered the Secretary of State to undertake schemes to support social and economic development in the colonies. For the first time, Britain agreed to spend large sums on the social and economic development of her colonies. The Colonial Office would no longer have any difficulty in forcing colonial governors to support the university idea since London would pay for it with funds from the CD&WA.

Before the Act even became law, MacDonald began to set in motion the necessary steps to implement it. The question of the provision of university facilities to Africans was vigorously renewed. Since the Colonial Development and Welfare Act provided the much-needed funds for social development and research, the ACEC and the Colonial Office were now offered the necessary financial instruments to pursue the higher education scheme. The Colonial Office swiftly began to abandon its traditional policy of informal influence in favour of formal control of the social, political and economic affairs of the colonies.[22] From then on, directives as regards educational policy in the colonies would emanate from London and not from the colonies. African colonial governments were merely expected to execute projects approved by the Colonial Office. The ACEC now became a powerful body whose recommendations would not only be readily approved by the Colonial Office but which also could be speedily executed in the colonies with the funds from the CD&WA. Thus, shortly after the passage of the Bill in May 1940, the ACEC set up a sub-committee under the chairmanship of Mouat Jones to review the recommendations of the West African Governors' Conference held in August 1939.[23]

Just as the Colonial Development and Welfare Act passed through Parliament, and as the Mouat Jones sub-committee began its work, the war tilted dramatically against Britain as the German *blitzkrieg* swept through the Low Countries and France collapsed in May–June 1940. For the next twelve months Britain, almost alone in Europe except for imperial support from the dominions, India and the colonies, faced the real danger of invasion. In these crisis conditions, the fortunes of war dampened the colonial reform initiative. Although the ACEC continued to work on the university question, war conditions began to stifle efforts towards colonial reforms begun under MacDonald. In fact, in May 1940, before the CD&WA became law, the Treasury had begun to push the Colonial Office for its suspension and for concentration on matters more nearly relating to the conduct of the war.[24]

But Lord Lloyd, who had replaced MacDonald as Secretary of

State, resisted the idea of complete suspension arguing that 'it might be construed in the Colonies as a gesture of despair'.[25] Furthermore, he reasoned that on political grounds an outright suspension would invite fierce criticism at home and in the colonies. But the Treasury would not easily agree. As a compromise, Lloyd assured Treasury that he would make it clear during the third reading in Parliament that the war crisis would make progress much slower than MacDonald had earlier suggested. Thus, as Flint points out, the period 'from May 1940 to the end of 1942 must be seen as one of retreat ... from the reform policies set in motion by Malcolm MacDonald ....'[26]

The exigencies of war, especially the threat of defeat from May 1940, put the reform process on the back-burner. Discussions on higher education foundered as well. The Colonial Office was now expected to mobilize colonial economies, manpower and production in the service of the British war economy rather than in schemes for social development. Colonial governors were informed that the war crisis demanded 'not only the postponement of progress but some curtailment of existing social and other services'.[27] Projects begun in the colonies, such as the Makerere Higher College scheme, slowed down as others became stagnant. From 1938, when the higher college opened to students, until 1940, the only 'progress' Makerere recorded was the link it established with Oxford University. With the help of personal faculty friends such as Reginald Coupland and Margery Perham, Governor Mitchell lobbied Oxford for the association.[28] This external link, as envisaged by the De La Warr Commission, was an important step toward the attainment of the ultimate goal of a university college. However, nothing of any real importance resulted from the Makerere–Oxford connection.[29] Ashby rightly blamed it on the war.[30] Shortage of staff, poor library facilities, narrow sources of student intake, accommodation problems and other related difficulties continued to plague Makerere during the war.

But the ACEC continued to deliberate on the university question even though the vagaries of the war hampered serious efforts at implementation. The Colonial Office preferred that higher education issues should be kept alive even when Britain faced the danger of defeat. The fear of African post-war reactions and the need to maintain peace in the colonies during the war began to occupy an important position in British official thinking. For one thing, the war brought the colonial peoples face to face with the powers of Europe, and battlefield experiences had begun to demonstrate the mortality of the latter. The doctrine of 'White' superiority was soon to come under serious question. The war shattered the myth of 'British imperial invincibility' since for the first time the British 'appealed for the loyalty of their subjects rather than assumed it as a matter of right'.[31]

The war that the British asked Africans to fight was a fight against racial discrimination, injustice, oppression and Nazism. Africans believed, therefore, that the ideals of racial equality and social justice would be extended to them as soon as the war ended. Indirectly, the war tended to question the whole concept of colonization as it equally legitimized nationalist movements. The ACEC knew this and the Colonial Office was conscious of it. Hence Bishop Grace, a member of the Mouat Jones sub-committee of the ACEC, was merely stating the obvious when he reminded the Colonial Office that

> Our African friends will be loyal in the war, even though on the lowest level it will be from the fear of Hitler; but we must not hide our eyes to the fact that there are many grievances that the Africans still feel against us, and much will spring to the fore immediately the strain of war is over.[32]

Among the grievances Bishop Grace highlighted was the neglect of education. Since the success of the colonial development envisaged by MacDonald depended on the leadership of a well-educated class, a class which was pitifully small, it became clear that the university question remained imperative in the reform process.

The significance of Grace's communication with the Colonial Office was that even though the tide of war had turned against Britain, the ACEC remained steadfast in its support for colonial education. Although the frequency of their meetings was seriously affected, members continued to relate ideas to the possible post-war situation in the colonies. In December 1940, the Mouat Jones sub-committee on the recommendations of West African governors submitted its Report to the ACEC. The Mouat Jones Report was as radical as Currie's proposal of 1933. Its views diametrically opposed those of the West African governors. The sub-committee disagreed with the pessimism of the governors, noting that 'we are more optimistic than the Conference appeared to be'. The Report rejected the opinion of the governors that a West African university idea belonged to the remote future. Instead, they pointed out that 'progress will be embarrassed unless essential preliminary steps towards the creation of a university are taken in the immediate future'.[33]

As for the pyramidal growth in the colonial educational structure advocated by the governors, the Mouat Jones sub-committee rejected that view as 'historically ill-grounded and practically not feasible' since 'the lower layers can be neither well-founded nor brought to completion without the simultaneous erection of the top storeys'. Significantly, the sub-committee's Report employed the analogy of a volcano, to argue for the interdependence between all strata of educational institutions. A volcano 'built up its cone in all stages at once'.[34] In other words, university development should advance simultaneously with both primary and secondary education.

It is important to note that the pyramidal educational development theory had long been a fixed doctrine of African colonial governors. It served as a good defence for their opposition to the idea of a university, since in most territories primary and secondary education was quantitatively inadequate and qualitatively defective. The Mouat Jones group, however, disagreed with the governors' argument that secondary education, which should feed the proposed university, was in a low state of development. They felt that the number of secondary schools in West Africa 'is sufficient for the present needs and, if adequately and competently staffed throughout, forms a broad enough basis for further development of university work'.[35]

As observed in the Makerere Higher College scheme, this 'pyramidal imagery' of educational development theory so favoured by the West African governments, had been repudiated by Governor Mitchell of Uganda.[36] In one of his Makerere addresses, Mitchell insisted that the university should be seen 'as the roots and trunk of the educational tree, the pursuit of true knowledge the sap, and the schools the branches, the foliage and flowers'.[37] Mitchell was quick to acknowledge that progress in one stage depended on progress in other stages. Thus, though Mitchell used the milder evolutionary analogy of the tree, he nevertheless argued for the interdependence of all levels of education as represented in the ACEC's more dramatic 'volcano' analogy.

Based on the evidence available to them, the Mouat Jones sub-committee maintained that 'the time has probably come for the development of general post-secondary courses in Arts, and perhaps also in Science, at Achimota'.[38] Before the outbreak of the war the Prince of Wales College, popularly known as Achimota, had almost completed arrangements for affiliation with the University of London for its engineering programme, which was relatively well staffed and equipped.[39] The ACEC did not want the process to be arrested by the governors' reactionary attitudes. Furthermore, the sub-committee was uncomfortable with the governors' opposition to the inauguration or foundation of a law school in the region. It believed that provision for some study of law should be made 'to meet the needs of those who enter the Civil Service, or serve Native Administrations, in an administrative capacity'.[40]

However, one major recommendation of the governors which apparently appealed to the Mouat Jones sub-committee was their suggestion that a local Commission be appointed to examine the details of a co-ordinated scheme of higher educational development in West Africa. The complex nature of educational development in West Africa demanded investigation. The governors' proposal for a Commission presented an opportunity to look into the particular situation and problem. Even though the Mouat Jones group favoured immediate university development, they believed that there were several problems which should be examined before further action was taken.[41] Contending that the higher education of Africans should not be halted at the diploma and certificate level, the Mouat Jones Report affirmed that,

> While we are not convinced of the validity of the objections, we believe that further investigation of the question from more than one angle should be undertaken before such courses are brought into being.[42]

While agreeing to make recommendations for a Commission along the lines suggested by the governors, the Mouat Jones Report added that the new Commission should not be 'local' or official in composition. Rather, it should be an authoritative body since 'we are satisfied that the inquiry itself will need to be of greater scope, and that more fundamental questions are involved than could reasonably be imposed upon a local Commission'. It is significant that the ACEC picked up the governors' suggestion for a local Commission, presumably staffed by territorial education department heads and the like, and transformed it into a much broader imperial question. By insisting on an 'authoritative' Commission, the Mouat Jones sub-committee knew that its membership would be dominated by experts in the establishment and running of universities, the academic lobby itself. The ACEC was thus proposing to transfer the issue from the periphery to the centre. This is basically what the whole business of colonial reform was all about – seizing control for the centre to make and execute policy, and circumventing the resistance of local colonial service people to reform initiatives.

The Mouat Jones sub-committee recommended to the ACEC the appointment of a Commission 'at the earliest opportunity' since 'the findings of such a Commission would open the way for a definite line of advance in which all the governments of the four territories could co-operate wholeheartedly with definite aim and clear purpose'.[43] At its meeting in December 1940, the ACEC endorsed the recommendations of the Mouat Jones sub-committee, and, in turn, asked the Secretary of State to appoint the Commission 'at once, in order to review matters of urgency in this country and to submit on these an interim report, and proceed to West Africa as soon thereafter as might be practicable'.[44]

However, the critical stage of the war made it impossible for the Secretary of State to appoint the Commission. Apart from the difficulty of securing qualified and capable personnel for the proposed Commission, the Colonial Office had been directed to concentrate only on 'matters more nearly relating to the conduct of the war'. In fact, after the disaster in France in May–June 1940 and during the Battle of Britain, virtually all the reform programmes advocated by MacDonald were suspended and plans for research and inquiry scrapped. The Colonial Office was told that the war crisis prevented any further progress on colonial reforms.

MacDonald's departure from the Colonial Office to the Ministry of Health dealt another heavy blow to the reform movement by removing its most important driving force. Those who succeeded him, with the exception of Lord Cranborne, had little political influence with the Cabinet.[45] In any case, whatever influence each Secretary of State had on the Cabinet was overshadowed by the exigencies of the war following the fall of France. As Flint puts it:

> Whoever had been in command of the Colonial Office in the summer of 1940 could, at best, have fought only a rear-guard action in defence of colonial reform as the magnitude of the disaster in France made itself apparent.[46]

In the meantime, Professor Channon, who had served on the Mouat Jones sub-committee, submitted a memorandum on higher education in the colonies to the ACEC.[47] Channon's visit to Southeast Asia in 1938 as a member of an education commission to Malaya had deeply influenced his ideas about higher education in the British colonies. Written in 1940 'as a postscript to the official report' after his return from Malaya, Channon had submitted the memorandum to the ACEC unofficially as 'his personal views on the problem involved'.[48] The document reached the ACEC at a most inauspicious time when the tide of war had turned against Britain, and at the time the memorandum was not considered. However, the ACEC's ultimate endorsement of the somewhat radical Mouat Jones Report presumably convinced Channon of the expediency of his own ideas. Furthermore, after making considerable changes to the document, Christopher Cox felt that the Channon memorandum should be brought forward for discussion by the Committee.[49] As a result, in February 1941, the memorandum was considered by the ACEC .

Channon's memorandum made a bold plea for an entirely new approach to the question of higher education in the colonies. Introducing the memorandum, Channon explained that three principles had guided him in writing it. Firstly, the colonial peoples with all their diversity of background could only be brought into intimate relationship with each other and with the empire as a whole through the medium of English as a universal language. Accordingly, 'Universities everywhere had common ideals and a common purpose, and advantage should be taken of this fact to help the colonial peoples to maturity and to make them members of an imperial family.' Secondly, the imperial resources of Britain should be drawn upon for promoting the policy of imperial trusteeship. Presumably, Channon meant financial as well as intellectual resources. Finally, immediately following the successful conclusion of the war there would be a unity in the empire such as had never hitherto existed; every constituent part would be glad that it belonged to the whole. Predictably, this

> feeling of gratitude and thankfulness that spread through the peoples would rapidly be replaced however by a desire for further progress, and the peoples could rightly expect that plans for their future development should be disclosed to them.[50]

Here lies one of the most precise examples of what colonial

reform was all about – strengthening the empire by reforms and liberalization. Evidently, Channon was an imperial statesman. He believed in the expansion and survival of the British Empire. For him, the economic, social and political development of the colonial peoples should therefore be a necessary corollary in the process. 'The real progress of the peoples and their ability to stand on their own feet', Channon contended, 'will only be ensured by early and active help and encouragement in the development of the top of the educational structure, in order that an educated section of the community may emerge as soon as possible'.[51] Thus university development, seen as the key to colonial economic and social reform, was put forward as a fundamental method of strengthening the empire and creating the educated élite which would carry through the reform process.

Channon knew that one of the dilemmas which would confront Britain in the post-war era was how to make the colonies a viable part of the 'imperial family'. He noted that the colonial problems of the past arose out of the failure to realize certain misconceptions about the fundamental principles underlying the conception of university education.[52] A university, he further explained, should not dangerously be misconstrued as a mass production machine through which students of different mental calibre were passed. Instead, it should be seen as a place where carefully chosen students of adequate mental attainment were not only fitted to 'take their places in the different professions', but also 'given the outlook necessary for them to play their part as citizens in the much wider sense'. Channon pointed out that

> Failure to appreciate this elementary principle inevitably gives rise to political fears, and institutions of university type are then established only when it is imperative to produce men vocationally trained for some particular type of government post.[53]

Channon acknowledged that there was a genuine fear of the political and economic consequences of the production of a highly educated class among colonial populations, but he regarded these apprehensions as 'largely groundless, for they are based on a misconception'. Insisting that universities would certainly strengthen the empire and not help to liquidate it, Channon asserted that

> The widely varying conditions of the Colonies and Protectorates – the different stages of development of the peoples, the

variations in their economic, social and religious backgrounds, the diversities of climate – provide so many vivid contrasts, that it is extremely difficult to see how each may become a member of a family working for a common end rather than the adopted child of a somewhat unenthusiastic foster parent.[54]

Channon's memorandum fully supported the idea of colonial universities, as did the Currie Report of 1933, De La Warr's Commission of 1937 and the Mouat Jones sub-committee of 1940. However, the difference lay in Channon's argument that universities would consolidate rather than liquidate the British Empire.

The memorandum further reviewed the problem of finding staff for the proposed universities as well as the question of the supply of students. Suitably qualified staff or professors often refused appointments in the colonial colleges while those who accepted were often regarded as substandard academics who could not find such work in Britain. Channon also highlighted the issue of the employment of students of the proposed colonial universities. According to him, 'education tends, in some cases, to be regarded as a wayward and difficult child in colonial government circles'[55] because it often produced undesirable political and social results. Furthermore,

> [t]he attitude of mind often found in government and commercial circles regarding university development in the colonies appears to be a somewhat reluctant recognition that universities must ultimately be created; but this is usually combined with a hope that the day of achievement may be postponed for as long as possible.[56]

The question of standards also featured throughout the memorandum. He noted that 'some of the [colonial] peoples possess a quite remarkable facility for memorizing facts, without appreciation of their significance of application; they have much information but little understanding'. For Channon, the London external degree system as used in the colonies was fraught with this danger because its curriculum had not been modified to suit imperial needs.[57] He suggested that university institutions, empowered at this stage to award pass degrees only, should be developed in the colonies instead. The development of such institutions 'would materially assist the most desirable object of creating nationalist pride in the institution and would lay the foundations of intellectual equality among the native populations ...' Ostensibly, Channon believed that the stimulation of nationalism in the colonies was essential as a force for imperial consolidation, and that by removing racial discrimination (by proving the intellectual capability of Africans in universities) a 'better' nationalism would be nourished for the empire.

Channon insisted that before full university status was conferred upon colonial institutions it must be agreed by both government and other employers that 'the colonial degree is equivalent to the English, so that adequate opportunity of employment of graduates becomes available' and that '[t]his recognition can, however, only come when the universities at home accept the colonial degrees as exempting students from equivalent courses here'.[58] This view remains one of the first thoughtful comments on the lack of recognition of African qualifications. Hitherto, it was felt that Africans would still prefer British degrees to those which the proposed colonial universities would confer, because of the tradition of the non-recognition of local qualifications.

Finally, Channon emphasized the need for colonial universities to be brought into close association with British universities as a whole, and to benefit from the accumulated experience of all rather than that of a single university, a point which the De La Warr and Currie Reports had previously underscored. Channon, who was a graduate of the University of Liverpool, was not comfortable with the somewhat domineering influence in the colonies of the University of London through its matriculation and external degree system. He wanted to see other universities participate in the higher education of colonial peoples. Thus he applauded the recent association which the University of Oxford had established with Makerere Higher College, whereby Oxford would give advice regarding curriculum, and would send visiting lecturers to the college if and when occasion permitted. While recognizing the psychological stimulation this type of connection would offer the students of Makerere, Channon decried an extended method (often used by the University of London) whereby 'a particular university becomes [so] enthusiastic in its work for a given college, ... that it has the possessive rights of a foster parent in controlling the welfare of its adopted child'. In such a circumstance, difficulties might arise whereby

> the college may tend to follow the practices of its foster parent instead of moulding itself to suit local conditions; I can well picture also the possibility of difficult positions arising in a

conflict of interests of the parent universities at home regarding the development of their adopted colleges.[59]

Generally, Channon aroused a new consciousness of the problem of university development in the colonies, and his idea of an imperial university system was warmly welcomed by members of the ACEC. Channon's call for a broader view of the problems of higher education in the colonies, to be followed by direct policy, was something which appealed to most members of the ACEC. His warning that: 'We should endeavour to control future events rather than wait until the pressure of events makes it necessary to take action',[60] highlighted the danger of neglect in the face of potential post-war reactions by colonial peoples to British colonial reforms and development policies.

Channon's memorandum led the ACEC to suggest the appointment of an additional Commission, much wider than the one for West Africa, which would undertake the study of a plan to involve the universities of Great Britain in an overall scheme for university development in the colonial empire. The work of this second Commission, it was expected, would be in relation to the general problem and the means whereby universities in Great Britain could assist in the development of colonial universities.[61] Since the work of the larger Commission would encompass the entire British colonial empire, the ACEC appointed a sub-committee under the chairmanship of Channon to consider the nature and form of investigation to be undertaken.[62] That Channon would head this sub-committee was almost predictable. To a great extent, his memorandum had distinguished him in the ACEC as a key thinker on higher education in the colonies and he was soon to become the leader of the academic lobby in both the ACEC and the Colonial Office.

It was not until two years later that Channon's sub-committee submitted its report to the ACEC. This considerable delay was caused by the war situation which remained uncertain between May 1941 and November 1942. Ashby observed that the sub-committee had to work 'under gruesome conditions of blackout, bombing, and the anxieties of war' and in some cases 'discussions had to be postponed owing to the complexity of the problem and the impossibility of carrying out the necessary consultations with heads of African colleges at that [critical] stage of the war'.[63] Maxwell also agrees that the war crisis inevitably delayed the work of the

Channon's group. According to him, 'handicapped by the war conditions, they [the sub-committee] could not complete their task for two years'.[64]

Even in the ominous face of possible defeat, the idea of colonial universities lingered on in the Colonial Office. Although war difficulties set back development, other wartime events kept the flame of the concept of colonial universities alive. Between 1941 and 1942 Britain was virtually fighting a war for survival. The entry of the United States on the Allied side after the Japanese attack on Pearl Harbor hardly brought immediate relief to Britain. Rather, it provoked a protracted debate on the colonial question regarding self-government, democracy, and self-determination. American support for British war aims, as enunciated by President Franklin Roosevelt, centred on the notion of self-determination and self-government for the colonial peoples. Roosevelt wanted to ensure that American aid for the British cause was not alleged to be for the purpose of the territorial aggrandisement of Britain. Hence, after its entry into the war on the Allied side, US pressures began to demand some definite statements from Britain on 'self government' for the colonial peoples and a timetable for its implementation. Although it is not the purpose of this study to consider the details of the controversy, suffice it to say that it resulted in a realistic self-examination by the Colonial Office of the goal of British imperial policy.[65]

The fall of Britain's eastern empire, particularly Singapore, was viewed by imperial statesmen as something more than just a military failure. In reality, the disaster 'undermined faith in the quality of British administration' since the colonial peoples of the Far East had refused to rise in defence of the empire.[66] The Colonial Office could no longer avoid the need for a new policy, one which 'would seize the imagination and inspire confidence about the future'.[67] Margery Perham and other members of the academic lobby called for the revival of the reform process which had been initiated by MacDonald. For Perham, the colonial peoples had grasped 'the connection of poverty and subjection to ignorance, and there is no service for which they ask with the same passion as they do for education'.[68] Thus, despite the war, the university idea continued to be supported.

In Britain, as well as in the colonies, it began to be increasingly appreciated that the aftermath of the war would usher in a new relationship between Britain and her colonial peoples. Partly as a result of American prodding, Lord Hailey had introduced the new doctrine of 'partnership' with the colonies to replace the embattled and outdated principle of 'trusteeship'. The Colonial Office endorsed this new doctrine, not only because it conveyed the idea of equality and friendship between Britain and the colonies, but also because it would placate its Americans allies. In the colonies some governors began to brace up for the occasion. Governor Charles Dundas of Uganda was one such governor. In June 1942, he prepared a confidential memorandum meant for the local colonial service, a copy of which was transmitted to the Secretary of State, Lord Cranborne.[69] Dundas pointed out that at the end of the war

> Several forces will combine to impose in these respects reforms that will be in harmony with the spirit of the time. In the first place there is what I might call the Atlantic Charter spirit, the universal resolve that there shall, so to speak, be no under-dogs, a humanitarian doctrine that is the direct outcome of desperate resistance against tyranny. There is also the growing sentiment, born in England already before the war, for betterment of all conditions in our Colonies, and elimination of poverty, ignorance and subservient status among backward peoples.

There was no longer any doubt that Africans would exert more pressure for colonial reforms after the war. What mattered now was how to guide these inevitable post-war problems lest they run out of control. According to Dundas, 'thousands of Africans who have served in many lands remote from their own, and who have seen much and gained many ideas, will now exert a new influence which will result in a demand for new methods and treatments'.[70] Such demands, he noted, included education, employment of educated Africans in higher and better-paid positions in the public service, political representation, equality in all its ramifications and better conditions of livelihood. These demands 'will not come only, and probably not most forcefully, from Africans, nor only from our own nation, it will be universally voiced'. Under such circumstance, he further contended, Britain would no longer dictate to the Africans. To do so would attract African opposition because it would contradict the principle upon which Africans and the Allied forces fought and won the war. Quoting 'the old saw', Dundas wrote: 'Good government is no substitute for self-government.' Thus he called upon British officials in Africa and those in London involved in the formulation of colonial policies to 'adjust their minds' to these impending and inevitable changes to avoid being 'intellectually behind the spirit of the times'.[71]

In his covering note to the Secretary of State, Dundas pointed out that his memorandum was 'intended only to stimulate a more liberal spirit and broader outlook in preparation for future developments' among local officials.[72] He noted the persistence of 'a rather too narrow and unimaginative attitude in certain local quarters', and insisted that such 'somewhat ultra-conservative outlook ... threatens to be ultimately stultifying'. Having witnessed 'the far reaching reactions of one war on Africa and African mentality', Dundas confessed,

> I am apprehensive that the new post-war situation may come as a shock to some who, having long lived in the undisturbed atmosphere of Uganda, so far little flurried even by conditions of war – may not be prepared for changes that I regard as inevitable and I have desired to rouse their attention to a situation with which they may be confronted and of which they should be forewarned.[73]

Dundas hoped that his memorandum would arouse the positive interest of the Colonial Office. He was also convinced that, given the more liberal tenor of the time, his initiative would not be misplaced. Cranborne sent Dundas a personal letter of commendation, praising his initiative. The Secretary of State acknowledged the 'radical change of outlook which has taken place' in London 'since the outbreak of the war' and 'a steadily increasing interest in the affairs of the Colonies is apparent in the Mother Country'.[74] The tone of Cranborne's response to Dundas's views clearly demonstrated the changing attitudes in London.

From November 1942 the fortunes of war turned in favour of the Allied forces, and the cabinet reshuffle of that month installed Oliver Stanley as the Secretary of State for the Colonies. Lee and Petter have observed that this period witnessed the shift of emphasis 'from fighting for survival to preparing for peace', which ultimately 'influenced the mood and agenda of the Colonial Office'.[75] Simultaneously, colonial reform, which had been put on the back-burner since May 1940, began once again to receive a new impetus. Furthermore, the shifting of the fortunes of war in favour of Britain gave more hope and strength to officials of the Colonial Office and the ACEC. The ideas of the Colonial Development and Welfare Act began to be revived. Stimulated by the interest which Stanley placed on the issues relating to reforms and the provision of universities in the colonies, the Channon sub-committee began to work enthusiastically. By February 1943, the head of the West African Department, A. J. Dawe, was complacent enough to state that 'war pressures and uncertainties had subsided to a degree where it was necessary to start serious post-war planning for West Africa'.[76] In February 1943, at Stanley's request, Channon accepted part-time duties at the Colonial Office to speed up the production of his sub-committee's report and assist in following it up.[77]

In March 1943 Channon's sub-committee submitted an interim report to the ACEC. Introducing the Report, Channon apologized for the delay in carrying out the assignment. This was as a result of the late arrival for informal discussion with the sub-committee of Mr Stopford, the Principal of Achimota College, and Mr Turner, the Principal of Makerere College. Channon's group considered it necessary to sound out these men in order 'to determine the form in which the colonies would best receive help and reactions to the proposals of the type described in the Channon Memorandum'.[78] The sub-committee also awaited receipt of the reactions of the home universities to the proposed scheme of higher education in the colonies.

In any case, the interim Report formally recommended the appointment of a more authoritative Commission to consider the general question of higher education in the colonies. This was endorsed by the ACEC. Ensuring that the increasingly influential academic lobby was fully involved, Channon argued that the personnel of the proposed Commission 'would need to include considerable representation of the home Universities'.[79] The question of the desirability of another Commission being appointed for West Africa was also reviewed in the light of the all-embracing terms of reference that the general Commission would be given. After considering the whole series of very important particular problems that a West African Commission would investigate, the ACEC formally endorsed the need for two Commissions to be appointed simultaneously. In addition, the need for overlapping membership in both Commissions was raised. The ACEC endorsed the idea, pointing out that 'it would be necessary for the Commission that went to West Africa to have in mind the ideas at which the general Commission had arrived as a result of their preliminary deliberations'.[80] Channon's group promised to produce another comprehensive report on the whole problem – a diagnosis of the present position and a discussion of lines of enquiry which the proposed Commission might pursue.

In May, Channon's group presented its final Report to the ACEC, which called for immediate action on the plans to deal with the general question of higher education in the colonies. The prospect of an early end to the war, and the British Government's pledge of self-government for the colonial peoples within the framework of the British Empire, gave a new drive to the university question. Accordingly,

> there will be a spontaneous and rigorous impulse for self-development among the colonial peoples in the immediate post-war period and preparations must be made to satisfy this impulse. Long-term plans must be made now so that the course of the future events may as far as possible be pre-determined. Unless such plans are so prepared, pressure of events will later compel action to be taken, and action taken under pressure lacks the ordered sequence necessary to success.[81]

Almost in complete agreement with the educational philosophy of Governor Mitchell that the establishment of a university should go hand in hand with those of primary and secondary schools, Channon's Report maintained that 'the progress of education at any level is not an independent thing; it depends in its turn of events proceeding at the different levels above and below it'.[82] Quality teachers for the primary and secondary schools had to be produced by higher educational institutions. Good students who would be admitted into the various universities also had to be produced by quality teachers. In other words, no one segment of the educational process should be neglected. Progress should be simultaneous.

The Report noted that 'the basic problems of higher education are common to all territories wherever they may be, and that they require a common type of solution'. It therefore concluded that 'a clear statement of policy regarding these general problems is needed now, for in its absence more difficult and perhaps insoluble ones will arise later'. 'Once a general policy has been formulated', the Report further stated, 'adaptation to the local conditions is a relatively easy matter.'[83] On the method of approach, the Channon sub-committee's Report stressed the need for the home universities to lend their intellectual resources in the development of colonial institutions. British universities should forge an intimate relationship with the colonial universities, and guide them to constructive development. The need for qualified staff and the policy of secondment of 'good men of varying seniority in teaching and research' was also highlighted. A policy of secondment would enable teaching staff to return to their posts in home universities after their service in the colonial institutions. It would equally ensure that only qualified staff taught in the colonial universities in order to maintain graduate standard.

Rehashing Channon's memorandum, the Report argued that the continued application of the present external degree methods in the colonies was unsound and could undermine the real purpose of higher education. It viewed the curriculum as 'largely unrelated to the background and educational needs of the peoples', and questioned the imposition of a syllabus designed for a British degree in conditions differing so radically from those in Great Britain. Furthermore, it questioned the wisdom of a system whereby 'a College has no part in the examining and the external University has no part in the teaching'.[84] The Channon sub-committee advocated substantial modifications in curriculum and in the method of conducting examinations.

As a substitute for the University of London external degree system, the Report suggested the creation of 'an academic body representative of all the Universities of Great Britain with powers to award degrees in the Colonies'. This body, which should be known as 'The Colonial University', should also include representatives from the colonial colleges. It was expected that they would act as 'joint trustees' until colonial universities had developed and received their charters. The sub-committee believed that this arrangement 'might overcome the possible difficulty of the students of West Africa regarding the new degree as an inferior substitute for the London degree'.[85]

Considering the political, psychological and educational implications of a realistic approach to the university question, Channon's group insisted that the 'very success of our own propaganda leaves us with no option but to go forward ... giving the lead rather than being pressed into action'.[86] The Report further stressed the effects of the new consciousness at home and the impact of the Atlantic Charter and other pronouncements on the colonial peoples. Accordingly, 'advantage must be taken of the new outlook at home, and the expectations of the Colonies must be moulded to fruitful and constructive purpose'. Believing that the problems of university development in the colonies 'must be investigated now, and that plans must be made ready', the Report called for a more authoritative enquiry. As the sub-committee stated:

> We ourselves are incapable of doing more than to provide a sketch of the problem as a whole; its solution must lie in more expert hands, and its political and educational importance with their wide implications are such that we consider an authoritative enquiry to be essential.[87]

When the ACEC considered the Channon sub-committee's Report in July 1943, it viewed the argument as both persuasive and progressive. This is hardly surprising. The academic lobby within the ACEC had sought to influence or initiate a forward policy for schemes of higher education in the colonies for so long. Thus, when Channon's sub-committee presented the far-reaching and radical proposals for an immediate formulation of a policy framework for university development, the ACEC swiftly endorsed their Report. The ACEC reiterated its earlier resolve that an authoritative Commission should be appointed immediately to consider the problem of higher education in all the British colonies, and reaffirmed 'the importance and urgency of immediate action' in the whole business.[88]

Although preceded by other Commissions and sub-committees, such as those of James Currie, De La Warr and Mouat Jones, the Channon Report, as Maxwell observed, 'played a vital part in generating some of the principal ideas and in persuading authority of the need for a constructive policy'. It was, particularly,

> the germ of the idea of an Inter-University Council, though De La Warr had suggested that 'it might be helpful if someone in London could be chosen to represent the common interests of the African Colleges', for example in such matters as securing the recognition of their diplomas.[89]

Similarly, Ashby has described the Report as 'the pacemaker for all subsequent development in higher education overseas' which rehashed 'in a more systematic and comprehensive way the ideas which Professor Channon had embodied in the memorandum ...'.[90] Professor Huxley viewed the Report as 'a piece of intellectual lend-lease', while Creech Jones found its argument 'irresistible' and the case for immediate action 'overwhelming'.[91]

The Channon Report rather overwhelmed the achievements of the preceding investigations. It should be recognized, however, that several advantages helped the Channon Report – advantages which its precursors had lacked. The Report appeared at a more auspicious time when the tide of war had turned in favour of the Allied forces. Secondly, the ACEC was now dominated by British academics, led by Channon himself, who were determined to push forward the interests of the academic lobby. Thirdly, Oliver Stanley, who had become the Secretary of State for the Colonies, was another 'MacDonald' in respect of his drive for reforms and higher educational development in the colonies. Fourthly, the Colonial Office had taken full control of the colonial policy-making process and implementation hitherto left to British officials on the spot. Additionally, funds had become available through the CD&WA for a sustained scheme of colonial development. By 1943 the support of home universities could also be more confidently counted upon, as demonstrated by unofficial discussions with Franklin Sibly, Chairman of the Vice-Chancellors' Committee and John Stopford, Chairman of the Universities Bureau.[92]

Clearly the events which informed the pre-1939 efforts at university schemes in the colonies differed from those which guided policies from the 1940s. Although the Currie Report of 1933 recommended the establishment of university facilities in Africa, it was not until the West Indian riots that a realistic effort towards the socio-economic and political development of the colonies was begun under MacDonald. Although the outbreak of the Second World War stultified progress of the CD&WA, the university question received a new impetus when the threat of defeat began to recede. Not only did it become necessary to maintain the peace in the colonies during the war, it also became very important to mobilize the colonial peoples in support of the war effort. The possible effect of the aftermath of the war on the colonial peoples had begun to worry officials of the Colonial Office. To prepare for post-war problems and ensure that the attendant changes were wisely regulated, policies needed to be planned during the war. Additionally, since the success of eventual 'self-government' and colonial development required a large body of educated Africans, the university question became more relevant. Thus the proposed Commissions on higher education – one for West

Africa and the other for all the British colonies – were designed to give practical purpose to post-war reconstruction.

NOTES

1. Emudong, 'The Evolution of a New British Colonial Policy in the Gold Coast, 1938–1948', p. 37.
2. Sierra Leone Archives (SLA), Colonial Secretary's Office (CSO), *Open Files On Education*, Memoranda on Higher Education by the Governments of Nigeria, Sierra Leone and the Gold Coast for the governors' conference scheduled for August 1939.
3. SLA, CSO *Open Files on Education*, Memorandum by the Nigerian Government, 1939. The forward policy recommended by the Makerere Commission was that immediate steps should be taken to establish universities in British African territories.
4. Ashby, *Universities: British, Indian, African*, p. 202.
5. SLA, CSO *Open Files on Education*, Memorandum by the Gold Coast Government, 1939.
6. Hailey, *An African Survey*, p. 1288. These 'considerations' could also be characterized as 'racial' merely coded in 'political' language.
7. *Report of the Committee Appointed by the Governor of the Gold Coast Colony to Inspect the Prince of Wales' College, Achimota, Accra, 1939*. Members of the inspection team included Hans Vischer and the Director of Education for the Gold Coast, Mr G. Power.
8. CO 847/18/9 Recommendations of the West African Governors' Conference, August 1939.
9. Refer to the *Report of the Committee Appointed by the Governor of the Gold Coast Colony*, p. 140; see also Ashby, *Universities: British, Indian, African*, pp. 201–2.
10. Ibid.
11. Ibid. Apart from Yaba Diploma in Medicine, other certificates were only valid in territories where they were awarded. They were not recognized in London which was the root of the hatred for Yaba felt by emergent 'nationalists', and the consequent yearning by West Africans for 'respectable' and recognizable London University qualifications.
12. It should be recalled that Hans Vischer had earlier visited West Africa, though unofficially, on behalf of the Colonial Office to lobby for co-operation and co-ordination among the three main educational institutions. As an influential member of the ACEC, and the Colonial Office 'expert' on education, the governors chose Vischer as the possible chairman of the proposed local Commission to show that they were being 'reasonable' and 'willing' to co-operate. It was a shrewd move.
13. Ashby, *Universities: British, Indian, African*, p. 204. This three-year term limit was followed by ineligibility for re-election for a year.
14. Channon was a Professor of Biochemistry at Liverpool University and Fellow of University College, London; Anderson was formerly a Professor of History at Elphinstone College, Bombay, India; Macmillan and Perham were both imperial historians at the Universities of London and Oxford respectively; and Cox was a Fellow of Oxford University and former Director of Education in the Sudan.
15. Davidson was formerly a Director of Education in Tanganyika and later became the Assistant Education Adviser to the Secretary of State in 1941.
16. See Ashby, *Universities: British, Indian, African*, p. 204.
17. Refer to *Statement of Policy on Colonial Development and Welfare Act*, February 1940, Cmd. 6175 as cited in R. D. Pearce, *The Turning Point in Africa: British Colonial Policy 1938–48*, Frank Cass, London, 1982, pp. 19–20; Stephen Constantine, *The Making of British Colonial Development Policy, 1914–1940*, London, 1984; J. M. Lee and M. Petter, *The Colonial Office, War and Development Policy: Organisation and Planning of a Metropolitan Initiative, 1939-1945*, London, 1982; and D. J. Morgan, *The Official History of Colonial Development*, Vol. 1, London, 1980.
18. Parliamentary Debates (House of Commons), Vol.361, col.42, 21 May 1940. MacDonald stressed that the new Bill 'breaks new grounds' as compared to the Colonial Development Act of 1929. While the Act of 1929 was devised 'to solve our own unemployment problem' the proposed Bill was expected 'to help colonial development for its own sake'.
19. Parliamentary Debates (House of Commons), col. 42, 21 May 1940. Robert Shenton (*The

Development of Capitalism in Northern Nigeria, University of Toronto Press, Toronto, 1986, p. 113) has further observed that the Bill was an attempt to demonstrate to the international community that Britain was still a trustworthy and humane colonial power.
20. G. Padmore, *Africa: Britain's Third Empire*, Ennis Dobson Ltd., London, 1949, p. 158.
21. Benedict B. Naanen, 'Economy and Society in Eastern Nigeria, 1900–1966: A Study of Problems of Development and Social Change', Ph.D. Thesis, Dalhousie University, Halifax, 1988, p. 230.
22. See Patrick Kakembo, 'Colonial Office Policy and the Origins of Decolonization in Uganda, 1940–1956', Ph.D. Thesis, Dalhousie University, Halifax, 1990, pp. 16–17, and Allister Hinds, 'British Imperial Policy and the Development of the Nigeria Economy, 1939-1951', Ph.D. Thesis, Dalhousie University, Halifax, 1985, pp. 1–30.
23. Other members of the sub-committee were G. Anderson, E. Burney, H. J. Channon, H. M. Grace, C. M. W. Cox, E. R. J. Hussey and W. M. Macmillan.
24. The Act became law on 17 July 1940.
25. Parliamentary Debates (House of Commons), col. 725, 2 July 1940. For the correspondence, see Morgan, *The Official History of Colonial Development*, Vol. I, pp. 87–8.
26. John E. Flint, 'On the Defensive: Retreat from Reforms, 1940–42', Manuscript, 1992, p. 2.
27. CO 323/1755/7450/2 f.82, Circular Telegram of 5 June 1940 as cited in ibid., p. 6.
28. This association arrangement began in early December 1939 and was completed in January 1940. It allowed for the establishment of a Makerere Council at Oxford charged with rendering any assistance which the College might ask for, and to specify visitation for the purpose of inspecting and advising on academic matters. See CO 822/105/16 Reginald Coupland to Governor Mitchell, 8 December 1939.
29. Refer to A. M. Carr-Saunders, *New Universities Overseas*, George Allen & Unwin, London, 1961, p. 244. The only noticeable result of the association was the placing of the coat of arms of Oxford University over the main entrance to the College where it is still to be seen.
30. Ashby, *Universities: British, India, African*, p. 210.
31. Michael Crowder, 'The 1939–45 War and West Africa' in J. F. Ade Ajayi and Michael Crowder (eds), *History of West Africa*, Vol. 2, Longman, London, 1974, p. 612, and refer also to Chinweizu, *The West and the Rest of Us*, Random House, New York, 1975, pp. 101–115.
32. CO 847/20/1 Bishop H. M. Grace to the Under-Secretary of State for the Colonies, 24 July 1940. Grace was a member of the ACEC, and he was raising this important issue in an unofficial capacity.
33. CO 847/18/9 Report of the ACEC sub-committee on the Recommendation of West African Governors' Conference, December 1940.
34. Ibid.
35. Ibid.
36. See CO 822/99/20 'A Governor's Views On Education in East Africa: Thinks University Should Come First', Extract from the *East African Standard*, dated 18 August 1939.
37. Ibid.
38. CO 847/18/9 Report of the ACEC sub-committee on the Recommendations of the West African Governors' Conference.
39. Refer to Wise, *A History of Education in West Africa*, pp. 113–114.
40. CO 847/18/9 Report of the ACEC sub-committee on West African Governor's Conference, December 1940.
41. Such problems involved employment – how far colonial governments were ready to admit African graduates to higher posts; and the types of qualifications and courses these proposed universities would offer.
42. CO 847/18/9, Ibid. The objection was the likelihood that graduates, on the strength of their qualifications, would expect employment of a kind which would not be available to them. By 'more than one angle', the Mouat Jones committee was obviously referring to the ACEC's viewpoint which ran counter to those of the governors.
43. Ibid.
44. CO 847/18/9 Extract from the Draft Minutes of the ACEC Meeting, 12 December 1940.
45. Lords Lloyd and Moyne had consecutively presided before Cranborne took over.
46. Flint, 'On the Defensive: Retreat from Reform 1940–1942', pp. 2 and 4.
47. H. J. Channon, 'Some Observations on the Development of Higher Education in the Colonies', 1940 as reproduced in Ashby, *Universities: British, Indian, African*, pp. 481–492.

48. Ashby, p. 206.
49. CO 947/1 'ACEC Discussions on Channon's Memorandum', February 1941. Cox had perused the document and offered some suggestions to Channon after which the former introduced the final draft to the ACEC.
50. Ibid.
51. Channon, 'Some Observations of the Development of Higher Education in the Colonies', as in Ashby, *Universities: British, Indian, African*, p. 485. For the colonial peoples to 'stand on their own feet', Channon was obviously not referring to complete independence as occurred in the 1960s. Rather, he was thinking along the line of Dominion status which would make the colonies viable components of the British Commonwealth.
52. Channon in ibid., p. 481.
53. Ibid., pp. 481-2.
54. Ibid., p. 490.
55. Ibid., p. 485.
56. Ibid., p. 481.
57. Channon insisted that 'it is of the greatest importance that the curriculum should govern the examination, rather than the examination should determine the curriculum...', ibid., p. 488.
58. Channon in Ashby, ibid., pp. 486-7.
59. Ibid., pp. 490-91. Channon's remarks appeared prophetic. These difficulties would indeed trouble the colonial universities when they finally emerged.
60. Ibid., p. 492.
61. CO 987/1 Minutes of the ACEC Meeting, April 1941.
62. Other members of the sub-committee were Sir Fred Clarke, Julian Huxley, B. Mouat Jones, W. M. Macmillan, Miss M. Perham and R. A. M. Davidson
63. Ashby, *Universities: British, Indian, African*, pp. 207-8.
64. Maxwell, *Universities in Partnership*, p. 7.
65. Lee and Petter, *The Colonial Office, War, and Development Policy*, p. 120.
66. Wm. Roger Louis, *Imperialism at Bay 1941-1945*, Clarendon Press, Oxford, 1977, p. 7.
67. Lee and Petter, *The Colonial Office, War, and Development*, p. 121.
68. Margery Perham to *The Times*, 14 March 1942 as reproduced in Perham, *Colonial Sequence 1930 to 1949*, Methuen & Co. Ltd., London, 1967, pp. 225-233.
69. CO 847/23/9 Charles Dundas, 'Memorandum By His Excellency the Governor on the Post-War Attitudes Towards Social and Administrative Policy in Africa', June 1942.
70. Ibid.
71. Ibid.
72. CO 847/23/9 Charles Dundas to Lord Cranborne, June 1942.
73. Ibid.
74. CO 847/23/9 Secretary of State to Governor Dundas, 30 July 1942.
75. Lee and Petter, *The Colonial Office, War and Development Policy*, p. 147.
76. CO 554/132/33718/1943 as cited in ibid., p. 151.
77. Channon himself was acting as Adviser on Education to the Secretary of State for the Colonies at the crucial period in 1943; Sir Christopher Cox was then on an extended tour in Africa.
78. CO 987/1 ACEC Discussion on the Interim Report of the Channon's sub-committee on Higher Education, March 1943.
79. CO 987/1 ACEC Discussion on the Interim Report of the Channon sub-committee on Higher Education, March 1943.
80. Ibid.
81. Report of Channon sub-committee on Higher Education in the Colonies, 1943 as reproduced in Ashby, *Universities: British, Indian, African*, p. 495.
82. Ibid., p. 596.
83. Ibid., p. 504.
84. Ibid., p. 509.
85. Ibid., p. 512. This was the view expressed by the Principal of Achimota College at a meeting with the members of the Channon's sub-committee.
86. Ibid., p. 523.
87. Ibid., p. 524.
88. CO 987/1 ACEC Resolution on the Report of the sub-committee on Higher Education, July 1943.

89. Maxwell, *Universities in Partnership*, pp. 7-8. The origins and functions of the Inter-University Council (IUC) will be highlighted in the next chapter.
90. Ashby, *Universities: British, Indian, African*, p. 208.
91. CO 987/1 ACEC Discussion of the Report of the Channon's sub-committee on Higher Education, July 1943.
92. CO 987/1 ACEC Discussion on the Channon's Interim Report, op. cit. Both Sibly and Stopford agreed that an authoritative enquiry was essential and recognized that the home universities had serious obligations towards the colonies.

5 The Asquith and Elliot Commissions, 1943–46: Laying the Foundations for University 'Imperialism'

From November 1942, when Oliver Stanley took over the affairs of the Colonial Office, matters relating to colonial development began to receive new impetus. Specifically, he considered university education as 'one of the most important questions in connection with the post-war reconstruction and development of the Colonial Empire ...'.[1] Under the new dispensation, which rested on colonial economic, social and political development, and coupled with pressures from the African intelligentsia, the objective of universities in the colonies became clearer. It was apparent that development in the colonies after the war would certainly require the collaboration of an educated African élite with skills. Since this class was pitifully small there was an urgent need to expand it if real progress was to be expected. Here the desire of the African educated élites to take control and the determination of the Colonial Office to allow them a measure of responsibility coincided.

The appointment of the Asquith and Elliot Commissions on higher education in July 1943 became an essential first step towards British colonial post-war planning. It marked a turning-point because, for the first time, the question of university development in the colonies became a matter of high policy. The Asquith Commission was expected to survey the higher educational needs of the whole British colonial empire, to look into the general question of the principles which should guide the development of universities, and how the process might be assisted by universities and institutions in the United Kingdom. The Elliot Commission – limited to British West Africa – was more directly concerned with investigating the existing conditions of higher education, the needs of the territories and how these needs could best be met by university development. The groundwork for the university scheme was complex and required careful planning; Stanley gave the project his utmost attention, personally working out the details while the great events of the war were turning against the Axis. Ashby portrayed the picture succinctly:

> While the Allied general staff worked out a greater and more dramatic strategy in Casablanca and Washington and Quebec, Stanley and his advisers were devising ways to mobilize the British universities to carry higher education into the colonial empire.[2]

The members of the Commissions were chosen after a series of informal discussions between the Colonial Office and the ACEC. In most cases, Stanley was directly involved, with Channon acting as ACEC spokesman. Since his memorandum, Channon had assumed a prominent position in London on matters of higher education in the colonies. In fact, in early February 1943, Channon was seconded to the Colonial Office to help advise Stanley on how the two proposed Commissions would function. Stanley was preparing his speech for the July debate in the House of Commons, and wanted to be able to announce the new policy to establish universities which would train Africans for self-government. From the onset, both the ACEC and the Colonial Office recognized the special role British academics would play. Those to be appointed to the proposed Commission should therefore demonstrate standing and influence among British academics. The opportunity had finally come for the academic lobby to influence significantly British imperial policy.

Since the findings of the two Commissions would relate to each other, and to ensure co-ordinated efforts from the beginning, the Secretary of State readily endorsed the ACEC's idea of overlapping membership. When they were appointed in mid-1943, Professor Channon and Dr J. F. Duff became members of both Commissions.[3] Considering the broader question and the general principles of higher education, the Asquith Commission held most of its sittings in London with occasional visits, usually in small groups, to various colonies. The Elliot Commission, on the other hand, spent some time in West Africa because its members were investigating the particular problem presented by that region. When the two

THE ASQUITH COMMISSION

Oliver Stanley endorsed the Channon sub-committee's Report on the setting up of a general Commission on higher education in March 1943. But before he could proceed, he decided to sound out the views of the British universities which were expected to play a major role in the whole process. The Colonial Office therefore initiated discussions with the universities, prominent amongst which were Oxford and Cambridge. The University of London became somewhat apprehensive when the appointment of the Asquith Commission began to be rumoured in April 1943. The University's major concern was that its traditional role in the colonies through the external degree programmes, which had long been a source of pride, might be disregarded by the Colonial Office in the new enterprise.

Writing to Alexander Carr-Saunders of the University of London School of Economics, the Principal of the University, Harold Claughton, confessed that he was 'rather perturbed about our relationship with the Colonial Office'.[4] He feared that 'matters may be maturing too fast in other directions whilst we are being left out in the cold'. Deeply distressed about official dislike for the workings of the London external degree system,[5] Claughton was convinced that 'much was going on behind the scenes' between the Colonial Office and other institutions, such as Oxford and Cambridge Universities. Claughton further affirmed that his fears 'were somewhat intensified over the week-end (and this you must keep to yourself)' when a Colonial Office man told him: 'I wish I could tell you what is going on behind the scenes but of course my lips are sealed'.[6] Claughton wanted Carr-Saunders to give his own assessment of the situation. Carr-Saunders was a powerful name both in the academic world and in Colonial Office circles, and, clearly, the Principal was looking for 'inside influence' with the Colonial Office. Carr-Saunders was on no less than three Colonial Office Advisory Committees,[7] and Claughton knew very well that there was not much Colonial Office policy of which Carr-Saunders was unaware.

The University of London was clearly ambitious in this matter, and wanted primacy in the whole business. The University was alarmed that the Colonial Office had not accorded it a role in the proposed development of colonial universities. Dominating university education in the colonies through its external degree scheme, London was outraged that Oxford and Cambridge Universities had been in serious consultation with the Colonial Office. Oxford, which had always proclaimed its 'imperial mission', remained an academic as well as institutional rival to London, even if not directly in relation to external degree programmes.[8] This rivalry had accounted for the derisory Oxford–Makerere links in 1940, the aim of which had been to challenge London dominance of colonial education.

One way or the other it seemed as if a 'scramble' for educational influence in the colonies was in the offing. The idea, in fact, was for joint co-operation among British universities. There was nothing conspiratorial in the discussions between the Colonial Office and the other universities, as later events would show. The Colonial Office wanted to sound out, and possibly induce, the support of all the home institutions towards the work of the contemplated Commission. The Secretary of State finally approached the University of London in May 1943. From then on, London University's efforts were guided by its ambitions, which were ultimately fulfilled as future events would demonstrate.

In his letter to the University of London, also transmitted to the other home universities, Stanley formally outlined his intention to set up an authoritative Commission on higher education in the colonies. He told them that he would need their help in order to implement the government's policy of extending university facilities to the colonies. Accordingly, 'I am troubling you with this letter in the hope of enlisting your sympathy towards a project for furthering higher education in the Colonial Empire.'[9] Reminding the various vice-chancellors of the government's deep commitment to 'quickening the progress of Colonial peoples towards a higher level of social well-being and towards the ultimate goal of self-government', Stanley maintained that it was 'essential to the success of this policy that the supply of leaders from the indigenous people themselves should be rapidly increased'. He pointed out the urgent and fundamental need to enlarge university facilities without which those leaders could not be created.[10]

Stanley outlined two phases in the project for which assurances of interest among the home universities would be of great importance. The first was the preliminary task of investigation, while the second would arise after the Commission had reported. In relation to the first phase, he suggested that the proposed Commission must not only include the amplest representation of the United Kingdom universities but also count on their assistance in giving valuable evidence throughout the sittings of the Commission. Stanley insisted that he would not 'launch' the Commission unless he felt assured that he could include in its membership 'some men of high distinction in our University life who would command confidence as exponents of university opinion upon the subject at issue'. With regard to the second phase he noted that, while it was 'impossible to anticipate what suggestions the Commission might put forward for eliciting the aid and interest of the Universities in the cause of higher education in the Colonies', it 'would be heartening to know that the Universities would feel disposed to examine sympathetically any practical suggestions which the Commission might make'. Thus he declared:

> I naturally could both expect more than an expression of general goodwill and a readiness to approach any suggestion which the Commission put forward in a helpful desire to assist if possible the achievement of the wider aims in view.[11]

Acknowledging that the war had greatly stimulated the aspirations of the colonial peoples towards a fuller means of self-expression in both political and cultural spheres, the Secretary of State surmised that 'when the story of their contribution to the war effort is told, it will place beyond question their right to receive the best contributions towards their future advancement which this country can offer them'. The colonial peoples expected Britain to provide them with that background of education and knowledge in the furtherance of the declared aims of a higher level of social well-being and self-government. The development of universities in the colonies constituted one of the most important steps to be taken in the post-war years. Such universities would be developed into active centres of both teaching and research, equal to those of universities in the United Kingdom.

Additionally, Stanley made an analogy between the past role of the home universities in 'training and nourishing' imperial administrators, and the new role of rearing local colonial leaders of the future. Here, Stanley was implicitly contrasting the former role of Oxford and Cambridge in training old colonial rulers with the new role of the University of London in rearing colonial 'nationalists'. Finally, as a mark of confidence and flattery, the vice-chancellors were advised to treat the matter as confidential until the Secretary of State was in a position to announce the appointment of the Commissions in the House of Commons.[12]

The University of London was, of course, delighted to co-operate. The Vice-Chancellor, Professor Frank Horton, assured Stanley that 'this University, itself the pioneer through its External side in extending facilities for higher education throughout the Colonial Empire, would not be backward in its interest in any agreed schemes planned in the cause of higher education in the colonies and for the wise development of Colonial Universities'.[13] The University was ambitious, and clearly desired to employ its external degree traditions to displace its rivals in the inter-university 'scramble' for influence in the colonial higher education schemes. Meanwhile, responses from other universities were similarly sympathetic. It would have been surprising for any of the home institutions to turn down this call for understanding and participation in the higher education of British overseas subjects, where the University of London had hitherto dominated through its external degree system.

With such assurances of co-operation from the home universities, Oliver Stanley felt confident to put education, especially university education, at the centre of his 13 July 1943 speech in the House of Commons. Noting that 'we are beginning, rightly, to think of, and prepare for, peace', he reiterated the British Government's commitment to the social, economic and political development of the colonies. Issuing his famous declaration about the object of British imperial policy, Stanley affirmed:

> we are pledged to guide Colonial people along the road to self-government within the framework of the British Empire. We are pledged to build up their social and economic institutions, and we are pledged to develop their natural resources.[14]

Acknowledging that critics of empire both in Britain and abroad had often concentrated on political evolution he stressed that it was by success in that field, success in advancing these colonial territories towards 'self-government', that 'critics are apt to test both our sincerity and our efficiency'. But success in 'self-government' must 'have solid social, and economic foundations' without which 'they will bring to those whom it is designed to benefit nothing but disaster'. Significantly, Stanley emphasized educational advance and economic development 'as the twin pillars upon which any sound scheme of political responsibility must be based'.[15]

Self-government and economic development must depend on a large body of trained professionals such as agriculturists, engineers, doctors, teachers, veterinary surgeons, and technicians. Stanley stressed the immense part colonial universities would play not only in the training of these professionals but also in the area of research. To encourage the constructive growth of colonial universities he emphasized the need for guidance and help from home universities, and further envisaged a partnership or 'an intellectual Lend-Lease between the universities at home and the Colonial centres of higher education'.

Expressing his confidence that from his 'preliminary and unofficial inquiries' the home universities were ready to take on the task, Stanley then announced the appointment of a Commission on higher education in the colonies, under the chairmanship of Cyril Asquith,[16] with the following terms of reference:

> To consider the principles which should guide the promotion of higher education, learning and research, and the development of Universities in the Colonies; and to explore means whereby Universities and other appropriate bodies in the United Kingdom may be able to co-operate with institutions of higher education in the colonies in order to give effect to these principles'.[17]

Simultaneously, he also set up another Commission for West Africa under Walter Elliot which will be discussed later in this chapter. Stanley could not yet give the House of Commons the full list of members of either Commission. However, he declared that he would like to see some overlapping membership between the two Commissions since their work 'will be closely linked'.[18]

There were no objections in Parliament to the appointment of these Commissions. This demonstrated the extent of political transformation taking place in Britain during the war. The war witnessed a coalition in which Labour's participation in the government made it difficult for the Conservatives to do anything of serious political import to which Labour had strong objections. Paul

Addison has shown how normal British party politics almost halted in the interest of national unity. Furthermore, he noted that from this period onward there was a huge Leftward swing in British opinion, particularly from November 1942.[19] Henceforth British Parliamentary debates became influenced if not dominated by Labour ideas. It was during this period that Stanley presented his address on the goal of British imperialism as well as the appointment of the two Commissions on higher education. Stanley was extremely anxious to create an agreed bipartisan colonial policy to avoid any party politics or divisions. He was aware that for colonial reforms to succeed it was essential that inter-party bickering be avoided.

By August the list of members of the Asquith Commission was ready, after consultation with the ACEC, 'with an eye to their standing and influence among British academics'.[20] There were sixteen members in all including the chairman. These were A. M. Carr-Saunders, Donald Cameron, H. J. Channon, Fred Clarke, J. F. Duff, Lord Hailey, James Irvine, Richard Livingstone, R. Marrs, Lilian Penson, Margery Perham, R. E. Priestley, J. A. Ryle, R. V. Southwell and J. A. Venn.[21] Although the membership of the Commission included celebrated political officers – Hailey and Cameron – the academic lobby dominated the membership, since the outcome of the Commission's investigation and the success of the whole scheme would depend on their effort.

The Asquith Commission met for the first time on 21 September 1943. In his opening address, the Chairman of the Commission began by emphasizing the politics of the whole enterprise. He reiterated the Secretary of State's pledge 'upon more than one occasion' to accelerate so far as possible, and to the utmost of his power the progress of the colonial peoples towards the ultimate goal of self-government. 'It is obvious that a pre-requisite to that progress', Asquith stated,

> is an advance in education, and ... it seems to me in our terms of reference, that the Government considers that there is no more hopeful means of providing a way to self-government than the extension and improvement of higher education.[22]

He reminded members that the Commission's task would fall under three broad sections. One would be a survey of the existing facilities for higher education in the colonies. Another demanded the formulation of general principles which should govern the development and extension of facilities. Finally, they must suggest practical proposals for giving effect to these principles.

For Asquith, 'the necessary advance cannot be made by the unassisted efforts of the Colonies themselves which suffer from great difficulties and handicaps, in the lack of adequate staff and finance.' Additionally, he highlighted the problems in the colonies which hindered experienced faculty members of home universities from taking up positions in the colonial educational institutions. Such difficulties include 'unpleasant surroundings, ... the lack of necessary research laboratories, libraries and so forth'.[23] Any meaningful progress would depend on the goodwill of the home universities. Asquith then notified members that the response from the British universities to the project had been 'both sympathetic and encouraging'.

Addressing the defective nature of the existing colonial educational system, Asquith argued that it 'has leant strongly towards the vocational side ...; it has not been directed consciously to evolving those civic qualities or qualities of leadership which will have to be developed if self-government is to follow'. Clearly, the Chairman's observation touched on the root of the larger question. Hitherto, it had been an aberration to train the colonial peoples as leaders. Since they were supposed to be educated as perpetual subjects, colonial education had been consciously modelled towards the training of those who would occupy the various intermediate positions in the colonial service. Such positions included clerks, typists, technicians, laboratory and medical assistants and other subordinate cadres. Deliberate attempts had been made to avoid the production of politically conscious elements whom the British feared as naturally troublesome and capable of upsetting the system of indirect rule. Asquith was fully aware of the central political question underlying the task given to his Commission; it amounted to a complete change in the assumptions which had governed political and constitutional thinking in the pre-war period.

Significantly, the Chairman reminded the Commissioners that Britain had entered the fifth year of the war and that 'opinions are fluid and the public is prepared to accept radical changes to an extent for which it is not prepared in peace-time'. Consequently, 'proposals which go to the root of the problem would be much more likely to be acceptable at this time, than at almost any other.'[24] Asquith's statement was an accurate assessment of British opinion. With the huge swing of opinion towards Labour-style radical policies following wartime exigencies, Asquith felt that the initiative must be seized to push the colonial university question. He was not confident that after the war these reforms could be carried out with an appropriate urgency since the peacetime politics of compromise and rhetoric would dilute the whole business. From November 1942 (beginning with the victory at Alamein), policies which might well have been rejected in peacetime began to be accepted.[25] Fortunately, it was during this period that the Asquith group was working, and the Chairman urged the Commissioners to make whatever radical recommendations they deemed relevant now that opinions were fluid.

Before the inaugural meeting rose, it mandated the Chairman to write to British universities to solicit their advice and co-operation during the course of the Commission's work. It was also considered important to sound out the views of local colonial administrations through the Secretary of State. In October, Asquith approached the British universities asking for their goodwill, advice and help in looking for ways to associate British universities with the new colonial institutions.[26] A month later 'Annexure II' was circulated to governments, vice-chancellors and principals of colleges in the colonies via the Secretary of State.[27]

The Annexure included, first, the questions of modification of curricula and syllabuses to suit local needs, the issue of secondment of staff of British universities to the colonial institutions and the problem of sabbatical study leave for staff of the colonial colleges. Secondly, it proposed that before the colleges reached a degree-granting stage, their students should sit for external degrees which would be of high standard and relevant to local conditions (with standards determined by external examiners collaborating, either by visiting or otherwise, with the staff of the colonial colleges). Thirdly, the Annexure suggested that the colleges should be constituted not only as centres of teaching, but also of research. This question of research was advocated by the ACEC, officials of the Colonial Office and the University of London, who all believed that only research could produce the much-needed local curricula in the colonial institutions. Fourthly, it was proposed that the Commission would address the issue of qualification for entrance into the colleges, the possible fees to be charged and the numbers, subjects and values of scholarships. Fifthly, views were asked for on: the method of government of the existing colonial colleges and the adequacy of staff and finance; the scope of studies required as a preparation for careers in the government administrative services; and the general policy regarding the rate and nature of the development of professional courses such as medicine, engineering, agriculture and social science. Finally, the Commission wished colonial governments to sound out the desire of the peoples, not presently served by any institutions, for new centres of higher education after the war.[28]

The responses to the Annexure from the African governments revealed that, while forced to accept a policy imposed from London, there was a distinct lack of enthusiasm. The Gold Coast Government, for instance, had reservations about the role of the London University external degree, apparently thinking that the plan would entail simply the establishment of colleges working for the existing external degree. The view was that 'External syllabuses cannot be adequately adjusted to local needs' because

> the necessity for preserving general uniformity between the External examinations at centres all over the world makes it impossible for the syllabuses to have more than a limited local adaptation.[29]

The Gold Coast Government argued that even though it would take some time to build up an adequate standard for the proposed university 'this time should not be exaggerated'. In line with the view of the Asquith group, it considered research 'of the greatest importance'. Without such research, the Government further observed, 'the teaching in a university would have little more than a general bearing on the political, economic and social life of the people of the region it serves'.

Ostensibly very much concerned about adaptation and standards, it would appear that the anxiety shown by the Gold Coast Government was related to its resistance to clear-cut Africanization of the colonial service. Despite the fact that it had been forced to accept the idea of university development, the colonial government stressed the 'need for a measure of caution in the turning out of graduates until there is a reasonable hope of the country being able to absorb them'. It concluded that it could only proceed on the university project 'at as great a rate as financial and other circumstances of the colony permit' and that 'any West African university which is established should restrict its degree courses to those fields in which the likelihood of local employment is greatest'. In admitting students to courses such as agriculture, engineering, education and medicine, 'the college authorities should relate the number of entrants to the prospective number of vacancies that are likely to be available'.[30] The vacancies envisaged were normally those of assistants and intermediate positions. Basically, the position of the Gold Coast Government had not changed much even in the face of the emerging wartime liberalism in Britain. It still believed in the pre-war educational policy of a carefully regulated production of educated Africans in order to preserve the indirect rule system.

In its response to the Annexure, the Nigerian Government agreed with the memorandum submitted by the Acting Principal of Yaba Higher College, W. A. Thorp.[31] It recognized the need for an exchange of staff between the new colonial colleges and British universities and, unlike the Gold Coast, preferred the imposition of British standards on the Nigerian peoples. Nigeria's main difficulty, according to the Government, 'is that it has no standards comparable with those of more highly developed countries'. Thus it insisted that the problem of inferiority and inefficiency of the Nigerian labour force could only be solved by the 'importation of the standards and of the actual workmen and professional men of European countries'. Furthermore, the Government observed that

> The more closely Nigeria is tied to external standards the better is the chance of cultivating a desire for the best as opposed to something which is just good enough to pass muster.[32]

Evidently the Nigerian colonial regime was less reluctant than the Gold Coast. The Yaba College controversy and the view of the Lagos intellectuals that British standards should be adopted in the College had compelled the Nigerian Government to become more open to the idea of further education for Africans.

Besides, the Government had come to realize that high standards were related to skill. In a sense, the economic impact of a university was becoming clearer to the regime. Perceptively, therefore, it warned that 'great social problems loom ahead in Nigeria' in the immediate post-war years unless economic research which 'is perhaps even more urgently needed' was emphasized. The position of the Nigerian Government on the economic aspect of university training and self-government remains striking. African proto-nationalists during the inter-war years and particularly the period preceding the Second World War hardly gave any serious thought to economic development. Thus the NCBWA focused upon the electoral process for the members of the Legislative Councils in the 1920s. What mattered to them was how to enter the colonial administration on a par with the Europeans. Even those Africans who wrested political power from the Europeans from the 1950s committed the same blunder of thinking that political independence would automatically assure economic development. On independence, lamentably, it was discovered that the 'nationalists' possessed no blueprint with which to tackle the attendant economic problems.

Supporting the idea of secondment and the idea of the colonial college staffs visiting London for study leave, the Nigerian Government presumed that the policy 'would help to readjust mental standards and ... self-confidence' which would be difficult to achieve in isolation. It was in such isolation, the Government further concluded, that teachers in Nigeria sometimes found they were setting standards for their students 'which could not be met in European schools'. Furthermore, it advised that research work should not be confined to the applied sciences.

Viewed from another perspective, it would appear that the Nigerian colonial government was as apprehensive as the Gold Coast regarding the issue of employment for graduates who would qualify in the administrative courses of the envisaged West African university. The Government regretted the Commission's stress on administrative studies rather than the productive sciences fearing that such emphasis would make the new universities merely vehicles for training Africans for administrative posts in the colonial service. It insisted that Nigeria 'is less in need of African administrators than the men who will see that the country produces something to be administered'.[33]

The administrations of Sierra Leone and the Gambia were somewhat indifferent to forging ahead with the university schemes. Following closely the Nigerian views on the efficiency of its workforce, the Sierra Leone Government stated that African 'possessors of a Pass Degree have proved less efficient on the whole in the General Clerical Service than youths admitted at an earlier age and of the School Certificate standard'. Basically both Sierra Leone and the Gambia preferred to offer scholarships to a few bright students to study overseas since they lacked the resources for any expanded local university schemes as envisaged by the Commission.[34]

Responses from African governments revealed their elemental resistance to Africanization of the colonial service. Clearly, the various governments were fundamentally uneasy about the admission of Africans to higher posts. Lord Hailey's powerfully expressed views in his Report of 1941, that Africanization should be the key policy for winning over the educated élite, and should precede the granting of more elected representation in the Legislative Councils, were endorsed strongly by the Colonial Office.[35] British officials on the spot were less enthusiastic about the whole idea and hence did virtually nothing before 1945, despite the very serious shortage of human resources at the higher level of colonial administration (with British men of military age having left for the armed forces) which Africans could have filled. The fear was that admitting more Africans into the higher cadre of the colonial service would mean not only their own gradual displacement, but also the disintegration of the indirect rule system which had offered them so much stability and honour. Thus, when the Gold Coast Government desired that college authorities should relate their number of graduates to the possible vacancies and the Nigerian Government insisted that the country was not much in need of administrators, they were essentially venting their resistance to Africanization.

Regardless of the stance of colonial governments and officials, the wind of change had begun to blow. The Asquith Commission was committed to give practical effect to the question of extending fully fledged university facilities to the colonies. For their part, the various colonial administrations barely had any choice but to carry out orders issuing from London. Centralization and control of colonial policies, resulting mainly from the exigencies of the war, had placed the Colonial Office in the vanguard. Colonial governments could only offer suggestions, which the Colonial Office was not bound to accept. Irrespective of the lukewarm responses of the local administrations to the Asquith Annexure, the overriding consideration remained that the British Government was now committed to establish and pay for universities in the colonial empire in order to foster the economic and social development necessary for the realization of the ultimate goal of self-government.

With the support of the Colonial Office, the Asquith Commission from the beginning consulted closely with the University of London. This was to give 'practical purpose' to the basic principles which should guide the foundation of colonial universities as well as the nature of curricula and syllabuses. London had, through its external degree programmes, established viable contacts with the colonies in relation to university education. Fortunately for the Colonial Office and the Commission, the University of London was enthusiastic about this enterprise and its own possible expanded role in the scheme. It could not have been otherwise. The University did not want to be relegated to the background in the new project having pioneered degree programmes in the colonies for so long. Well-placed senior faculty in London now took steps to seize the initiative on the new overseas colleges.

In December 1943, Fred Clarke, the Director of the University of London Institute of Education and a member of the ACEC as well as the Asquith Commission, drafted a confidential memorandum to the Principal of the University, H. Claughton, in which he initiated the discussions which ultimately resulted in the formulation of the scheme of 'special relationship' between the University of London and the proposed colonial institutions.[36] This scheme would confer on the University of London the right and responsibility to regulate the academic standards of the colonial institutions, and to foster their 'healthy' development into fully fledged, degree-awarding universities once they were established. Although Clarke claimed that the memorandum covered only his 'personal view of the situation', there is no doubt that he was echoing the wishes of both the Colonial Office and the Asquith Commission. Accordingly, Clarke told Claughton that

> the commission appears to be rather strongly desirous that a way may be found of adapting the University of London external degree to the needs of such institutions ... where facilities for higher education are now being developed, but where the conditions for full university status cannot yet be satisfied.[37]

However, what agitated the Asquith Commission from the start about the application of the London external degree arrangement was how to reconcile relevance and quality – the necessity for adaptation to indigenous needs and conditions, and the necessity to maintain degree standards at a level equivalent to those in Britain. It is noteworthy that the same issue had troubled the Currie, De La Warr, Mouat Jones and Channon groups variously in their earlier investigations. Stressing the extent of the problem, therefore, Clarke reminded the Principal that Africans were likely to react passionately against adaptation to local conditions since they would naturally feel that something of a lower standard was being foisted upon them. As he put it:

> They may well look askance at any modified form of the London degree, adapted to local conditions, even if the point of equivalence were beyond all doubt. They would probably reject altogether any form of degree which left room for doubt and would prefer to take the external degree as it stands, even if that should mean a considerable amount of private study.[38]

The point which Clarke failed to make, however, relates to the reason why Africans demonstrated such predilection for London and British degrees in the first place.[39] It should suffice to say that this preference was particularly strong given the employment and wage discrimination in the colonial service against those African graduates who secured their qualifications locally. Local graduates were 'disappointed to find their qualifications considered inferior to their fellows who secured their education in an overseas university'.[40]

Be that as it may, Clarke then outlined the sort of arrangement over adaptation which the University might contemplate in the circumstance of a formal request from the Commission. He pointed out the need for some modification of the curriculum and syllabus 'to meet local conditions', and the participation of the local institution 'both in the framing of courses and in the conduct of examinations'. Under the scheme, Clarke further noted that

> While the actual degree awarded could hardly be other than the London External, it is hoped that the practical working of it could be sufficiently internalized to give the necessary training for autonomy for each institution.[41]

After almost a century of indoctrination that Africans were inferior either intellectually, creatively or in abstract thinking, it was essential that the curricula of proposed colonial universities should approximate that offered in the United Kingdom. It was necessary, not only to build self-worth in African students but also to establish in the colonial administrations the principle of equality, for salary and other purposes, of Africans trained locally and expatriates educated overseas. Furthermore, the adaptation to local needs and conditions required a far greater amount of research than the British envisaged, much of which would come from Africans who after their first degree would continue in graduate research. Once such Africans joined the staff of the proposed universities, they would provide the impetus for the adaptation to local needs. Local African communities would be far more prepared to follow such adaptation than one designed and implemented by expatriates whose motives always remained suspect. Consequently, planners of the future colonial universities were correct in their desire for adaptation but were ill-advised to try to determine what those modifications should be.

In any case, if British universities were to be fully effective in nourishing and guiding the growth of new universities in the colonies through visits, secondment of staff, and research, Clarke asserted that it was imperative to 'develop some common organ through which these functions can be discharged'. This, he suggested, would be in the form of 'a Colonial Council or Committee with a properly organised secretariat'.[42] This idea eventually led to the establishment of the Inter-University Council for Higher Education in the Colonies. Clearly, Clarke had outlined two major ways in which the University of London was to be involved in the entire business; namely, as a member of the proposed Colonial Council and as the pivot of the special relationship scheme. The place of the University of London in the Commission's work remained vital. In the words of Clarke:

> The well-established prestige of the London degree and the great body of experience that has been built up in the working of it do seem to offer the best guarantee that here is the most suitable nursery already built and equipped, for the task of leading to maturity, growing institutions which are already showing such vigour and promise.[43]

Given the trend of unofficial discussions on the subject and feeling confident that the university would give sympathetic consideration to the responsibility with which the Commission hoped to place upon it, Cyril Asquith now wrote formally to the Vice-Chancellor of the University of London.[44] He sounded out the University's willingness to undertake what he admitted would be 'a massive responsibility', namely: the adaptation of its syllabuses and curricula to the specific needs of the different colonial institutions; sending out examiners; allowing staff of overseas colleges to take part in examining; and more importantly 'to enter into partnership with institutions thousands of miles from London'.⁴⁵ Thus the Asquith Commission formally invited and authorized the University to formulate the scheme of special relationship which, despite its shortcomings, was to dominate the practical implementation of the higher education project in the colonies. It marked the genesis of 'university imperialism', with London University as the institutional powerhouse and the various colonial colleges as its offspring. The Senate of the University responded swiftly to Asquith's letter. According to the Vice-Chancellor,

> the University of London would be proud to share in the general responsibilities contemplated for the universities as a whole, which the Commission has suggested that it should undertake.⁴⁶

It is not surprising that the University of London jumped at this invitation to what appeared an onerous task. It had always desired and lobbied for a controlling role in the project.

The University quickly set in motion its own programme of action. It was delighted that both the Colonial Office and the Asquith Commission neither wished to ignore nor obliterate the degree arrangement it had already put in place in the colonies. The tone of discussions had convinced the University that the Colonial Office was eager to employ the University's degree-granting system to develop institutions of university standard in the colonies. Furthermore, London had become more confident that its influence in colonial higher education would not be undermined by the increasing interest in the new scheme shown by Oxford and Cambridge. The University of London now began to outline the conditions upon which it might offer its degrees to overseas universities when formally requested to do so.

Although the University of London had age-old experience of external degree programmes in the colonies, which the Colonial Office and the Asquith Commission had recognized, Ashby observed that the problem of the new scheme 'was a novel one'. Syllabuses now had to be adapted to local conditions without arousing any suspicion; degrees had to be awarded, without depreciation of the currency, to remote colleges in non-European societies; and teaching staffs of the colonial colleges had to be encouraged to take part in the examining and marking of papers and be allowed to propose syllabus modifications.⁴⁷ The new scheme envisaged by the Colonial Office and the Asquith group was a remarkable deviation from the existing external degree arrangement long practised and controlled by London which had no consideration for its relevance to local conditions. Nevertheless, the University agreed to adjust its syllabuses and examinations to suit the type of adaptation recommended by the Colonial Office and the Asquith Commission. It could not ignore the political aspects of the university question upon which Stanley and Asquith had placed a high premium.

In July 1944 Cyril Asquith wrote again to the Vice-Chancellor of the University of London to thank the Senate for its 'sympathetic consideration' of the advice and help which the Commission had sought from it. He noted that the Commission was delighted that the University had agreed to take part in a scheme 'whereby the development of higher education in the Colonies would be promoted by the joint efforts of the Universities of Great Britain', and had additionally agreed 'to conduct examinations for the award of degrees to students of Colonial Colleges'.[48] Regarding the 'joint efforts' arrangement, Asquith informed Horton that the Commission was recommending that 'there should be established in this country an inter-university organization', the nature of which 'has yet to be defined but the home universities as a whole would have representation on it', which would have a permanent secretariat. The duty of this body should be

> to foster the development of the [colonial] Colleges in every way possible, and among its many functions will be those of giving advice on matters of general policy and on the provision of material facilities, and of providing help in obtaining members of the staff of high quality.[49]

This followed closely the ideas outlined in Fred Clarke's unofficial memorandum to Principal Claughton, so Horton was already aware of the plans. Clearly, the functions contemplated for the inter-university body were so wide that they dwarfed those of similar councils which existed in the United Kingdom. Its proposed power seemed at odds with London's intended role as the vanguard of university imperialism.

Asquith, however, assured the Senate of the University of London that in contemplating the inter-university body the Commission recognized that, in all questions affecting the award of degrees, London 'must have unfettered control and that the university must satisfy itself that the conditions it considers to be requisite to students to become candidates for degrees have been satisfied by the Colonial Colleges'. In any case, direct contacts between examiners and the colonial colleges remained vital in the Commission's view, not only because of the need to relate courses to local conditions but also to foster interaction with the staff of the colonial institutions. Under the existing London external degree system, most of, if not all, the examiners had never visited the colonies or met the students they would be examining. Standards were set in London with no regard to the socio-cultural milieu from which the students came. Thus the Commission felt that modifications were essential. According to Asquith,

> The Commission attaches greatest importance to devising direct contact between the Colleges and their examiners, not only from the point of view of educating the members of the staff in the duties of examining and the standards to be achieved but for the valuable discussions which would result as to the suitability of the examinations and curricula to local conditions.[50]

As a result of the prominent role assigned to it by the Commission, the University of London set up a special Senate Committee on Higher Education in the Colonies in October 1944 under the Chairmanship of Alexander Carr-Saunders, who was himself a member of the Asquith Commission.[51] This committee was charged with preparing a scheme for a special relationship between the University and the colonial colleges. In his further communication with Asquith, the Vice-Chancellor laid down the duty of the committee: 'to develop the new relationship with the Colonial Colleges and to co-operate with their staffs and with the proposed inter-university organization in the fostering of university education in the Colonies.'[52] Thus from the onset the Senate of the University became actively involved in the process. This, according to Ashby, had a beneficial effect ensuring that 'all the tortuous and time-consuming motions of academic diplomacy which are essential before a university can be persuaded to agree to anything, had already been completed before the Asquith Commission submitted its report'.[53]

Since its function involved the formulation of general principles which should guide the ordered foundation of universities in the colonies, the Asquith Commission sat mostly in London while sending delegations to the various colonial territories from time to time to evaluate the state of the existing facilities for higher education. By May 1945, after two years of hard work, the Asquith Commission submitted its Report to Oliver Stanley, who in turn presented it to the House of Commons in June. In July, the Report was published as a Command Paper. The Asquith group had already secured the co-operation of the University of London in a special relationship with the colonial institutions to supervise their academic work. It was also assured of support from all the British universities in the form of membership of the proposed inter-university organization. When the Report appeared it became a blueprint for how universities were to be developed in the British colonies.

In August 1945 the Labour Party came to power, having won a landslide victory in the July election, and George H. Hall (later Viscount Hall) replaced Stanley as the Secretary of State. Under the new administration, the university question was still a matter of high policy. The goal of British imperial rule – ultimate self-government for the colonial peoples – had been defined along bipartisan lines. The Colonial Office remained resolved to follow the principles laid out by the Asquith Commission without further delay.

Almost predictable in its recommendations, the Asquith Commission urged the immediate creation of university colleges 'so situated that ... the remaining areas of the Colonial Empire shall be served by one of them'. Stressing the urgency and practicability of the 'immediate setting up of university colleges', the Asquith group insisted that 'there should be no undue delay in converting these colleges into universities'.[54] Since East Africa would not be covered by the Elliot inquiry, the Asquith Commission recommended that Makerere College be developed to full university college status to serve the whole of the region.[55] Although the Report cautioned that 'no step could be taken which could more gravely prejudice the interests of these institutions than the premature grant of degree giving powers',[56] the Commission was clearly as convinced as the Colonial Office that action needed to be taken immediately to avoid unpleasant post-war political and social consequences.

It was proposed that the 'Inter-University Council' should include representatives of all existing universities of Great Britain and the Colonies, to provide the machinery for close co-operation between them and the proposed institutions and foster 'the development of Colonial Colleges in their advance to university status'.[57] The decision to set up the Inter-University Council demonstrated a sense of foresight; it was through this organ that many of the Commission's recommendations and the actual establishment of the colonial university colleges were implemented, as will be seen later.

Equally conscious that the development of higher education in the colonies must depend upon the grant of substantial financial aid from Great Britain, the Commission recommended the setting up of a Colonial University Grant Advisory Committee to advise the Secretary of State.[58] Since this body would advise on the allocation of funds, the Asquith Commission felt that the proposed Inter-University Council should not act in that capacity. Here, the Commission merely adopted the British system of a single national University Grant Committee, which had been reorganized in 1943, distinct from other regulating bodies. With these proposals all seemed set for the task of the actual establishment of university colleges in the colonies, with financial aid from the CD&WA expected to provide the initial funding.

Since members of the Commission were conscious of the political importance of their task, the Report stressed that there should be a good mix between liberal and vocational education. They realized that in order to form a balanced judgement on political matters the new universities should not only pursue courses which would prepare students for particular jobs, but also undertake humane studies (arts and social sciences) which could prepare them for administrative responsibility. The quality of education to be provided by the proposed institutions was now related to the role the educated African was expected to play in the new order, predicated on economic and social development, and self-government. The Asquith Commission fully realized that for the colonies to become viable independent nations their leaders would need the kind of intellectual integrity and acuteness which only high quality education could nourish.[59] The new colonial education policy prescribed by the Report was intended to prepare the colonies for responsible self-government within the British Empire.

Generally, the Asquith Report was not out of touch with the current of the time. It re-echoed the need for a reconsideration of British imperial policies and attitudes, and stressed the fact that the social and economic development of the colonies was not intended to liquidate but rather to consolidate the British Empire. The policy of imperial partnership had, since the war, become desirable partly to appease international pressures and partly to assuage colonial peoples' agitations and aspirations. Addressing the colonial social and economic welfare question had been recognized as the only sure way of maintaining the peace and political stability in British imperial territories in the post-war era. The Asquith Commission remained conscious of this goal throughout its deliberation. No doubt its proposals pleased the Colonial Office. It was also in harmony with the desire of the British academic lobby both within and outside the ACEC. Outlining the general attitude taken by the Secretary of State on the Asquith Report, the Chairman of the ACEC had noted that Hall

> regarded this document as fully justifying the hopes which were entertained when this Commission, representative of authoritative university opinion, was appointed, and he was commending it warmly to Colonial Governments and to all those concerned in the Colonies with development of education.[60]

As a necessary step towards the effective realization of the Commission's recommendations, the Colonial Office moved immediately to establish the Inter-University Council for Higher Education in the Colonies (IUC), as proposed by the Asquith Commission. Having secured a firm promise from the British universities of their willingness to co-operate with the Colonial Office, and to help in the foundation of universities in the colonies, Hall finally appointed the IUC in February 1946 under the Chairmanship of James Irvine with Walter Adams as Secretary.[61] Other members were A. M. Carr-Saunders (University of London), W. Hamilton Fyfe (Aberdeen), R. G. Baskett (Belfast), R. Priestley (Birmingham), J. A. Venn (Cambridge), Ivor Jennings (Ceylon), James Duff (Durham), J. J. Macmurray (Edinburgh), N. Morris (Glasgow), N. Bentwich (Jerusalem), B. Mouat Jones (Leeds), J. G. Wright (Liverpool), R. Galea (Malta), W. J. Pugh (Manchester), W. T. S. Stallysbrass (Oxford), R. H. Stroughton (Reading), L. E. S. Eastham (Sheffield), Ifor Evans (Wales), and Christopher Cox (ex-officio), the Secretary of State's Adviser on Education.

With the exception of Carr-Saunders, Baskett, Macmurray, Wright and Stroughton who were high calibre academics, the rest of the members of the IUC were vice-chancellors and principals of British universities.[62] This 'deliberate design', according to Maxwell, was 'to ensure that the IUC could speak with authority on the policy and practice of university development and could give a balanced overview rather than a medley of specialist opinions'.[63] Interestingly, none of the members was an expert on African or Asian affairs, except Christopher Cox who was a former Director of Education in the Sudan. This deficiency was ameliorated by the co-option of Margery Perham, Lilian Penson and T. H. Davey.[64]

Whether to create a new area of research or to exercise some kind of authoritative political influence, the British academic lobby had regularly sought a role in the policy-making process of imperial Britain. The inauguration of the IUC, composed solely of British academics, was thus a triumph for the academic lobby. On 8 March 1946, the IUC held its inaugural meeting. The address sent to the Council by the Secretary of State confirmed his acceptance of the principle that the IUC should exercise a full measure of independence in its operation. Accordingly,

> I appreciate the jealous care with which the Universities guard their autonomy and freedom from governmental interference. I am sure that in such freedom you can better discharge the great tasks you have undertaken.[65]

The two principles – independence and the right to communicate directly with colonial institutions – were the fundamental issues stressed by British universities during their preliminary negotiations with the Colonial Office about the formation of the Council.[66] Apparently, the home universities were aware of how political considerations might be manipulated to override or even jeopardize matters of academic expediency, especially when concerned with British colonies. By conceding these powers to the Council, the Colonial Office conferred upon it an unrestrained and unregulated authority to take control of almost all major policy matters in relation to the foundation of universities in the colonies. This was remarkable because it placed the universities almost outside the control of both the Colonial Office and the colonial governments, except in the matter of financing which was regulated by the Colonial Office. Here, ironically, was a case of a liberal ethos being implanted into a generally authoritarian system to appease the academic lobby.

However, the Secretary of State placed no funds at the disposal of the Council for salary supplementation for overseas service or the extension of the projects relating to higher education in the colonies.

The Colonial Office endorsed the view of the Asquith Commission that the Council 'would have greater influence with the Colonial institutions' if its functions 'were confined' to purely academic matters rather than financial administration'.[67] In November 1946, therefore, the Secretary of State set up the Colonial University Grants Advisory Committee (CUGAC), under the Chairmanship of Hector Hetherington,[68] to administer the funds under the CD&WA which were to be used to finance the activities sponsored by the IUC.[69] Even though the Secretary of State gave the IUC the power and autonomy to carry out its responsibilities, he reminded them of the commitment of the British Government 'to quicken the social, economic and political progress of the Colonial peoples and to guide them towards the ultimate goal of self-government'. Linking the pledge to the question of the provision of universities for Africans and almost repeating Stanley, Hall pointed out that the success of the British Government's policy would depend on

> the emergence, in the Colonial territory of increasing numbers of educated men and women with the technical training, the ability and desire to serve their communities as leaders in every sphere of public life in a sustained effort of partnership with us.[70]

Responding to the Secretary of State's message, the Chairman of the Council, Irvine, assured him that members were impressed with the importance of the task allotted them in the conduct of what he called a 'great educational experiment'.[71] Expressing the Council's delight that the task placed upon them would provide the colonial peoples with many of the educational opportunities that would constitute a sure basis for self-government, Irvine noted that their work would also 'have important repercussions on the policy of Home Universities and thereby will have an effect on public opinion in this country regarding the nation's duty to the Colonies'. Furthermore, he noted that their assignment 'will be one of the greatest of the factors enabling our country to fulfil its duty to the Colonies of the Empire'.[72]

With the appointment of the IUC and the arrangement with the University of London to sponsor university colleges in the colonies, the stage was set for the development of the British university system in the colonies. Thus, paradoxically, in an attempt to develop institutions essential for 'self-government', a kind of imperial framework of control was imposed. This encapsulates the entire phenomenon of the decolonization process, which was accompanied by what historians have called the 'second colonial occupation'.[73] It took far more human resources and money to decolonize than to colonize, and far more governance than in the old days of minimal government and indirect rule.

THE ELLIOT COMMISSION

The Walter Elliot Commission for Higher Education in West Africa was appointed simultaneously with that of Asquith's in July 1943.[74] In his speech in the Commons, Stanley declared that British West Africa was one area which needed 'detailed investigation' because it 'presents a number of difficulties'. Such difficulties included: the existence of a number of centres of education of various standards, doing different work; the great distances separating the colonies; the great contrasts not only between territories in social, economic and political development but also within each territory between development on the coast and inland; and the lasting effect of the war upon the conditions of the territories.[75] It was decided that only a special inquiry could effectively address these problems. By August 1943 the list of members of the Elliot Commission was complete. There were fourteen in all: H. J. Channon, J. R. Dickinson, J. F. Duff, Geoffrey Evans, Julian Huxley, A. Creech Jones, B. Mouat Jones, K. A. Korsah, I. O. Ransome Kuti, Eveline Martin, Margaret Read, E. H. Taylor-Cummings and A. E. Trueman. Their terms of reference were:

> to report on the organization and facilities of existing centres of higher education in British West Africa, and to make recommendations regarding future university development in the area.[76]

Like Asquith's, the membership of the Elliot Commission was dominated by British academics. However, unlike the Asquith Commission it had three African members – K. O. Korsah of the Gold Coast, I. O. Ransome Kuti of Nigeria and E. H. Taylor-Cummings of Sierra Leone.[77] The inclusion of African members was a particularly significant step by the Colonial Office for it clearly demonstrated how British attitudes towards the colonial peoples had changed dramatically during the war. It showed the British

159

commitment to the new imperial policy of partnership which had replaced trusteeship. The opinion had gained ground that Africans could, as a matter of right, play some part in the making of colonial policies relating to their own social, economic and even political well-being.

However, the persistent West African agitation for universities cannot be disregarded in any analysis of why the Elliot Commission was appointed. By the late 1930s the question of university education for Africans had become a burning issue among the emerging African 'nationalists'. It was not unlikely that the appointment of the Elliot Commission was intended to pacify the now very vociferous West African educated class. Certainly, the British were not unaware of the age-old demands of West Africans such as Horton, Blyden, Casely Hayford and, more recently, Nnamdi Azikiwe for the establishment of universities.[78] It was felt that a special investigation of the higher educational needs of West Africa, even if somewhat belated, would serve to ameliorate these demands. Moreover, the Colonial Office now felt that it was West Africa's turn to have a Commission since a similar body had examined higher education in East Africa in 1937 under Lord De La Warr. This was notwithstanding the fact that West Africa was more advanced in the acquisition of Western education than any other British region in tropical Africa.[79]

The Elliot Commission began its work with preliminary sittings in London to clarify matters of general principles before proceeding to West Africa. Thereafter, the Commission spent the whole of 1944 visiting the four British West African territories – the Gold Coast, Nigeria, Sierra Leone and the Gambia. Throughout its inquiry the Elliot Commission discovered that public opinion in West Africa was solidly in support of a fully fledged university in the region with high academic standards. What became a major concern to the Commission was the question of where to site the proposed university, given that each of the territories was apparently uneasy over the matter. But this did not provoke a heated debate, presumably because of the costs involved. Even though the colonies were aware that funds were available from the CD&WA, it was not clear to them exactly how the university project would be funded. Hence, while giving evidence to the Elliot Commission, the Asantehene (King) of Ashanti in the Gold Coast stated that,

> as it is now, we the people have no money to establish a university ourselves and so must look up to the Imperial Government if a

university we must have .... We live in the land of gold but not on gold.[80]

For some reason, however, the Gold Coast and Sierra Leone did not worry as much as Nigeria over the site question at the time the Commission was gathering information. In his oral submission to the Elliot Commission, for instance, the Asantehene had declared: 'Yes, my people would not mind where the university is, so long as it is in British West Africa and they have access to it'.[81] Similarly, in response to a Gold Coast journalist, Fara Abrahams, who asked the Elliot Commission whether the territory had any claims to the site of the proposed university, K. O. Korsah (the Gold Coast representative on the Commission) asserted that,

> We in the Gold Coast are broadminded over this question. Which ever country is best qualified for the university, let her have it. All we want is a university for higher education in West Africa.[82]

In fact, the Gold Coasters were quite convinced that their territory would be the only possible site for the proposed university given that compared to the others – Sierra Leone's Fourah Bay and Nigeria's Yaba – Gold Coast's Achimota College was the most advanced in terms of courses and infrastructural facilities at the time. Additionally, Achimota was already preparing candidates for the engineering degree (external) of the University of London and was thus the most likely to receive approval as the best site. To the Gold Coast people, the question of site was more or less a foregone conclusion in favour of the Gold Coast, and they therefore considered it unreasonable to make it the main issue in their submissions to the Commission.

As for Sierra Leone, although the war had caused the requisitioning and transfer of Fourah Bay College to a wretched location at Mabang, outside the city of Freetown, its people were equally as confident as the Gold Coasters that they had a better claim to the possible site for the proposed university. Since Fourah Bay College had established an enviable reputation as the only institution in Africa affiliated to a British university (Durham) since 1876, and with fully fledged degree-awarding status, albeit only in Theology and Arts, Sierra Leone felt that the College could not be relegated in any circumstance. In fact, all the African representatives on the Elliot Commission were graduates of Fourah Bay and hence the assumption gathered force that they would naturally put the College first. The site problem, therefore, was not taken seriously in their oral evidence to the Commission. It is probable that the governments of both the Gold Coast and Sierra Leone played down the site issue because the larger question relating to funding of the proposed university still remained hazy. Apart from the problem of funding, the Sierra Leonean Government was also concerned about the supply of students for the proposed university, given the poor state of the colony's primary and secondary schools.

However, Nigeria presented a different case. The colonial government chose to support local nationalism on the issue of demanding a university in Nigeria. Most of the memoranda submitted by Nigerians to the Elliot Commission demanded that the proposed West African University be sited in Nigeria. Obviously, the people of the territory were apprehensive of the politics which would pervade the question of site once the preliminary issues were settled. Nigeria appeared worse off in the existing situation. From the time of its foundation, Yaba College had been discredited by the Nigerian intelligentsia as a substandard institution designed to train subordinate staff for the various colonial government departments. Worse still, because of the exigencies of the Second World War the College had been requisitioned by the army, and its students sent to Achimota and the Government College in Umuahia.[83] In other words, Nigeria had nothing approximating the advances already attained by Achimota or Fourah Bay Colleges to commend it as a suitable site at the time of the Commission's visit. Nigeria was thus more uneasy than the other territories about where the new university would be located.

The Ife Branch of the Nigerian Youth Movement (NYM), in its memorandum, urged the Commission that 'under any circumstance, a university of equal status with any British university and with an African bias, should exist in Nigeria'.[84] Similarly, in his own submission, presumably on behalf of the government, the Nigerian Acting Director of Education, C. R. Butler, contended that 'Nigeria was the most suitable site for a West African University for many reasons, not the least of which was that there was greater demand for higher education here than in any of the Colonies' and that 'the standard of education in Nigeria was definitely higher than that of the Gold Coast'.[85] The CMS Yoruba Mission agreed that 'the time was ripe for a university of West Africa and Nigeria was the most suitable site'.[86]

THE ASQUITH AND ELLIOT COMMISSIONS

For a highly placed colonial official such as the Nigerian Director of Education to take this kind of position suggests that the era of territorial patriotism and parochialism, inter-colonial and intra-regional jealousy and bickering had begun. It would come to a head over the site question. The Nigerian colonial administration saw the site question as transcending mere petty politics. In reality, gaining the site was conceived as a measure of advanced educational attainment as well as an index of effective administration. It was natural that the Nigerian colonial government would be much concerned with the issue. Nigeria had a huge land mass and a dense population compared to the rest of the colonies. The Nigeria administration was conscious of the fact that the question of the supply of students for the new university could sway the Commission and thus place the territory in the top position as an ideal site. However, the poor state of Yaba College and its notoriety among the educated élite created some anxiety among Nigerian officials that Achimota might better impress the Commissioners because of its better infrastructural facilities, or Fourah Bay because of its reputation.

The Elliot Report was ready in May 1945, and was presented to Parliament in June 1945 simultaneously with the Asquith Report by Secretary of State Oliver Stanley.[87] The Elliot Commission produced two reports – a Majority Report[88] and a Minority Report[89] – because the Commissioners fundamentally disagreed among themselves on certain issues. The Majority Report recommended that two university colleges should be established immediately in West Africa, one at Ibadan in Nigeria and the other at Achimota in the Gold Coast, and that Fourah Bay College in Sierra Leone should be reorganized to attain university college status at a later date. They reasoned that 'already the demand for skilled and responsible men and women has exceeded the training capacity of the existing educational institutions in British West Africa', and that 'no single university institution, however excellent, could adequately supply these wider influences to the other colonies from one site in West Africa' because these territories 'are not only themselves of wide extent; they are ... separated from each other by long distances, and by other states and governments'.[90] When reorganized, according to the Majority opinion, Fourah Bay College should serve Sierra Leone and the Gambia. The standards of the various stages of the courses proposed, they further advised, should be those of the British universities. With regard to funding, the Majority Report recommended that 'at first the greater share of the expenditure should be met from the Colonial Development and Welfare funds'.[91]

The Minority group disagreed. Instead, it recommended the establishment of only one 'comprehensive unitary university college for the whole of British West Africa' in Ibadan,[92] Nigeria. The choice of Nigeria as the site of the new university was because of the vast population of the territory compared to the other colonies. It was presumed that Nigeria could supply the highest number of students for the university. Additionally, the Minority Report proposed the establishment of three Territorial Colleges in Nigeria, the Gold Coast and Sierra Leone. In other words, both Achimota and Fourah Bay would be reconstituted into territorial colleges while an entirely new one would be established for Nigeria. The Territorial Colleges, accordingly, would provide academic courses to the intermediate level – to train teachers for the primary and secondary schools, to train social workers, and to act as the main centres from which the extra-mural activities throughout each territory were to be organized.[93] To create three university colleges concurrently, the Minority reasoned, 'will defer for a considerable time the provision of the type of university education which we would wish to see established as soon as possible'. Furthermore, the Minority group contended, the proposals of the Majority

> do not pay sufficient attention to the question of the number of students likely to be available, nor to the difficulties of making the necessary provision of staff, equipment and finance; they involve a diffusion of effort and resources when all the circumstances suggest to us the urgent need of concentration, if realization is not to be indefinitely postponed; they make what we regard as a provision for quantity when we would prefer one of the higher quality, more soundly based.[94]

The arguments of both factions appeared sound, and perhaps this accounts for why they could not reach a compromise. While the Minority seemed to have been more concerned about possible delay and the financial cost from imperial funds of providing for three university colleges simultaneously, the Majority were persuaded by political considerations. The latter appeared to have been more influenced by the possible political uproar should either Achimota, Yaba or Fourah Bay be elevated to a university college at the expense of the others. The fact that the three African members of the

Commission endorsed the Majority view was indicative of the West African desire for more than one university.[95] But, more fundamentally, the division resulted from different judgements of how far the colonial reform movement could go. To both groups, British imperial policy was in transition but the extent of the transformation remained hazy and thus debatable.

While the Minority believed that asking for three universities at the same time might delay and possibly jeopardize the whole project, since the resources demanded were so huge (in money and manpower), the Majority group was more radical and premonitory. They realized that British opinion had swung Leftward since the war, and that Treasury had become less parsimonious. They were convinced that the idea of three universities would be accepted. Surprisingly, Creech Jones, a powerful advocate of radical colonial reforms in Parliament, supported the Minority opinion as did Channon who had championed the cause of higher education in the colonies. It seems then that the larger question transcended funding. It was related to quality, standards and the urgency of the whole question. The Majority judgement was that the emerging trend of territorialism and nationalism would prove an insurmountable obstacle to the success of a unitary West African university sited in any one colony. Channon and his group disregarded this factor. The Majority group was more far-sighted, as events would prove.

While the Elliot proposals were specifically relevant to West Africa, the Asquith Report provided the general framework on the principles which should guide the establishment of universities in the colonies. The Inter-University Council was set up to formulate policies while the University of London was given the authority to regulate the academic affairs of the new universities under the special relationship scheme. Both the University of London and the IUC were to ensure that the academic standards and pattern of development of the new colonial universities would be essentially British. While Makerere in Uganda would become a university under the Asquith plan, the Elliot Report, despite the duality of its recommendations, advocated one or more universities for West Africa. Thus the policy framework for universities in Africa was complete. Generally, educated Africans were pleased that the degrees to be awarded by the new universities would be equivalent in reputation to those of the United Kingdom, and hence the stage was perfectly set for British 'university imperialism' in Africa.

IMPERIALISM, ACADEME AND NATIONALISM

NOTES

1. Stanley to Channon, 23 February 1943 as cited in Ashby, *Universities: British, Indian, African*, p. 211.
2. Ashby, ibid.
3. Duff was the Vice-Chancellor of Durham University. The full list of all the members of both Commissions is given later in this chapter.
4. University of London Archives and Palaeography, London (ULAP), AC 11/1/1 H. Claughton to Alexander Carr-Saunders, 1 March 1943.
5. Note that Channon, who was now very powerful in the Colonial Office and the ACEC as well as in the Asquith Commission, had deeply criticized the London external degree system. Claughton's fears may, after all, have been well-founded considering that Channon was from the University of Liverpool.
6. Ibid.
7. Lee and Petter, *Colonial Office, War, and Colonial Development*, p. 178. Carr-Saunders was a member of the Colonial Office Research Committee, the Social Welfare Committee, and Social Science Research Committee.
8. Neither Oxford nor Cambridge Universities had developed the external degree programmes in the colonies as the University of London had.
9. ULAP, AC 11/1/1 Stanley to the Vice-Chancellor of the University of London, 29 May 1943.
10. Ibid.
11. Ibid.
12. Ibid.
13. ULAP, AC 11/1/1 Frank Horton to Oliver Stanley, 1 June 1943.
14. Parliamentary Debates (House of Commons), Vol. 391, col. 47, 13 July 1943.
15. Ibid.
16. Ibid. Cyril Asquith was a judge and the son of the Earl of Oxford and Asquith, knighted judge of King's Bench, Lord Justice of Appeal (PC), scholar of Winchester and Balliol College, Oxford, and a Fellow of Magdalen College.
17. See the terms of reference embodied in Cmd.6647, *Report of the Commission on Higher Education in the Colonies*, HMSO, June 1945, p. A2.
18. Parliamentary Debates (House of Commons), Vol. 391, col. 54–57, 13 July 1943. The idea of an overlapping membership was suggested in Channon's Report and endorsed by the ACEC.
19. See Paul Addison, *The Road to 1945: British Politics and the Second World War*, Jonathan Cape, London, 1975, pp. 13–21, and Kenneth O. Morgan, *Labour in Power, 1945–1951*, Clarendon Press, Oxford, 1984, pp. 229–269.
20. Eric Ashby, *Universities: British, Indian, African*, p. 428 (footnote 42).
21. Apart from Hailey and Cameron, who were career administrators, the rest of the members of the Commission were British academics. Interestingly, there was no clergy in the Commission, the first time that missionary interests were ignored in such a colonial educational body.
22. CO 958/1 Minutes of the First Meeting of the Asquith Commission on Higher Education in the Colonies, 21 September 1943.
23. Ibid.
24. Ibid.
25. See Addison, *The Road to 1945*, pp. 13–21, and Morgan, *Labour in Power*, op. cit.
26. CO 958/1 Cyril Asquith to British Universities, October 1943.
27. CO 958/2 'Annexure II: Points on which the Asquith Commission would Appreciate the Views of the Governments, Vice-Chancellors of Universities and Principals of the Colleges of the Dependencies', November 1943.
28. Ibid.
29. CO 958/2 Comment from the Gold Coast Government on Annexure II despatched through the Secretary of State, 17 November 1943.
30. Ibid.
31. CO 958/2 Comments by the Nigerian Government on Annexure II as Required by the Asquith Commission, November 1943.

32. Ibid.
33. Ibid.
34. CO 958/2 Comments for the Governments of Sierra Leone, and the Gambia on Annexure II, November 1943.
35. National Archives of Nigeria (NAI) RG/H1 Lord Hailey, *Native Administration and African Political Development*, Report to the Secretary of State for the Colonies, 1941.
36. ULAP, AC 11/1/1 Fred Clarke to H. Claughton, 6 December 1943.
37. Ibid.
38. Ibid.
39. For a detailed analysis of this issue, see Chapter 3.
40. University of Ibadan Archives (UIA), Provisional Council File, *The University College Report, 1948–1952*, 1952, p. 3.
41. ULAP, AC 11/1/1 Clarke to Claughton, 6 December 1943.
42. Ibid.
43. Ibid.
44. CO 958/1 Cyril Asquith to Frank Horton, 10 March 1944.
45. Ibid.
46. CO 958/2 Horton to Asquith, 24 May 1944.
47. Ashby, *Universities: British, Indian, African*, p. 213.
48. ULAP, AC 11/1/1 Cyril Asquith to Frank Horton, July 1944.
49. Ibid.
50. Ibid. He assured the University that its expenses in connection with the conduct of special examinations would be defrayed by the British Government.
51. ULAP, AC 11/1/1 Minutes of Senate Meeting, University of London, 25 October 1944.
52. ULAP, AC 11/1/1 Frank Horton to Cyril Asquith, 4 October 1944.
53. Ashby, *Universities: British, Indian, African*, pp. 213–214.
54. Cmd.6647 *Report of the Commission on Higher Education in the Colonies*, HMSO, June 1945, pp. 10–13.
55. Ibid., p. 13. The Asquith group knew that the Elliot Commission would be recommending the establishment of universities in West Africa, thus they felt that East Africa should be included in any arrangement.
56. Ibid., p. 13.
57. Cmd.6647 *Report of the Commission on Higher Education in the Colonies*, p. 30.
58. Ibid., p. 54.
59. Ibid., pp. 10–11.
60. CO 987/2 ACEC Discussions on the Asquith Report, 1945.
61. Irvine was a distinguished chemist and the Vice-Chancellor of the University of St. Andrews. He was also a member of the Asquith Commission. Walter Adams was formerly a history lecturer at the University College of London and Secretary of the London School of Economics and Political Science.
62. Carr-Saunders was the Director of the London School of Economics and Political Science, Baskett was a Professor of Agricultural Chemistry, Macmurray was a Professor of Moral Philosophy, Wright was a Professor of Veterinary Surgery, and Stroughton was a Professor of Horticulture.
63. Maxwell, *Universities in Partnership*, p. 11.
64. Perham was Reader in Colonial Administration at Oxford, Penson was a Professor of Modern History at the University of London and a member of the Asquith Commission who later became the Vice-Chancellor of the University. T. H. Davey was a Professor of Tropical Hygiene at the University of Liverpool.
65. CO 987/3 Text of a Message from the Secretary of State to the Inter-University Council, 8 March 1946.
66. Maxwell, *Universities in Partnership*, p. 9.
67. Cmd.6647 *Report of the Commission on Higher Education in the Colonies*, p. 33.
68. Hetherington was formerly a Professor of Philosophy at Liverpool and the Chairman of the Committee of Vice-Chancellors and Principals of British Universities.

69. In 1945 the sums voted by Parliament under the CD&WA of 1940 were superseded by a new Act which allocated the sum of £120 million for ten years. This new Act was the brainchild of Stanley to speed up colonial reforms just as MacDonald initiated the Bill of 1940. Out of the allocation for social and economic development, £4.5 million was set aside for higher education. See Ashby, *Universities: British, Indian, African*, p. 429.
70. CO 987/3 Text of Secretary of State's Message to the IUC, March 1946.
71. CO 987/3 Irvine to the Secretary of State, March 1946.
72. Ibid.
73. Refer to Bill Freund, *The Making of Contemporary Africa*, Indiana University Press, Bloomington, 1984, pp. 192–202. John Lonsdale and Anthony Low also employ the same terms in their writing. See D. A. Low and Alison Smith (eds), *History of East Africa*, Vol.111, Clarendon Press, London, 1976.
74. See Parliamentary Debates (House of Commons), col. 47, 13 July 1943. Walter Elliot was an MP for Kelvingrove and Minister of Health before his appointment as Chairman of the Commission.
75. Ibid.
76. Refer to the terms of reference as stated in Cmd.6655 *Report of the Commission on Higher Education in West Africa*, HMSO, June 1945, p. 2.
77. Korsah was a prominent Gold Coast lawyer, Middle Temple. While Ransome Kuti was the President of the Nigerian Union of Teachers, Taylor-Cummings was a medical practitioner in Sierra Leone.
78. It may be noted that Azikiwe, on a visit to London in 1943, was consulted by Oliver Stanley on the university question. A Nigerian, Azikiwe was among the few Africans who, in the 1920s, had gone to the United States for advanced education. Returning to Nigeria in 1934, he discovered that British opposition to university education for Africans had become even stronger. In 1937, Azikiwe published his book *Renascent Africa*, which was highly inspiring and provocatively critical of colonialism, racial prejudice, and the British educational system in Africa. Resentful of what he called British miseducation of Africans, he called for the establishment of universities in Africa to emancipate Africans mentally and to re-educate them to the real needs of a renascent Africa. Azikiwe later became one of the foremost Nigerian nationalists, the first African Governor-General, and then President of an independent Nigeria.
79. Carr-Saunders, *New Universities Overseas*, pp. 30–32.
80. National Archives of Ghana, Accra (NAGA) NP 22/1, *The Gold Coast Observer*, 25 February 1944, 'Visit of the Elliot Commission to Sir Osei Agyeman, Prempeh II, Otumfuo the Asantehene of Ashanti on the 3rd of February 1944'.
81. NAGA, NP22/1 *The Gold Coast Observer*, 25 February 1944.
82. NAGA, NP22/1 *The Gold Coast Observer*, 28 January 1944.
83. See Adewoye, 'The Antecedents' in J. F. Ade Ajayi and Tekena N. Tamuno (eds), *The University of Ibadan, 1948–73*, pp. 12–15.
84. *The Daily Service*, 26 February 1944, p. 4.
85. *The Daily Service*, 12 February 1944, p. 1.
86. *The Daily Service*, 15 February 1944, p. 4. From the early 1930s when British academics began to dominate the ACEC and pushed for a university for Africans, missionary influence increasingly declined. Missionary bodies could not fund universities and, moreover, the literary nature of the education they provided had come under attack both in Africa and London.
87. Cmd.6655 *Report of the Commission on Higher Education in West Africa*, HMSO, June 1945.
88. The Majority Report was signed by Walter Elliot, J. R. Dickinson, J. F. Duff, B. Mouat Jones, K. A. Korsah, I. O. Ransome Kuti, Eveline C. Martin, E. H. Taylor-Cummings, and A. E. Trueman.
89. Those who signed the Minority Report were H. J. Channon, Geoffrey Evans, Julian S. Huxley, A. Creech Jones, and Margaret Read.
90. Cmd.6655 *Report of the Commission on Higher Education in West Africa*, pp. 52–54.
91. Ibid., p. 128. They stated that the share to be met by the West African Governments should increase until they ultimately bore the whole expenditure.

92. Ibid., p. 155. 'Ibadan', the Minority faction argued, 'is West Africa's largest native town, and one of character, situated in attractive country.' With almost one million people, Ibadan was viewed as the largest catchment area for the future students of the proposed university. Ironically, the Ibadan people possibly demonstrated the least interest in Western education of any major city in British West Africa.
93. Ibid., p. 159.
94. Ibid., p. 141.
95. They might have either been apostles of territorial nationalism or were apprehensive that their *alma mater* had no chance of being elevated to a university college, and hence they went with the majority.

6 Colonial Territorial 'Nationalism' and the Implementation of the Asquith and Elliot Schemes

The end of the Second World War and the victory of the Labour Party in the British election in mid-1945 afforded a favourable atmosphere for a new stimulus to colonial reforms. Just before the Labour election victory, the Coalition Government passed the 1945 CD&WA, which increased the funds available for colonial investment to £120 million over the next ten years. Out of this sum, £4.5 million was set aside for higher education.[1] Roger Louis observed that such a colossal increase from the 1940 Act in the face of British wartime debt, adverse balance of payments, and domestic financial austerity, 'was truly the turning point in British commitment to improving economic efficiency and production, and to raising the standards of health, education, and welfare in the colonies'.[2] With the increased funds now available, and the conducive political climate, the Colonial Office swiftly moved to implement the Asquith and Elliot schemes.

But crises soon erupted. While London was strongly disposed towards the establishment of a comprehensive unitary university for West Africa, as the Elliot Minority Report had suggested, each of the three larger territories vehemently demanded its own institution as the Majority Report anticipated. Territorial 'nationalism' became a potent factor. The mood in the region sharply contrasted with that of the 1920s when the NCBWA, under the leadership of Casely Hayford, had clamoured for a unitary University of British West Africa. The Colonial Office finally succumbed to African 'nationalist' pressures. For the first time, organized groups of educated leaders, each of them expressing a sense of 'national interest' based on the colonial territory rather than the pan-British West Africa perspective of the pre-war period, agitated successfully for a major modification of a new colonial reform initiative. Their success not only expanded the scope of the policy for new universities, but was also a turning-point which demonstrated that 'nationalists' could affect and shape the detailed implementation of the new policies.

Soon after the publication of the Asquith and Elliot Reports in July 1945, the first Labour Government to control a solid majority in the House of Commons was elected. In August, George Hall replaced Oliver Stanley as Secretary of State for the Colonies while Creech Jones, one of the signatories to the Elliot Minority Report, became the Parliamentary Under-Secretary of State. Hall was a stolid trade unionist who, despite his years as Parliamentary Under-Secretary in the wartime Coalition Government, was neither particularly well informed, nor held pronounced views on colonial issues (except those relating to labour, working conditions and trade unions). Creech Jones, on the other hand, was perhaps the most well informed of all MPs on colonial and especially Caribbean and African matters. As a leading figure in the Fabian Colonial Bureau, Creech Jones was the regular recipient of detailed research reports, and kept up frequent personal correspondence with a host of African and Caribbean leaders. For almost ten years he had been Labour's acknowledged 'authority' on colonial affairs in the House of Commons. Not surprisingly, the Colonial Office became very much inclined towards the implementation of the Minority Report suggestions.

In October 1945, three months after the publication of the Elliot Report, Hall sent out a despatch to the governments of Nigeria, the Gold Coast, Sierra Leone and the Gambia, to inform them of his decision, after a careful consideration of the arguments of both the Majority and the Minority factions.[3] Having considered the recommendations of the Majority group in favour of three centres of higher education in West Africa, and the strength of local sentiments, Hall concluded:

> I have, however, been much impressed by the arguments and criticisms contained in the Minority Report in favour of the development, at any rate to begin with, of a single University College for West Africa, and those arguments appear to me to carry so much weight that I feel no hesitation in stating at once that in my opinion the general policy advocated in the Minority

> Report is the one which, in the best interests of the peple [sic] of West Africa as a whole, we should make every effort to bring into effect as soon as possible.⁴

Even though the higher educational needs of West Africa would call for the development of additional university institutions at a later date, Hall further pointed out that, 'at the present stage the speedy development of a full range of university facilities is a consideration of the greatest importance'. He argued that for West Africans to take their share, to an increasing and effective extent, in the plans for the development of their countries, and to make satisfactory progress along the road to self-government, 'it is essential that the development of higher education should be promoted at the quickest pace compatible with the attainment of adequate standards'. This, Hall stressed, could only be effectively achieved by 'concentrating at the outset upon the establishment of a single university institution on the lines advocated in the Minority Report'.⁵

Furthermore, the Secretary of State stated that he subscribed to the Minority view that the proposed West African University should be founded in Nigeria 'at the earliest possible date'. As a safeguard against the university becoming dominated by Nigeria, he acceded to the Minority view that the College should be governed by a Council 'fully representative of the four West African Territories'. Leaving the more detailed recommendations, such as the proposals for the establishment of three territorial colleges and research institutes, for consideration in due course, Hall advised the governors that they should publish his despatch or use whatever appropriate means to disseminate its content in order to 'ascertain the trend of public opinion' and reactions.⁶

Admittedly, the arguments of the Minority were powerfully articulated in the Elliot Report. But those of the Majority were no less forcefully enunciated and Hall hardly gave sufficient credit to the opinions of the latter in his despatch. There was no doubt that the Minority group did not want the university question to be delayed simply because of the demand, simultaneously, for multiple institutions. It was also clear that they were seriously concerned with the problem of securing sufficient funds, competent staff and qualified students. However, what remained baffling was why the Colonial Office now ignored the issues of the great distances separating one British West African colony from another, and the contrasts between them in social, economic and political development – an argument Stanley had made in Parliament in 1943 as the compelling reason for a separate West African Commission under Elliot.[7] It was ironic that while recognizing the emerging spirit of territorialism and nationalism in the colonies, championed by the educated elements and sustained by the local governments, Hall ultimately chose to endorse the Minority Report.

Hall hardly acted of his own volition. As an 'expert' on colonial affairs, Creech Jones was certainly the driving force behind Hall's support for the Minority opinion. For so long, Creech Jones had pushed for reforms and a reordering of British imperial goals. Hall, on the other hand, had little experience of imperial issues and hence had to rely heavily on the advice of his Parliamentary Under-Secretary. No doubt, both Hall and Creech Jones wanted a West African University to be established immediately. However, they seemed to have been excessively persuaded by the purely academic arguments of Channon that three universities established simultaneously would only lead to the dissipation of scarce resources (qualified academic staff and funds), the supply of students and the maintenance of high standards. It is strange that as political men they did not focus more on the possible political repercussions of the adoption of the Minority recommendations, against which the Majority group had forewarned. No doubt Creech Jones did not want to lose face, having not only signed the Minority proposals but now also being placed in a position to implement the schemes. However, there is no question that both Creech Jones and Hall wanted the university project to get started quickly.

It is significant that Hall, in his despatch to the governments of West Africa, asked the governors to publish his comments in order to test public opinion. This was unconventional. It was not the usual method of governing colonies, at least not in the pre-war era. From 1938, MacDonald had centralized and concentrated authority in the Colonial Office, and the exigencies of the war necessitated the flow of directives from the Office to the colonies. Both colonial officials and the colonial peoples were expected to comply and they did so. But the end of the war ushered in a new spirit of partnership whereby the colonial peoples would play an increasing role in deciding their future development. The idea of the university was to foster and expand the class of educated Africans who would lead in this advance. By undertaking to test African opinion on his resolution Hall merely strove to demonstrate that British imperial attitudes towards the colonies had changed. Politically, however, this opened up the whole question, and gave educated elements the ability to affect the outcome. Such a procedure invited interested groups to organize and express opposition or support. Clearly, neither Hall nor Creech Jones anticipated the ensuing uproar because neither the Gold Coast nor Sierra Leone had insisted the location of the proposed university be in their territories (as Nigeria had done) when the Elliot Commission had collected evidence.

Accordingly, the various West African governments publicized the Secretary of State's despatch as well as the Report of the Elliot Commission. Predictably, the Gold Coast educated elements were upset. On October 1945, the territory's Central Advisory Committee on Education reviewed both Hall's despatch and the Elliot Report. Members frowned on the view of the Secretary of State and, instead, supported overwhelmingly the Majority recommendations. In November, therefore, they issued a statement in response. According to the Committee,

> Irreparable harm would be done by denying work begun at Achimota its natural growth and by denying, therefore, the educational system the step in its development which it is now ready to take and which is urgently necessary to it and to the Gold Coast.[8]

Several memoranda were also submitted to the Government of the Gold Coast from various educational, political and social organizations, and interest groups. A memorandum presented by the Joint Provisional Council of Gold Coast Colony expressed unanimity in support of the Majority Report. Accordingly, 'the establishment of a unitary university in any single Colony of British West Africa – notwithstanding the largeness of its population – without the support of the sister Colonies is destined to be a fruitless venture', and there is no evidence that such support would be forthcoming since 'interest is the secret of success'.[9] Clearly this demonstrated the emerging spirit of territorial 'nationalism'. The Gold Coast traditional élites seemed to have sunk their traditional animosity with the educated class in defence of colonial territorial sentiments. Highlighting how the Minority proposals would diminish the regional educational achievement of both the Gold Coast and Sierra Leone, the Council concluded that

> to reduce, therefore, Achimota College and Fourah Bay College which have done so much preparatory work in Higher Education

in British West Africa to the status of Territorial Colleges as recommended by the Minority Report would be to frustrate the hopes and aspirations of the peoples of the Gold Coast and Sierra Leone.[10]

The memoranda of many professional bodies and interest groups such as the Gold Coast Bar Association, the Old Boys Association of Achimota College and the Gold Coast Teachers Union were all firmly in favour of the Majority Report. As a result of the outcry from interest groups and politicians against Hall's decision and the Minority proposals, a public rally was convened at the Rodger Club, Accra, in December 1945 to ascertain the strength of popular opinion. It was sponsored and overwhelmingly attended by the educated élite and, predictably, the rally unanimously endorsed the Majority Report.[11] At another public meeting held at the Hodson Club on 14 December it was declared that 'no university or university college could ignore the natural divisions and affiliations of the people for whom it is intended to serve'. The meeting decried the subordination of the natural and healthy development of higher education in the territories 'to financial considerations, as if they are overriding factors in the establishment of a university', while 'the human element is of minor importance'.[12] Furthermore, it was declared that 'democratic principles should govern all matters affecting the welfare and progressive development of all human beings' and thus the 'principle of self-determination would be applied in deciding the type of institutions we in West Africa require'.[13] Significantly, J. B. Danquah, the politician who had formed the Gold Coast Youth Movement in the late 1930s, took part in this rally. The protest played into his hands as the rally turned out to be a sort of leadership colloquium, inaugurating, in a 'democratic' fashion, the advent of the educated élite on the centre stage of colonial politics and the decision-making process.

It is noteworthy how political all this had become. The Majority Report foresaw the problem when they warned that West Africa, 'by the very nature of things, has developed with a high degree of decentralization', and that the various territories 'follow independent' lines of development.[14] There was no longer any sense of a single and indivisible 'British West Africa', as Casely Hayford and the rest of the educated elements who formed the National Congress of British West Africa envisaged in the 1920s when they demanded the establishment of a single university for the region. Interestingly, the West African educated élite now took pride in referring to the colonial frontiers established by the imperial powers as 'natural divisions'. Thus, the colonial state now took over the psychology of nationalism as the Gold Coast began to see itself as 'naturally' a distinct political entity, and linked its position on the university question as the right expression of 'self-determination'.

All this pointed to the extent of political awareness in the colonies at the end of the war. The African educated élite had imbibed the wartime slogans of 'self-determination' and 'democratic principles', and were ready to translate them into purposeful nationalist catch-phrases in the post-war era. The Colonial Office and many imperial statesmen had predicted these post-war effects on colonial peoples.

Seemingly swayed by what he termed the 'strength of public opinion', the Governor of the Gold Coast, Alan Burns, despatched a letter to the Secretary of State to relay the views of the 'people' of the Gold Coast. He had 'been impressed by the strength of public opinion and high level of discussion both in the press and in the resolutions and memoranda submitted ...' and had discovered that 'public opinion is overwhelmingly in support of the Majority Report'. Besides,

> [t]he people of the Gold Coast would wish their government to do everything in its power to ensure the uninterrupted development of Achimota on the lines recommended by the Majority of the Commission, even if this would mean a heavy contribution from the funds at the disposal of the Gold Coast to the capital and recurrent costs of these developments ... and that there would be strong opposition to the voting of public funds for any development of higher education in West Africa which did not include the immediate development of Achimota on the lines recommended in the Majority Report.[15]

What Burns was obviously hinting at was that even without any financial allocations from the CD&WA funds the Gold Coast could go ahead with the university scheme at Achimota. He pointed out that informed opinion in the territory was resolute in pressing their government to continue the development of Achimota into a university as had been envisioned by the former governor of the territory, Guggisberg, as far back as 1923.[16]

Throughout his tenure as governor, Burns had striven for a good relationship with the vociferous educated class, and to elevate his reputation by the advancement of the importance of the Gold Coast in regional affairs. The university question presented him with an ideal opportunity. By relentlessly underscoring the strength of public opinion, Burns wanted to demonstrate to the Colonial Office that the wartime centralization and control of the colonies from London would prove very fragile in the post-war era. Burns, like all other officials on the spot, disliked the wide powers which the Colonial Office had assumed between 1938 and 1945. Naturally, he informed the Office that he was merely reflecting public opinion after sounding out the unofficial members in the Legislative Council as well as prominent politicians such as Danquah. Significantly, Burns had offered funds both for the capital and recurrent costs of the Achimota University College project and had also threatened that such funds would not be voted for the single University College in Nigeria. This remained a shrewd political move, forceful enough to influence the Colonial Office. It later proved successful.

In Sierra Leone, as in the Gold Coast, the reactions of some sections of the people, particularly the Creoles, against the Minority Report and the Secretary of State's despatch was no less vehement. Sierra Leone possessed the highest number of well-educated people in West Africa – predominantly the Creoles – who lived in the Freetown area. However, educational attainment for the hinterland dwellers remained critically impoverished, and this segment of the population rarely clamoured for a university college. Christopher Fyfe has noted that 'only a tiny handful from the Protectorate reached secondary school level. The vast majority had no schooling at all, for there were not enough schools'.[17] Fourah Bay College, which had been affiliated to Durham University since 1876, had been the only institution in West Africa which offered a full university degree in Theology and Arts. Nigerians as well as the people of the Gold Coast and the Gambia had attended the College. For the Creoles, therefore, the College had come to symbolize their great achievement. Inevitably, the Minority Report, which reduced Fourah Bay to the status of a territorial college doing work for the intermediate programmes, teacher training, social-work courses, and extra-mural activities instead of degrees, was considered not only an insult to the long-established tradition but also an affront to Sierra Leone.

The Creoles were incensed. To them, 'to reduce the academic status of a college which has held the torch of enlightenment in West

Africa for well over a century is to destroy a historical monument' and certainly 'future historians will lament the attending tragedy if the academic status of Fourah Bay College is reduced'.[18] In its memorandum to the Government of Sierra Leone, the Fourah Bay College Council advised the governor to inform the Secretary of State that the people of Sierra Leone rejected the Minority Report in its entirety.[19] Bluntly stating their viewpoint on the difficulties which Sierra Leoneans and the people of the Gold Coast would face in attending a university in Nigeria, the old students of Fourah Bay, mostly Creoles, contended that 'there are barriers between the different Colonies which are not only physical but social and psychological'.[20]

However, unlike the Government of the Gold Coast which was inclined towards the Majority Report in response to 'public opinion' in the territory, the Sierra Leone administration of Hubert Stevenson failed to respond positively to local sentiments. The Government was very much aware that the educational priority of the majority of the population living outside Freetown was not necessarily university education. To the Sierra Leone administration, therefore, the provision of adequate facilities for primary and secondary training remained more crucial. While communicating the decision of the Sierra Leone Board of Education (which voted in favour of the Majority Report) to the Colonial Secretary, the Director of Education unmistakably reiterated his own position to which the Government of Sierra Leone equally subscribed:

> Tradition and local sentiment must inevitably carry some weight; but in a matter of this importance it is absolutely vital to face the facts, and to consider the question dispassionately and from a realistic point of view. I therefore support the Minority recommendation.[21]

Sierra Leone, however, contrasted with the Gold Coast in many ways. The territory had no money with which to defy the decision of the Colonial Office. Hence the Sierra Leone government knew very well that any full-scale university scheme for the territory would have to depend on substantial financial grants from London through the CD&WA funds. Appreciating that the Colonial Office would not concede to any local pressure not fully backed with material and human resources, the Government of Sierra Leone ignored the demands of its educated and interest groups. The Government refused to try to persuade Hall to develop Fourah Bay College into a fully fledged university. Sierra Leone Creoles could not make much impact. They were overwhelmed by government flaunting of the grim financial argument, coupled with the poor state of primary and secondary education in the interior. Furthermore, the policy of indirect rule had directed the attention of the colonial administration from the Creoles to the peoples of the interior. Official attitudes were quite openly anti-Creole and in favour of the chiefly Temne and Mende and their requirements for primary education. Burns of the Gold Coast appeared to have been breaking the tradition of indirect rule while Sierra Leone and, to an extent, Nigeria, were less inclined to do so.

In Nigeria, public reactions to both the Elliot Report and the Secretary of State's decision in favour of the Minority was naturally not as vehement as the fierce protests in the Gold Coast and Sierra Leone. The Government did not feel any compunction to respond to Hall's despatch until June 1946. Nigeria's complacency was informed by the belief that the territory would certainly have a university no matter which part of the Elliot Report – Majority or Minority – was ultimately approved. As Governor Arthur Richards put it, 'public opinion over the question has not shown any marked strength of feeling one way or another, perhaps because Nigeria stands to get a university whichever Report is eventually adopted'.[22]

Ostensibly, the Nigerian Government was favourably disposed towards the Minority Report. Even though the governor pointed out that the desire of the Gold Coast and Sierra Leone to preserve and develop their local institutions 'is natural and reasonable', he nevertheless stressed that 'it is essential to distinguish between local sentiments and academic efficiency'.[23] None the less, the governor stated that there were certain interest groups such as the Nigeria Union of Teachers (NUT) which supported the Majority recommendations. This was based on professional and sympathetic grounds. The NUT called upon the Secretary of State to implement the Majority proposals without delay. Accordingly,

> The Nigeria Union of Teachers deprecates any steps that might result in the retardation of the progress already made by the University College at Fourah Bay and Achimota College which have for seventy and twenty-four years respectively pioneered higher education in West Africa ... while naturally appreciating the good things envisaged for Nigeria in both the Majority and Minority Reports of the Commission....[24]

After digesting all these reactions from West Africa, the Colonial Office realized that the problem transcended the Minority reasoning. Colonial and territorial 'nationalism', as the Majority faction predicted, was becoming overpowering. What now plagued the Colonial Office was how to garner, for the proposed unitary university of West Africa, the support and co-operation of the other territories, given the outpouring of emotions over the Minority Report. London realized how resolute the Gold Coast educated élite, now backed by their government, had become in launching the Achimota university scheme. The colony had the necessary resources to support its claims, and the educated elements and politicians had seized the initiative. Compromise became necessary. In July 1946, Hall despatched another letter to the governments of the four British West African territories.[25]

In his letter Hall stated that he had been 'urged to give due weight to local political considerations as well as those which are primarily educational and practical' and that

> a beginning in the founding of University Colleges should now be made in two, if not three of the territories concerned or that arrangements should be made by certain of the existing Colleges so that the foundation of a federal University of West Africa may now be laid.

While still resolved that a unitary university college, as recommended by the Minority, should be established in Ibadan, Nigeria, as soon as possible, Hall felt that whatever decision he took 'must be such as to secure a wider measure of consent from the people of all the territories and to enjoy the co-operation and goodwill of local feeling in the task ahead'.[26] Therefore, he suggested that there should be certain facilities in the Gold Coast for post-intermediate studies, and that, as a temporary measure until the University of West Africa at Ibadan was fully developed, Achimota should continue teaching for the B.Sc. (Engineering) degree. He concluded: 'I hope that the proposal I now make will secure their cooperation not only in promoting and encouraging the facilities in their own country but for the University College of West Africa.'[27]

As insignificant as the modification appeared, no such concession was extended to Sierra Leone. The Colonial Office knew that the colony could not support a fully fledged university for lack of resources. Even combined with the Gambia, Sierra Leone could not supply an adequate number of students. Governor Stevenson resisted Creole pressures and would not lobby London for a university college as did his Gold Coast counterpart. Furthermore, the Elliot Report had observed that 'at the present time the chief educational need in Sierra Leone and the Gambia is for better qualified teachers in the secondary and primary schools especially in the hinterland'.[28] As a result, Hall did not feel compelled to offer any compromise to Sierra Leone, other than to elaborate upon the proposed territorial college which should serve the colony and the Gambia. Accordingly, he maintained that the territorial college 'should conform to the scope and purpose set out on pages 158–9 of the Elliot Report and should be sited in or near Freetown'.[29] Furthermore, Hall hoped that the CMS authorities would be willing to associate themselves closely with this college and that 'the name Fourah Bay, so long associated with higher educational effort in Sierra Leone, should be given to it'. Responding to the Creole desire for the reorganization of Fourah Bay to attain a university college status at a future date, as the Majority of the Elliot Commissioners proposed, Hall insisted:

> I do not feel justified at this stage in encouraging at the College post-intermediate studies where the resources for the satisfactory university life and practice cannot be present, or in making available, from Imperial sources, financial or other assistance for the continuance or transference to the new institution of the present degree courses at Fourah Bay.[30]

While the Colonial Office position on Fourah Bay infuriated the educated elements in the colony, the Government of Sierra Leone continued to argue that, unlike the Gold Coast, it had no financial resources to pay for a fully fledged university college. As the governor remarked, 'the controlling factor in regard to setting up a university college in the Gold Coast was not the constitutional position but the fact there were adequate financial resources available'.[31] Pointing out further that there would be very heavy expenditure on primary and secondary education, the governor enjoined Sierra Leoneans to 'take advantage of the university standards to be made available in the Gold Coast and Nigeria'.[32]

Driven by the force of territorial 'nationalism', the various interest groups took their fight to the Legislative Council as they prepared for a confrontation. Since Sierra Leone possessed no financial base to disregard the instructions from London, the few unofficial members of the Legislative Council, who were mostly Creoles, were politically crippled. They could not pass a bill to challenge the Minority Report, as was the case in the Gold Coast, and the governor regarded a constitutional battle over the question as potentially futile. Clearly, the larger issue involved funds and the educated elements understood that. In these circumstances, the position of the Colonial Office would hold sway, despite the strength or weakness of informed local opinion.

Unlike Sierra Leone the Gold Coast was determined upon a show-down. The Gold Coast possessed all the right ingredients with which to confront the Colonial Office effectively. It had both a genuine case for which to fight and a supportive governor. Furthermore, the colony had an informed public led by the clamorous educated élite which insisted that a territorial college would not suffice and that a full-scale university must be established. To the educated elements, therefore, Hall's compromise despatch of 6 July fell short of their expectations. The inaugural session of the Gold Coast Legislative Council held on 24 July 1946 was almost entirely devoted to Elliot's Report and the Secretary of State's despatch of 6 July. Angrily reacting to what Hall considered a concession to the Gold Coast, C. W. Tachie-Menson observed that 'the Despatch allows, but at the same time does not encourage, the Gold Coast to develop either Achimota or any new centre of Higher Education in the Gold Coast into a University College'.

Almost rehashing Burns' 1945 position, Tachie-Menson rejected Hall's proposition and affirmed that the Legislative Council 'shall not support the expenditure of Gold Coast Revenue on any development of Higher Education in West Africa which does not contemplate the immediate development of Achimota on the lines of the Majority Recommendations'.[33] In demonstration of how resolute the Gold Coast politicians were over the question, Tachie-Menson subsequently moved a motion requesting the governor

> to appoint a representative Committee to advise him on this matter to the end that the views to be submitted by the Governor [to the Secretary of State] may reflect the clear and undoubted wishes of the people of the Gold Coast on a subject so deeply concerning the future of the country.[34]

The motion was seconded by Nene Mate-Kole who felt that the appointment of the committee was absolutely necessary in order to 'implement and justify those strong views with competent speed and effective expression'.³⁵ No one, including the official members, spoke against the motion. To do so would have not only alienated the African educated élite and politicians but would have certainly offended the Government. Clearly, Burns was not displeased that the unofficial members were raising a row over the matter.

Seizing the initiative provided by Tachie-Menson and Mate-Kole, J. B. Danquah presented a powerful and emotional speech in favour of the motion. As he affirmed,

> The Gold Coast is not Nigeria, and never could be. Achimota is not Yaba or Ibadan, and never could be.... There are nations in West Africa as there are nations in Europe. There are peoples among black Africans as there are peoples among white Europeans.... For purely cultural reasons ... this Gold Coast, a proud little country with a good reason for being proud, will never, can never and shall never be proud of a university situated at Ibadan and not Achimota.³⁶

Danquah's speech illustrated explicitly how the university question was a catalyst to territorial/colonial nationalism, jealousy and parochial politics. It represented a sharp contrast with the 1920 pan-West African 'nationalism' championed by Casely Hayford and the NCBWA. In the post-war years African 'nationalists' such as Danquah were positioning themselves in their various countries for leading roles in the possible 'self-government' which might soon follow. The new premium which the Colonial Office placed on the role of an educated élite under the current colonial development policy was seized upon by the 'nationalists' to carve out 'empires' for themselves. Seeing himself as a rising 'Black star', Danquah's political and mass followership depended on how he could whip up public sentiments of this 'proud little country' against Hall's decision.

Tachie-Menson's motion was ultimately carried by the Council, willing to show its commitment to fight for 'the people's cause'. In August, Alan Burns accordingly appointed a twelve-man committee under the Chairmanship of Kenneth Bradley, the territory's Acting Colonial Secretary. The task of the committee was very simple. Influential interest groups in the colony wanted their own university college, and nothing less. In November 1946, three months after its appointment, the Bradley Committee submitted its report to the

Government.[37] The Bradley Report reiterated the determination of the Gold Coast to have a university college. It recommended the immediate development of a Gold Coast University College which 'should evolve from the existing university courses at Achimota'. Since it was the view of the committee that the Achimota site 'could not be satisfactorily adapted for permanent use', it identified a separate site for the proposed university college on and around Legon Hill, some two-and-half miles from Achimota and eight miles from Accra, and recommended that it be secured.[38]

As to the question of funding for the proposed university college, the committee considered that the capital cost of approximately £750,000 over a ten-year period 'can be made available from the Colony's surplus balances' while the recurrent costs 'should be met from endowment, which should be built steadily as the resources of the Colony permit'. Furthermore, Bradley's group noted the assurances given by the people, while the committee was collecting evidence, that they were prepared to make sacrifices for higher education even if it implied higher taxation.[39] Regarding the nature of financial contribution the Gold Coast should make towards the proposed university in Nigeria, the committee recommended that 'this contribution should take the form of generous *per capita* grants in respect of government-sponsored Gold Coast students attending that university college'.[40] The Bradley Report represented a blueprint for what was soon to become the University College of the Gold Coast.

The turn of events in the Gold Coast overwhelmed the Colonial Office. Either London would accept a second university college in the Gold Coast or the Gold Coast government would unilaterally build one, as the Bradley group had recommended. In December 1946, seeking to end the feud, the newly formed Inter-University Council for Higher Education in the Colonies (IUC), sent out a delegation to West Africa under the leadership of William Hamilton Fyfe, the Vice-Chancellor of the University of Aberdeen.[41] Initially the IUC group was to investigate the situation in each territory and the action necessary to implement the Secretary of State's decision on the Elliot Report as outlined in Hall's despatch of 6 July. This was another practical step by London to implement the Asquith and Elliot plans for Africa. Earlier, in July 1946, an IUC delegation under the Chairmanship of A. M. Carr-Saunders had visited Makerere College in Uganda to inspect its facilities in relation to upgrading to university college status. Finding the site of the college excellent the delegation observed, however, that some facilities should be improved.[42] Generally, the delegation concluded that 'indispensable foundations for a college of a university standing have been laid' at Makerere, and advised that a rapid effort should be made to build 'on those promising foundation'.[43] As a necessary first step, the Secretary of State appointed Dr W. D. Lamont as the Principal to see Makerere Higher College through this transitional process.[44]

Before the Hamilton Fyfe delegation left for West Africa, the Bradley Report reached the Colonial Office. The content of this Report obliged the Secretary of State and the IUC to instruct the delegation to pay particular attention to the claims of the Gold Coast. The delegation first arrived in Nigeria to inspect the site of the proposed University College. On 28 December 1946 Hamilton Fyfe

> pushed his way through the undergrowth into the 'bush' a few miles north of the town of Ibadan ... until he reached a clearing where it was possible to see a few yards ahead. He planted his walking-stick firmly into the ground and said: 'Here shall be the University of Nigeria'.[45]

Thereafter the delegation left for the trouble-spot – the Gold Coast. The discussion between members of the Hamilton Fyfe group and the various interested bodies convinced the IUC delegation that immediate steps should be taken to establish degree courses there, 'if necessary with local resources'. As to whether the proposed college would enter into the special relationship scheme with the University of London or retain an unmodified external degree arrangement, the IUC group favoured the former which was also readily acceptable to the Gold Coast Advisory Committee on Higher Education. Ultimately, when the delegation submitted its report in January 1947, it recommended the establishment of 'two university colleges in West Africa, one in Nigeria and one in the Gold Coast, each providing courses for degrees in arts and science within the terms of the special relationship with the University of London'.[46] In view of this new arrangement, the delegation advised that the term '"West African" would not be appropriate for either college' since its use might 'perpetuate some of the grievances engendered in the majority–minority debate'. Instead, they recommended that a place name be adopted for each of them.[47] Although the delegation recognized the possible shortage of 'adequately qualified staff willing to serve on the West Coast', the Hamilton Fyfe group felt that 'it would be wrong to take a merely defeatist attitude'.[48] On funding, they referred to the Bradley Report which expressed the ability and willingness of the Gold Coast to provide both the capital and recurrent funds for its university and recommended that

> the main proportion of funds available for West Africa from the higher education allocation under the Colonial Development and Welfare Act should be used for establishing the college at Ibadan.[49]

The IUC delegation had modified the Colonial Office and British Government policy on the number of university colleges which should be founded in West Africa. There is no doubt that the delegation based its recommendation not necessarily on academic expediency but mainly on the strength of local sentiments which could no longer be resisted. This is why the Colonial Office had found itself almost powerless to implement the university project in West Africa. Furthermore, the Secretary of State could neither veto nor ignore the recommendations of the delegation because it had given the IUC wide powers, including independence from government interference in the discharge of its functions. Given the impasse created by the stubborn opposition of the Gold Coast to the Minority Report and Hall's refusal to approve a second university college, the intervention of the IUC was a saving grace. The Colonial Office ultimately yielded and the Gold Coast initiative was a success. Significantly, it was a triumph for African 'nationalists' who discovered that their opinion now seriously mattered under the new dispensation. From then on they would begin to seize further initiatives.

Hamilton Fyfe's group also revised the conception of the territorial college as outlined in the Elliot Minority Report. Teaching for the intermediate examinations, thereby serving as 'feeders' to the university colleges, would no longer be one of their primary functions. Instead, the delegation proposed the creation of 'regional colleges' in Nigeria, the Gold Coast and Sierra Leone 'to provide a coherent and complete training, and not merely part of the training to be completed elsewhere'.[50] In other words, the new regional colleges should be in the nature of polytechnics – to relieve the university colleges of some vocational courses, and to supplement efforts in secondary education. The IUC delegation wanted to make this clarification in order to remove the regional colleges from its sphere of responsibility. 'Since the regional colleges are not and never will be university institutions', the delegation opined, 'we presume that any responsibility for their development ... will only indirectly concern the Inter-University Council.'[51] Since the delegation had proposed that the regional colleges be assisted financially from the CD&WA allocation for higher education, it made a strong representation to the British Government to provide substantial funds for the colleges which were separate from university funds.[52]

The visit of the IUC delegation to Sierra Leone and its consequent report on Fourah Bay College created more indignation there. The Hamilton Fyfe group did not support the claims of the colony for a university college and the scope of the regional colleges proposed by the delegation would further degrade Fourah Bay College (if certain courses taught by that institution were transferred to the regional colleges). However, the group suggested that the Fourah Bay College site at Mount Aureol be extended until the new regional college took effect. It further recommended that a grant-in-aid from the CD&WA funds should be made to Fourah Bay to keep the Durham degree arrangement going until university courses began in Nigeria and the Gold Coast. Such financial help would only be necessary if the CMS was unable to maintain the college degree work for that interim period with the assistance of the local government. Considering the tense political situation in Sierra Leone, the IUC delegation could not recommend an immediate halt to degree work at Fourah Bay. As they stated,

> It would be a ludicrous climax to all the public discussions of West African higher education during the past years if the only institution on the West Coast in which students can obtain British degrees were to expire before degree courses are provided elsewhere on the Coast. This would arouse great and justifiable indignation locally and create a very embarrassing political situation.[53]

Although the claims of Sierra Leone for a university college were not supported by the IUC delegation, these interim compromises were steps which later permitted the eventual development of Fourah Bay into the University College of Sierra Leone. But it was clear that progress would be slow given all the difficulties. What is important to note is how local pressures were affecting the whole process of Colonial Office decision-making. African reactions were beginning to dictate the details of policy implementation.

In March 1947, the IUC endorsed the report of the Hamilton Fyfe delegation to West Africa, and advised the Secretary of State to approve a second university college for the Gold Coast. While the Colonial Office was considering the question, Governor Burns of the Gold Coast announced at the opening of the March 1947 Budget Session of the Legislative Council that the Gold Coast was proceeding with the establishment of its own university college. A second university college in West Africa had become a *fait accompli*. The Colonial Office knew this, and to continue to argue otherwise would be foolhardy. In his despatch of 16 August 1947 to West African governments, the Secretary of State, Arthur Creech Jones, who had taken over the mantle from Hall in a cabinet reshuffle, 'agreed in principle to the proposal that a University College should be established in the Gold Coast'. However, he added that his acceptance in principle of the arrangement 'was based on the assumption that the greater part of the cost of establishing and maintaining the College could be met from Gold Coast funds'.[54] Giving approval for another university college was a climb-down by Creech Jones, who had consistently favoured the Minority idea of a unitary University of West Africa.

The turn of events since 1945 demonstrated that those who signed the Elliot Majority Report were more far-sighted than the Minority signatories, including Creech Jones. In recommending more than one university college, the Majority fully understood the strength of local sentiments, and the influence of emerging colonial territorial nationalism. They also realized the ambitions and strength of African educated elements. Creech Jones was clearly late in recognizing these factors, but that he eventually did marked a significant triumph for the African educated élite who used the university issue as a test case for later vigorous nationalism. Accordingly,

> I recognized, however, that any successful educational advance must depend on active and informed popular support and, in view of the strong public demand in the Gold Coast for the establishment of a University College there and of the necessary financial support, I have agreed in principle that a University College should be established in the Gold Coast.[55]

Creech Jones further endorsed the recommendation of the Hamilton Fyfe delegation that neither of the two university colleges should adopt the term 'West Africa'. The Nigerian college now became known as the University College of Ibadan (UCI), while the other became the University College of the Gold Coast (UCGC). In the meantime, the Secretary of State had appointed Dr Kenneth Mellanby as the Principal-designate of the UCI, Nigeria.[56] In July 1947, Mellanby left for Nigeria to examine the problems relating to the establishment of the college. Later in the year, David Balme was appointed the Principal-designate of the newly approved University College of the Gold Coast.[57] Thus by the end of 1947 a major step had been taken for the establishment of two university colleges in West Africa. Mellanby from London and Balme from Cambridge would imprint upon their respective colleges the attitudes, organizations and academic culture reminiscent of the institutions from which they came. Ibadan would exhibit the legacy of the University of London while Legon (the University College of the Gold Coast) would bear the stamp of Cambridge.

As for Fourah Bay College, the Secretary of State reaffirmed his unwillingness, despite the strong representations made to him by the CMS, the Methodist Missionary Society, Durham University and other influential interest groups within and outside Sierra Leone, to support the development of Fourah Bay as a university college. Creech Jones felt that Sierra Leone did not possess the resources to build and maintain a university college and that the funds available from the CD&WA could not provide for a third university in West Africa. As he asserted,

> I do not believe that Sierra Leone in its present stage of development can undertake the necessary recurrent financial commitment to maintain a University College of the required quality and it is certainly not possible to contemplate assistance from the Colonial Development and Welfare Vote for three university colleges in West Africa .... I believe that the needs of Sierra Leone can best be met by the University Colleges established in Nigeria and the Gold Coast and the regional college on the lines suggested by the Inter-University Council.[58]

Agreeing with the proposal of the IUC delegation, Creech Jones conceded that in recognition of the role of Fourah Bay College as the only institution providing degree courses in arts and commerce in

West Africa these programmes 'will continue until the university colleges in Nigeria and the Gold Coast are in a position themselves to provide such degree courses'. During this interim period, the Secretary of State agreed to make available to Fourah Bay a measure of financial assistance if this was seen to be required to enable the college to continue with its activities.[59] Not surprisingly, this did not appease the Creoles and other interest groups in Sierra Leone. They opposed the arrangement because it fell short of what had been granted to the other contending territories. Since the Gold Coast had been given a university college, it was clear that nothing would pacify Sierra Leone's élite other than the immediate reorganization and development of Fourah Bay towards ultimate university status. For Sierra Leone's educated elements, therefore, the matter had not been laid to rest and resistance persisted.

Meanwhile, as Sierra Leoneans were protesting against the content of the Secretary of State's despatch of 16 August 1947, events were moving rapidly in both Nigeria and the Gold Coast. Mellanby had been mandated to ensure that classes started at the UCI in January 1948 by adapting the former 56th General Military Hospital some five miles from the permanent site at Ibadan, which the Hamilton Fyfe delegation had approved. Lectures accordingly began in January 1948 with 108 students transferred from the Yaba Higher College. However, not all of these students were university candidates. They were mainly intermediate and teacher-training students who completed their programmes in the new university college. It was not until October 1948 that approximately 148 new university students were admitted for the various degree courses offered by the UCI. Thus, a university institution was established in Nigeria. The larger part of the financial support for capital costs, to the tune of £1,500,000 initially, was provided by the British Government from the CD&WA allocation to higher education in the colonies, as recommended by the Asquith Commission. The Nigerian Government bore the recurrent expenditure.[60] As agreed, the University College was tied to the University of London under the scheme of special relationship. The degrees the students took were those of the University of London.

In the Gold Coast, likewise, the Secretary of State officially approved the establishment of a university college for the territory. The appointment of David Balme as the Principal-designate in late 1947 and his arrival in the Gold Coast in January 1948 set the wheels in motion. Finally, in October 1948, classes began in the University College with 90 undergraduates taken from Achimota's post-secondary programme. During these foundation years the UCGC shared accommodation with the teacher-training department at Achimota. The rate of expansion meant that work had to begin immediately at its permanent site. Legon Hill, some three miles from Achimota, which the Bradley Committee had recommended, was chosen in preference to Kumasi, even though the Hamilton Fyfe delegation pointed out that the Legon Hill site 'has some serious disadvantages'.[61] Since Creech Jones refused to promise substantial financial support for the UCGC, the bulk of the funds required for the initial establishment were provided by the government and people of the Gold Coast. The Gold Coast Government provided the sum of £1,100,000, and the Gold Coast Cocoa Marketing Board gave £1,896,718 for the development of an agriculture department and associated sciences.[62] The Gold Coast later felt burdened by this financial arrangement in which the government and people were compelled to fund the UCGC while huge Imperial funds were being poured into the Nigerian UCI.

While the two new university colleges were being built in Nigeria and the Gold Coast, Sierra Leone was embroiled in protest against the interim measure proposed for Fourah Bay College by the Secretary of State. Maxwell has observed that Creech Jones' interim arrangement of August 1947 'met with a worse reception in Sierra Leone than his predecessor's [Hall's] refusal in July 1946' to approve a university college for the colony.[63] It was devastating to the Sierra Leonean educated class and other interest groups that Fourah Bay College, which had a long tradition of degree work, could be so relegated to a regional college to offer courses of merely secondary school or polytechnic character. Further representations were therefore made to the Secretary of State by Sierra Leone's paramount chiefs and other influential lobbies. But Creech Jones stood his ground and refused to alter the overall plan for higher education in West Africa any further. The IUC advised against any further concession to Sierra Leone, and the Secretary of State concurred. In the opinion of the IUC, any attempt to divert the CD&WA funds to Fourah Bay should be viewed as 'purely a political gesture, when justifiable educational claims elsewhere far exceeded the available resources'.[64]

Lobby groups came to realize that the main point at issue for the refusal of London to approve a university college for Sierra Leone was the lack of resources to build and sustain it. Thus a mass rally was organized in early 1948 which set up a committee 'to appeal to the people of Sierra Leone for funds to serve the College'. The committee was only able to raise the sum of £7,000[65] which could hardly provide a meaningful base for a university college. While this took place locally, a group known as the Friends of Fourah Bay continued lobbying the Colonial Office and the IUC for a sympathetic reconsideration of the Fourah Bay College case.[66] Meanwhile, in early 1948, Hubert Stevenson was replaced by George Beresford-Stooke as Governor of Sierra Leone. As his actions would demonstrate, this new governor appeared more sensitive to the Creole interests and the fortunes of Fourah Bay College than his predecessor.

The Colonial Office urgently desired to get the regional college for Sierra Leone and the Gambia off the ground. But given the intensity of local sentiment and opposition to the regional college idea progress seemed unlikely. Furthermore, the Sierra Leone Legislative Council was likely to refuse to vote funds for the new regional college in protest against the humiliation of Fourah Bay. These factors, coupled with the powerful pressures from the Friends of Fourah Bay in London, convinced the Secretary of State of the need for further concessions. In his despatch of October 1948, Creech Jones, after giving 'the very fullest weight to local opinion and aspirations', proposed what became known as a 'compromise solution'.[67]

By this arrangement, imperial funds from the CD&WA allocation were to be granted to Fourah Bay College for five years, in the first instance, provided that it became a composite institution, embracing academic work envisaged for the regional college, and a university department conducting the existing degree courses. This was on the condition that the university courses would not be expanded until reviewed by the Sierra Leone Government regarding '... the cost of continuing or expanding degree courses'. Even though he asserted that 'the responsibility of deciding the future of the College rests with the College authorities', Creech Jones further advised that before any full university scheme should be undertaken a Commission of enquiry drawn from both London and locally should be appointed, 'in four or five years' time ... to investigate and report on the educational requirements of Sierra Leone at all levels in the light of the funds available, including the question of the future of degree course teaching in Sierra Leone'. Stressing the importance he attached to the proposal for a Commission the Secretary of State concluded: 'I feel that acceptance of this proposal must be regarded as an essential part of the compromise which it is the purpose of this despatch to propose.'[68]

With this proposal Creech Jones demonstrated considerable political adroitness. He purposely set the interim period in order to allow tempers to cool in Sierra Leone, and to afford enough time for the two university colleges in Nigeria and the Gold Coast to take root. Furthermore, the Colonial Office desired that the regional college for Sierra Leone and the Gambia should be established immediately, even if under the Fourah Bay umbrella. Evidently, Creech Jones was buying time. He was not unaware that the tense political situation over the university question in Sierra Leone could derail the entire plan in both Nigeria and the Gold Coast. It appears that the Secretary of State's interim arrangement was more a divide-and-rule ploy than it was intended to establish a university college in Sierra Leone. As Maxwell aptly described it,

> Behind the decisions lay the expectation that in five years' time the current bitterness would have passed and that the legislative council, with by then a majority of members from the hinterland where school facilities were desperately poor, would not willingly devote an excessive share of educational resources to Fourah Bay College to meet the wishes of the Creole population of the Freetown area.[69]

In December 1948 the Fourah Bay College Council accepted the Secretary of State's compromise plan. This was on the condition that 'the position of the Degree courses in the new Fourah Bay College is safe-guarded by the division of the College into Departments', and as long as there was 'the possibility of developing out of the existing courses, honours courses in Arts as the University of Durham may approve and as soon as circumstances justify such a development', and 'provided that the enlarged Fourah Bay College should be largely autonomous'.[70] The Governor of Sierra Leone, Beresford-Stooke, despatched an urgent letter to the Secretary of State in which he accepted the observations and recommendations of the Fourah Bay College Council. According to him, it 'gives me particular pleasure to transmit to you the proposals by the Council to which this

Government can attach its general support, and which I can commend to your favourable consideration'.[71] Furthermore, Beresford-Stooke observed,

> In my view the report of the Council offers a basis on which an agreed solution of this problem can be reached. I trust that you will be able to accept in principle the recommendation made by the Council and that we shall then be able to proceed with plans for developing higher education in Sierra Leone.[72]

On receipt of the Council's views and the governor's comment, the embattled Secretary of State telegraphed to the Governor of Sierra Leone: 'I accept the modifications which the Council have suggested in the arrangement proposed in my despatch [of October 1948]'.[73] The speed with which Creech Jones gave his approval to the Fourah Bay Council's views demonstrated how relieved the Colonial Office was that a solution had been reached. Fourah Bay College had presented a perennial problem in British efforts to provide university facilities for Africans. Although the Gold Coast resistance to the Hall/Jones' decision in favour of the Elliot Minority proposal was much more ferocious, the opposition of the Creoles, albeit more subtle, was more protracted. Both encounters proved weakening to the Colonial Office's ability to face the university issue with vigour.

In February 1949 the Sierra Leonean Legislative Council gave its official approval to the new arrangement, and Fourah Bay College became reconstituted by Ordinance No. 1 of 1950. It became a composite college offering both degree courses and middle-level training of a polytechnic nature. Under the plan, the IUC, which had consistently avoided involvement in Fourah Bay, was glad to be relieved of any responsibility since Durham University and the newly appointed Advisory Committee on Colonial Colleges of Arts, Science and Technology (ACCCAST) took over the duty of providing advice and financial support. In September 1950 the sum of £450,000 was granted to Fourah Bay College from the CD&WA funds – £100,000 for recurrent and £350,000 for capital expenditure.[74] However, it took almost ten more years before the college could attain university college status. Advance was very slow. A Commission was appointed, and reported in 1954,[75] as required in the compromise plan. Sierra Leone finally got its own university college in 1959, but very belatedly, as the IUC and Colonial Office had foreseen.

The foundation of the two university colleges in Nigeria and the Gold Coast in 1948 influenced events in East Africa. In 1937 Makerere College had begun its long and sluggish march towards university college status as the De La Warr Commission envisioned. The Second World War was a stumbling block, but Colonial Office plans for post-war reconstruction in the colonies gave the college a new impetus. In September 1947, a year after the visit of the IUC delegation led by Carr-Saunders, the college applied to the University of London for admission into the special relationship scheme. This was not immediately approved because the University wanted further informal discussion with the college 'concerning its constitution, staffing, courses to be offered and other matters'.[76] Nevertheless, the IUC was determined to see Makerere College advance towards university college status as envisaged by the Asquith Commission. Its progress should, if necessary, be induced since within both college and government circles there was divided opinion on the wisdom of proceeding immediately with development towards university status.[77] However, in view of the progress made in West Africa, in November 1948 the College Council made a public statement to declare its stand on the university question. Accordingly,

> Both for educational and political reasons it is most important that ..., as early as possible satisfactory arrangements should be made between the University of London and the College authorities whereby students of the College can read for external degrees of the University.[78]

This statement confirmed the IUC desire to establish, as soon as possible, a link between Makerere and the University of London in the scheme of special relationship. The commencement of the two university colleges in West Africa in 1948 under the special relationship plan hastened events in East Africa. Negotiations on the modalities of the scheme with respect to Makerere began in London in January 1949, and in July of that year the Carr-Saunders IUC delegation revisited Makerere to assess its progress. Even though they observed that there might be a need for 'further negotiations on points such as Matriculation of the degree courses' and a reorganization of the College Council to ensure African representation, the delegation felt that Makerere should 'assume the status of a University College' without delay. The IUC group believed that the college was entitled to recognition as a university college and so greatly increased financial assistance should be extended to it.[79]

In November 1949 the college was duly accepted into the special relationship scheme with the University of London, with its name and status changed to the University College of East Africa. Professor Bernard de Bunsen was appointed the Principal of the new institution.[80] Educated at Oxford, de Bunsen vigorously pursued Oxford tradition at Makerere while maintaining the special relationship links with London. For the initial establishment, the sum of £1,250,000 from the CD&WA was granted to the college for capital expenditure.[81] Thus, a third university college was approved in Africa under the Asquith plan.

East Africa presented a sharp contrast with West Africa in that its educated elements were not as large and forceful in championing the cause of territorial nationalism as those of West Africa. From the beginning, efforts at higher education in East Africa had been centred at Makerere, while in West Africa various centres emerged in the different territories. Furthermore, apart from Uganda, none of the other East African territories had even a handful of African educated elements who could put pressure on the Colonial Office for separate university colleges. Worse still, none of the territories, apart from Uganda, possessed the resources to pursue any independent university project. Kenya's settlers were not interested in the issue since they preferred to send their children to England for university education. It was recorded that out of the total number of students at the University College of East Africa, Makerere, in 1954, there was only one European.[82] Obviously, despite its change of name, Makerere was still a Ugandan affair and a Ugandan institution, supported by the chiefly élite and a colonial budget surplus, with an ambition to become the Oxford of Africa.

In West Africa, the Gold Coast, like Uganda, had the resources but with an altogether more vociferous educated élite. Sierra Leone had no money but it possessed the largest number of educated Africans – the Creoles – as well as the only institution in West Africa which had offered degrees since 1876. Nigeria, although poorer than the Gold Coast, was the largest British West African territory both in population and land mass. It also had vocal educated elements. The Gambia, the smallest of all the territories, was the poorest in everything and hence did not present any demands. Obviously, the physical and human resources of the various British African territories correlated with the demand for universities.

Significant in all these events was the lobbying of the African intellectual élites, which led to very important changes in Colonial Office policy. This is central to the fundamental change which was occurring in the focus of imperial policy on the transfer of collaboration patterns from traditional to new and educated élites. Significant in this new collaboration was the willingness of the Colonial Office actively to seek the opinion of the educated élite thereby circumventing colonial establishments. Indirect rule was in decay and doomed. By reshaping, adjusting, and modifying its university policy, the Colonial Office demonstrated a sensitivity toward the educated élite quite unique in its history. It upset the gradualism and imperviousness of colonial establishments usually more attuned to the chiefly predispositions of indirect rule than to the Westernized élite. In this new colonial policy lay the link with decolonization.

Even when the change of attitude was not actually intended to lead to complete transfer of power, the expansion of the class of African educated élite and the relegation to the background of the traditional class boosted the 'nationalist' movements. The new élites, unlike the traditional one, had initiatives and demands of their own, and these had to be met as the price of their collaboration with the economic, social, and political development policy of the Colonial Office. The university issue became, therefore, one which touched deeply and fundamentally on élite class interests, because the universities were seen as the means by which their class could be enlarged and entry gained into government administration, education and other professions. Ultimately, it would lead them along the corridors of power into the control rooms of the colonial states.

NOTES

1. See Cmd.6713 *Colonial Development and Welfare*, HMSO, December 1945; Ashby, *Universities: British, Indian, African*, p. 429; and Pearce, *The Turning Point in Africa*, pp. 65–66.
2. Roger Louis, *Imperialism at Bay 1941–1945*, p. 101, see as well Lee and Petter, *The Colonial Office, War, and Development Policy*, pp. 215–217.
3. National Archives of Ghana, Accra (NAGA), ADM 5/3/122 Secretary of State to the Officer Administering the Government of Nigeria, the Gold Coast, Sierra Leone, and the Gambia, 1 October 1945.
4. Ibid.
5. Ibid. One other factor which he emphasized was the impossibility, with the existing resources,

of assembling a staff adequate in number and qualification for more than one university.
6. Ibid.
7. Refer to Parliamentary Debates (House of Commons), Vol. 391, cols. 54–57, 13 July 1943.
8. NAGA, ADM 5/3/122 Recommendations of the Gold Coast Central Advisory Committee on Education, 21 November 1945.
9. NAGA, ADM 5/3/122 Memorandum on Hall's Despatch and the Report of the Elliot Commission submitted by the Standing Committee of the Joint Provisional Council, 28 November 1945. This Council consisted of all the paramount chiefs in the Gold Coast Colony.
10. Ibid.
11. NAGA, ADM 5/3/122 Resolution Passed at a Public Rally held at Rodger Club, Accra, 3 December 1945.
12. NAGA, ADM 5/3/122 Resolution Passed at a Public Meeting held at the Hodson Club, Accra, 14 December 1945.
13. Ibid.
14. Cmd.6655 *Report of the Commission on Higher Education in West Africa*, HMSO, June 1945, p. 54.
15. Sierra Leone Archives (SLA), CSO Miscellaneous/Confidential Files on Education (General), From Alan Burns to G. H. Hall, 23 December 1945.
16. Ibid. Refer also to Gordon Guggisberg, *The Keystone*, London, 1924, p. 32.
17. Christopher Fyfe, *A Short History of Sierra Leone*, Longman, London, 1962, p. 167. In colonial Sierra Leone, the hinterland mostly inhabited by the Temne and the Mende was referred to as the Protectorate while the Freetown area where the Creoles lived was known as the Colony.
18. SLA, CSO Misc./Confid. Files on Education (General), *The Daily Guardian*, 17 October 1945.
19. SLA, CSO Misc./Confid. Files on Education (General), Memorandum from the Fourah Bay College Council to Sierra Leone Government, 17 November 1945.
20. Ibid. *The Daily Guardian*, 22 November 1945.
21. SLA, CSO Misc./Confid. Files, Memorandum from the Director of Education to the Hon. Colonial Secretary, Sierra Leone, December 1945.
22. SLA, CSO Misc./Confid. Files, From Governor Richards to the Secretary of State, 11 June 1946.
23. Ibid.
24. Ibid. The NUT's position was not surprising. Ransome Kuti, who presided over the Union, was a signatory to the Majority Report. Just as Creech Jones was pushing the Minority opinion in London, Ransome Kuti was equally demonstrating his strong support for the Majority view in West Africa. Kuti could not easily give up simply because Nigeria stood to gain in any circumstance. Besides, there were a large number of secondary school teachers in Nigeria who not only came from Sierra Leone and the Gold Coast but had also attended Fourah Bay or Achimota. Undoubtedly, they were a factor in the NUT's views.
25. CO 987/11 Secretary of State to the Governors of Nigeria, the Gold Coast, Sierra Leone and the Gambia, 6 July 1946.
26. Ibid.
27. Ibid.
28. Cmd.6655 *Report of the Commission on Higher Education in West Africa*, p. 69.
29. Ibid. Pages 158–9 of the Elliot Report describes the functions of the proposed Territorial Colleges. These have been stated severally in this discussion.
30. Ibid.
31. SLA, CSO Misc./Confid. Files, Colonial Secretary's Note on the Governor's Remark on the University Question, August 1946.
32. Ibid.
33. NAGA, ADM 5/3/122 Extract from Honourable C. W. Tachie-Menson's Speech at the Inaugural Session of the New Legislative Council, 24 July 1946.
34. Ibid.
35. NAGA, ADM 5/3/122 Extract from Nene Mate-Kole's Speech in the Legislative Council, 24 July 1946.
36. NAGA, ADM 5/3/122 Extract from Dr J. B. Danquah's Speech in the Legislative Council, Gold Coast, 24 July 1946.
37. DP/LA 1611/G5/G35 *Report of the Committee on Higher Education in the Gold Coast*,

August–November 1946, Government Printer, Accra, Africana Section, Balme Library, University of Ghana, Legon, Ghana.
38. Ibid., pp. 12–13.
39. Ibid., p. 14.
40. Ibid., p. 15.
41. Other members of the delegation were Professor H. H. Bellot representing the London Senate Committee, Professor T. H. Davey, Professor L. E. S. Eastham, and Walter Adams.
42. These facilities included the Library, teaching and residential accommodation, and improving both the scope and standard of courses in Arts and Science.
43. *Report of the Inter-University Council for Higher Education in the Colonies*, July 1946, p. 21 as cited in Maxwell, *Universities in Partnership*, p. 197.
44. Cmd.7331 *Inter-University Council for Higher Education in the Colonies, Report 1946–1947*, HMSO, February 1948. Dr Lamont was a lecturer in Moral Philosophy at the University of Glasgow.
45. Kenneth Mellanby, *The Birth of Nigeria's University*, Methuen and Co. Ltd., London, 1958, and republished by Ibadan University Press, Ibadan, 1974, p. 15. By calling it the 'University of Nigeria' and not of 'West Africa' the impression was created that the Hamilton Fyfe delegation had decided to recommend in favour of the University College of the Gold Coast even before the group visited the Gold Coast.
46. National Archives of Nigeria, Ibadan (NAI) MED/FED 1/10 CADW 33 *Report of the Inter-University Council Delegation to West Africa*, 21 December 1946–15 January 1947, p. 4.
47. Ibid., p. 5.
48. Ibid.
49. Ibid., p. 10.
50. Ibid., p. 14. They should be one of the most flexible organs in the educational system, quickly responsive to the employment requirements of government and of society.
51. Ibid., p. 16. The territorial colleges would rather be the concern of the ACEC. Contrary to the delegates' views that the colleges 'will never be university institutions', nearly all of them ultimately became such after the various colonies had attained independence.
52. Ibid., p. 17.
53. Ibid., p. 19.
54. NAI OX/A28 From Secretary of State to the Governors of Nigeria, the Gold Coast, Sierra Leone and the Gambia, 16 August 1947.
55. Ibid.
56. Appointed on 8 May 1947, Dr Mellanby was a University Reader in Medical Entomology at the London School of Hygiene and Tropical Medicine.
57. Balme was formerly a Senior Tutor of Jesus College, Cambridge and University Lecturer in Classics.
58. NAI OX/A28 From the Secretary of State to the Governors of Nigeria, the Gold Coast, Sierra Leone, and the Gambia, 16 August, 1947.
59. Ibid.
60. NAI, CSO 26/4197/Vol.1 *Proposals for the Future Financing of the University College, Ibadan*, Government Printer, Lagos, 1952, pp. 2–3.
61. See the *Report of the IUC Delegation to West Africa*, p. 12. Some of these disadvantages, the delegation stressed, were that it was a coastal belt with desert-like conditions, it was in the midst of non-African influences near Accra, which was on a hill 450 feet above sea level, and was thought to be 'artificial' as a centre of European administration and influences.
62. See the *Report of the Principal of the University College of the Gold Coast, 1948–1952*, Government Printer, Accra, 1952, pp. 28–30; and CO 1004/1 Governor of the Gold Coast to the Secretary of State, 22 February 1950.
63. Maxwell, *Universities in Partnership*, p. 177.
64. Ibid., p. 178.
65. Sierra Leone Collection (SLC), RS 378.664/SA97 Harry Sawyer and Eldred Jones, 'The Story of Fourah Bay College', 1960, p. 15.
66. Ibid., p. 16. Members of this lobby group seem to have consisted mainly of the former as well as current staff of Durham University who had long-standing connections with Fourah Bay College.
67. SLC, RS 378.664/G798 Secretary of State to the Governor of Sierra Leone, 20 October 1948.

68. Ibid.
69. Maxwell, *Universities in Partnership*, pp. 178–9.
70. SLA, CSO Misc./Confid. Files on Education, 'Observations and Recommendations of the New Council of Fourah Bay College on the Secretary of State Despatch', December 1948.
71. SLC, RS 378.66/SI 17 Governor of Sierra Leone to Secretary of State, 28 December 1948.
72. Ibid.
73. SLC, RS 378.66/SI 17, Secretary of State to the Governor of Sierra Leone, January 1949.
74. SLC, RS 378.664/F825 'Fourah Bay College – Past, Present and Future: A Memorandum from the College Council to the Fulton Education Commission', 1954, p. 9; see also SLC, RS 378.664/F74 C. P. Foray *An Outline of Fourah Bay College History, 1827–1977*, pamphlet, 1977, p. 22.
75. See the SLC, RS 370.9664/SI 17 *Report of the Sierra Leone Education Commission*, 1954.
76. Maxwell, *Universities in Partnership*, p. 198.
77. Although details and issues involved in this rift were not documented it would appear that government departments which insisted that Makerere should remain a higher college were concerned with the supply of middle-level manpower, while those who supported a university were the Ugandan chiefly élite. However, given the 'Oxford complex' of Makerere, the Baganda chiefs might have opposed an external relationship with the University of London, in their opinion a less prestigious institution than Oxford.
78. Ibid.
79. ULAP, AC 11/12/1 *Report of the Inter-University Council Delegation to East Africa*, July-August, 1949, pp. 42–48.
80. Professor de Bunsen was formerly a director of education in Palestine, and later Professor of Education at Makerere College. He was educated at Balliol College, Oxford.
81. Macpherson, *They Built for the Future: A Chronicle of Makerere University College, 1922–1962*, p. 102.
82. SLA, CSO Open Files on Education (General), Cmd.9515 *Inter-University Council for Higher Education Overseas, 1946–1954*, HMSO, 1954, p. 26.

Conclusion

It took almost one hundred years before the British could see their way to the provision of the necessary facilities for university education in Africa. The reason for this did not lie entirely in British lack of recognition of the positive role which higher education could play in the social and economic development of the colonial peoples. Instead, the larger question involved the place which the highly educated African was expected to occupy under a form of colonial rule which depended on the collaboration of traditional élites. The ideas which essentially informed the foundation of universities in Africa in the 1940s – the expansion of the class of African educated élite for colonial development – were fundamentally the same as those which frustrated it in the late nineteenth century.

Between 1860 and 1920 the agitation for the establishment of a university in Africa came almost exclusively from Africans such as Horton, Blyden, Johnson and Hayford. Except for Blyden's demand, which attracted the sympathy of Governor Hennessy of Sierra Leone, other demands made hardly any tangible impact in London. The Colonial Office failed to be persuaded mainly because the idea raised in Parliament in 1865 about 'self-government' for the colonies quickly evaporated, even before Blyden publicized the university question in a more sophisticated fashion. Had it been pursued sincerely, the idea of 'self-government' would have entailed the training of an African élite to take over and run the new African states along British lines – as in the 1940s colonial reform ideology. But the university question was clearly ahead of its time, since the notion of British withdrawal from Africa soon became moribund. The British

Treasury would have laughed at any request from the Colonial Office for funding of African university schemes.

Between 1860 and 1900 the CMS possessed a near monopoly on education in British African territories. Believing that successful proselytization must depend on effective control of educational institutions, the Society jealously guarded its dominance. It was quick to dismiss Blyden's demand for an indigenous and secular institution as an attempt to establish a 'godless' university.[1] Since the missionary bodies actually funded most of the schools, thereby relieving the Sierra Leone Government of the responsibility, African demands hardly received any serious official British attention. However, to consolidate its control, the CMS settled for the affiliation of Fourah Bay College to Durham University in 1876 for the award of external degrees in Theology and Classics. Essentially, this was meant to dampen African agitation and ensure that neither the local colonial government nor London would have any logical reasons to support Blyden and his group. It worked. Soon after affiliation, from the 1880s onwards, African demands for a university lost their vitality as the era of 'scramble and partition' set in.

The affiliation with Durham University occurred at the end of the period when British policy favoured a social policy of assimilation of Africans into European civilization, Christianity, and commerce. Horton, Blyden, Johnson and the archetypical 'Black Englishman', Samuel Crowther, were all products of this age. It was an age when some British officials, such as Governor Pope Hennessy and missionary personnel such as Henry Venn, believed that African 'inferiority' had resulted from the lack of opportunity.[2] For them, to encourage education, spread Christianity and promote trade and modern commerce would eliminate the differences between Africans and Europeans. Within this framework the logic of a university institution was obvious. Thus, the Fourah Bay affiliation was partly intended to cater to the assumptions of the 'civilizing mission'.

With regard to policy and overall goals, educated Africans did not differ in essentials from either secular or religious foreign officials. Blyden, who stressed adaptation, became a spokesman for African opinion. Although, as later events demonstrated, not all believed wholeheartedly in his advocacy of an Africanized syllabus, fearing that it would not only be interpreted as inferior to the education offered in Britain but would also serve to legitimize European racial claims. As a result, educated Africans, almost without exception, indirectly approved educational 'imperialism' and urged the British forward. Ironically, however, official British thinking underwent a profound change of opinion just as the affiliation of Fourah Bay occurred. Once Britain began to administer her appropriated territories, the idea of ultimate withdrawal from Africa became little more than a joke. Whatever assimilationist progress there had been was abandoned and replaced by a set of new and, in essence, racist ideas surrounding the concept of indirect rule and colonial occupation.

To justify colonial rule Africans were now considered as either genetically inferior – and therefore not fundamentally changeable by education and Christianity – or so many millennia behind Europeans in cultural development that they would take centuries to catch up.[3] Indirect rule was postulated on these new assumptions. The 'civilization' of Africans now became the 'White Man's burden' as European arrogance grew. Philip Curtin aptly noted that the new racism became 'the most important cluster of ideas in British imperial policy'.[4] Similarly, Basil Davidson has also pointed out how Africans were treated as inferior to Europeans under colonial rule, justified by a whole range of myths which supported 'White superiority'.[5] The belief followed that Africans would require possibly a thousand years to evolve, in their own time, at their own speed and along their own lines, to a 'civilized level'. The idea of an African university threatened the slow evolutionary gradualism of the indirect rule ideology, serving only to disrupt and undermine the system.

Educated Africans who had achieved fame in medicine and university education were now dismissed as unusual exceptions. Where they were given credit at all, it was shrouded in racism. Some officials contended that Africans possessed an exceptional power of memory without a corresponding ability to apply their knowledge in practice.[6] For a long time this theory was used by British officials as a justification not to hire well-educated Africans. Until these ideas began to change in the late 1930s – and they changed more rapidly in England than among the European rank and file in the African colonial service – there was no hope of undermining indirect rule or establishing universities.

The elevation of the African traditional élite over and above the educated class under the indirect rule policy caused the educated élite to abandoned their demand for a university to fight for recognition in the colonial administration. Realising that there was no role for them, they began to protest. This accounted for the meeting of the leaders of the West African educated élite in Accra, the Gold Coast, in 1920 under the auspices of the National Congress of British West Africa. In a sense, it was the original exclusion of educated Africans which helped to create the germ of the nationalist movement in Africa. In Uganda the two élites were one and the same and nothing approaching a nationalist movement took place there during the first phase of decolonization. Since British colonial officials collaborated with the traditional élites, African intellectual elements in West Africa were seen as adversaries if not actually subversive. It is no surprise that British officials refused to 'exert themselves to provide what the "educated and Europeanized natives" wanted, namely facilities for university education'.[7]

From the 1920s there were feeble efforts at the provision of higher educational facilities resulting in the foundation of Achimota College in the Gold Coast and Makerere College in Uganda – the two most financially secure colonies. The establishment of these institutions was essentially a response to the middle-level manpower needs of the colonial service, and not a benevolent official response to African demands for a university. It was American involvement in African educational matters under the auspices of the Phelps-Stokes Commission in the 1920s that forced the Colonial Office to issue, for the first time, an education policy for British African dependencies, and to establish the ACNETA. Nevertheless, university education remained anathema to indirect rule enthusiasts who did not want to see the expansion of the class of highly educated Africans for which no role existed under that colonial dispensation. Ironically, the expansion of the educated class, which British officials studiously avoided between 1920 and 1940, became not only necessary but ultimately constituted a matter of high policy in London in the 1940s.

African preference for overseas training against local qualifications has been misunderstood. In the mid-1930s, especially following the Yaba credibility question, Africans lost faith in official British attempts to establish institutions of higher learning. Suspicious of the motive of colonial education and fearing that a 'second rate' academic status was being foisted upon them, Africans preferred to obtain their qualifications overseas. Worse still, the non-recognition of African diplomas and certificates beyond the borders where they were obtained, coupled with government employment discrimination – in both wages and positions – against those who trained locally greatly encouraged the African predilection for British qualifications.[8]

CONCLUSION

In Uganda these comparisons did not exist since the educated élite and the British operated in almost two distinct administrative services. Within the Kabaka's government, Makerere standards, certificates and diplomas were usually the only ones which counted. Ugandans did not look upon them as inferior but rather equal to those obtained from Britain, even when they actually were not. In West Africa, however, colonial regimes degraded the local qualifications from Achimota and Yaba and hence the African intelligentsia also maligned them. Thus, while East Africans looked up to Makerere with awe, West Africans viewed Achimota and particularly Yaba with disdain and Fourah Bay's reputation revolved only around its theological foundations.

The attempt by the Gold Coast Government in 1935 to 'Africanize' the Achimota curriculum was resisted by the local intelligentsia.[9] The feeling of the educated élite was that special courses constituted an attempt to keep Africans indefinitely in subordinate intellectual and social positions. Even in Uganda, informed opinion pushed for changes which would increase rather than lessen the Western character of African education.[10] Thus 'mental colonization' was inaugurated by British officials hostile to 'assimilation' and, ironically, imposed by Africans upon themselves. It became logical for British officials to employ the argument of African opposition to local standards to convince the Colonial Office that the university scheme should not be embarked upon.

Since under indirect rule the British did not need skilled African man-power, universities were not required. However, when decolonization got underway, the need for highly qualified African human resources became urgent and thus the rush to establish universities. Unfortunately, the view of universities as merely producers of manpower was transferred to African governments after independence. But manpower production remains only one function of a university; only part of its overall mission, which involves research in preserving and explaining the culture, in developing its languages, arts and theatre, in studying the diseases of the environment and improving agriculture, in examining forms of government, in criticizing policies and in analysing the social consequences of various economic policies.

The late 1930s witnessed early signs of a changing attitude in London when the academic lobby within the ACEC picked up 'Paragraph 19' of the recommendations of the East African Directors of Education and made it a matter of vital significance. Even though it was not a university institution, the foundation and endowment of the Makerere Higher College in 1938, following persistent lobbying from the ACEC, clearly marked a turning-point. For the first time, British funds were used for a scheme of higher education in Africa. For the first time, too, British official opinion in London began to shift demonstrably in favour of universities in the colonies. The causes behind this change of attitude are central to this book, and hence considerable attention has been given to them.

Driven by the academic lobby within and outside the ACEC, and by apprehensions that Africans might be forced to flood the United States for education unless university facilities were provided,[11] the Colonial Office enthusiastically embraced the Makerere project. Besides, the crises in British colonial territories as exemplified in the West Indian riots had unsettled the Office and demonstrated the urgent need for action. Pressures from imperial critics, some outside, but most within Britain, who argued that Britain was running a 'slummy' empire, coupled with what Emudong refers to as 'the anticipatory factor',[12] ultimately resulted in the Treasury breaching its traditional parsimonious policy. In London, by 1938, the argument gained ground that it was far more dangerous to British imperial prestige, politically and socially, to deny Africans access to university education than to satisfy that urge.[13]

What Africans desired was not a higher college which awarded certificates and diplomas which were not even recognized in London. Hence the funding of Makerere Higher College did not go far enough. However, it marked the gradual shifting of initiatives from African demands to an impetus emanating from London. Presumably, Ormsby-Gore's success in persuading the British Treasury to commit imperial funds to the Makerere Higher College scheme in 1938 encouraged his successor, MacDonald, to push further for the Colonial Development and Welfare Act. Treasury was right in its insistence in 1937 that it was 'being launched upon almost an uncharted sea'.[14] But soon after that 'sea' was to be charted with the coming of MacDonald and the passage of the Colonial Development and Welfare Act of 1940.

MacDonald's assumption of office in 1938 as Secretary of State gave new vigour to the already changing attitude in London. The ideas evidenced in Hailey's *African Survey* gradually began to convince the Colonial Office that an increasing role should be given to educated Africans in the political, economic and social affairs of the colonies. Determined to institute reforms from the start, MacDonald initiated the Colonial Development and Welfare Act of 1940 to provide funds for schemes of colonial development. Although MacDonald came into office with the spirit of reform and the idea of colonial 'self-government', it has been argued that he was basically compelled to launch the Bill because of the West Indian crises and the domestic and international climate of opinion, particularly after the outbreak of the Second World War. The establishment of universities constituted an essential part of the reform process.

With funds now available from the CD&WA, the Colonial Office moved to centralize colonial policy as it began to undermine the positions of British officials on the spot. It was this shift of power that made the opposition of the West African governors to the university idea inconsequential. Imperial statesmen felt that the war years were the ideal period to prepare for the post-war social, economic and political transformation of the colonial empire. Oliver Stanley's appointment as Secretary of State in November 1942 marked a watershed in the colonial reform initiatives. Not only did he revive the CD&WA (which had been placed on the back-burner between 1940 and 1942 when Britain faced the threat of defeat in the war), he also linked the role of universities effectively to the goal of training colonial leaders for post-war reconstruction and development in the colonial empire.[15]

The academic lobby had stressed consistently the role of the local educated élite in the reform process and they urged the Colonial Office that the time to train these leaders had come. Although the war stultified the reform process, with the turn of the tide in 1943, British confidence revived, and with it the desire to continue colonial reforms. This made the appointment, in 1943, of the two education Commissions – led by Asquith and Elliot – a matter of high imperial policy. Hitherto, the idea of any African university had been rejected because British officials had dreaded the expansion of educated elements disrupting indirect rule. By the 1940s that notion had begun to change, at least in London.

From the start, the Colonial Office was determined to use British universities, particularly London, to implement the university scheme in the colonies. This was understandable since the University of London had dominated existing higher education in the colonies through its external degree arrangements. Neither the Colonial Office nor the University of London wanted this fact to be discounted. For some time, too, the academic lobby had pushed for the recognition of its group interests in British imperial policy to little avail. These new schemes gave the academic lobby its opportunity. Dominating the two Commissions on colonial higher education, British academics strove to carve out an 'empire' for themselves. They succeeded. The Reports of the Commissions insisted that the proposed colonial universities should be excellent centres of teaching and research and that British universities should guide their development. This was the genesis of the Inter-University Council for Higher Education in the Colonies, consisting of representatives of British universities.

It was partly the intense pressures from the academic lobby which culminated in the actual establishment of universities in Africa; it was also its enterprise which inaugurated 'university imperialism' by transplanting British models to Africa. Since the University of London would award the degrees to graduates of the colonial universities, under the scheme of special relationship, the existing African intelligentsia were pleased. British degrees had become the hallmark of academic achievement which, in turn, served to initiate neo-colonial links between Britain and the subsequent African post-independent states.

By 1948 when the university colleges were eventually established in Africa, colonial territorial nationalism had begun to manifest itself in the continent, particularly in West Africa. The effects of the Second World War on the colonial peoples were underestimated in London. The British continued to believe that they could direct the affairs of the colonies from London. Thus the Elliot Minority Report had proposed a single unitary university college for West Africa believing that the pan-African spirit of Horton, Blyden, and Hayford's era would still hold West Africans' loyalties. They were mistaken. Territorial nationalism based on the colonial boundaries created by European powers had permeated the body politic of Africa's new élite. The overwhelming strength of colonial nationalism proved vital in forcing the Colonial Office to establish two university colleges (and preserved a third – Fourah Bay – from certain death) in contrast to its official policy. African educated elements had seized the initiative and would from then on influence decision-making emanating from London.

CONCLUSION

The transfer of collaboration from the traditional to the educated élites from the 1940s had profound effects both in London and the colonial empire. Once the educated élite had seen a sign of 'weakness' in London over the unitary university college feud, they would stop at nothing in pushing for further reform. Soon the wind of change (agitations for the transfer of political power) began to blow. Swiftly, educated élites transformed themselves into influential nationalists, began to build mass support, and took control of the decolonization movements in their various colonial territories. Ultimately, they overpowered the cautious evolutionary plans of the Colonial Office.

Thus, the university question was a central element to the whole process of British colonial reform and to the decolonization process which arose from it. The new universities were conceived as a means to facilitate a transfer of alliances from the traditional to modern (Western-educated) collaborators within the colonial system. In the end, they became nurseries for a new ruling class who would expand élite territorial nationalism into mass politics and take charge of the transformation of colonial units into independent states.

NOTES

1. Henry Cheetham (Bishop of Sierra Leone) to Henry Wright (Secretary of the CMS, London) 13 March 1873 as reproduced in Ashby, *Universities: British, Indian, African*, pp. 463–464.
2. E. A. Ayandele, *African Historical Studies*, Frank Cass, London, 1979, pp. 92–93.
3. See Charles H. Lyons, *To Wash an Aethiop White: British Ideas About Black African Educability 1530–1960*, Teachers College Press, Columbia University, New York, 1975, pp. 122–130.
4. Philip D. Curtin, *The Image of Africa*, Macmillan, London, 1965, p. 364.
5. Basil Davidson, *Modern Africa* (Fourth Impression), Longman, New York, 1991, p. 5. Refer also to Joseph E. Harris, *Africans and their History* (New Edition), Mentor Books, New York, 1987, pp. 13–28.
6. See CO 847/5/7 Note by E. R. J. Hussey, Nigerian Director of Education, on Draft Report of the sub-committee of the ACEC with regard to University Education for Africans, 1935.
7. Carr-Saunders, *New Universities Overseas*, p. 31.
8. See Chapter 3 for a detailed analysis of this issue.
9. CO 847/5/7 Acting Governor of the Gold Coast to the Secretary of State, 12 October 1935. See also Foster, *Education and Social Change in Ghana*, p. 167.
10. Refer to Pratt, 'Administration and Politics in Uganda, 1919–1945', in Harlow and Chilver (eds), *History of East Africa*, Vol. 11, p. 524.
11. See CO 847/3/2 Report of the ACEC sub-committee on 'Paragraph 19' of the Report of the Conference of East African Directors of Education, 1933.
12. Emudong, 'The Evolution of a New British Colonial Policy in the Gold Coast, 1938–1948', p. 37.
13. CO 822/83/11 Secretary of State to Secretary of Treasury, November 1937.
14. CO 822/83/11 Hale (Treasury) to Flood (Colonial Office), 18 December 1937.
15. See Stanley to Channon, 23 February 1943 as cited in Ashby, *Universities: British, Indian, African*, p. 211.

Epilogue

The history of the university colleges at Makerere, Legon and Ibadan after their foundation, and the subsequent development and proliferation of universities in the former British colonial territories in Africa after 1948, is a much broader subject than this author would claim to encompass in the present study. Nevertheless, having analysed the origins of the university idea among West Africans, its early rejection, its revitalization as part of the colonial reform process and its eventual realization, an epilogue which at least sketches in the main consequences of these decisions and their effects (or not) on subsequent university development is necessary if the reader is not to be left with more questions than answers.

At their foundation, the three university colleges – Ibadan, Legon, and Makerere – were tied to the apron-strings of the University of London through the scheme of special relationship. Worked out by the Colonial Office, the Asquith Commission, the IUC and the University of London, the scheme became a sort of imperial behest on higher education handed down to the colonies. Academic standards were regulated by the University of London, and the African élite were initially satisfied with the arrangement. Since London actually awarded the degrees, and given the quality of their staff, the new colleges rapidly gained international recognition as outstanding centres of teaching and research. Each of them strove to replicate the academic culture of London with little attempt at curriculum modification until the advent of mass nationalism in the late 1950s.

The academic standards, costs, teaching methods and the range of subjects taught at the new university colleges were guided by British notions of what constituted the ideal model. As Ashby observed, 'the fundamental pattern of British civic universities – in constitution, in standards and curricula, in social purpose – was adopted without demur'.[1] Beside the imposition of the academic standards of the University of London, the élitist social manners of Oxford and Cambridge Universities were also consciously transplanted in the new colleges.[2] According to Van den Berghe, the British intention from the beginning was to create in Africa a class of social élite 'patterned after the ideal of the Oxbridge gentleman-scholar'.[3] At Makerere, Ibadan and Legon, for instance, there was the practice of Oxford 'high table' culture whereby the lecturers and other distinguished persons ate at an elevated platform while the students dined at a low table. What a social stratification in display! In reality, the university colleges were only African in geographical location and in the composition of their student body. In every other respect, they were typically British.

Once British academic culture was imposed, Africans themselves soon became its most enthusiastic defenders. They continued to regard adaptation with suspicion. Chukwuemeka Ike has pointed out how, in its early years, Ibadan students proudly referred to the University College, as 'the University of London situated at Ibadan for purposes of convenience'.[4] Prior to the 1920s Blyden and Hayford had argued for a West African University deeply rooted in indigenous African life. But with the consolidation of indirect rule in the 1920s, coupled with the racial assumption that Blacks were intellectually inferior, Africans sought to dispel such stereotypes by seeking to compete with Europeans in educational attainment. Hence university education adapted to suit African conditions became suspect. It was viewed as an attempt to legitimize the racial claims of Whites. British colonial officials in Africa further accentuated the African predilection for British qualifications by a policy of discrimination – in employment, wages and positions – against those trained locally. Yaba medical diplomas and certificates, for instance, were not registrable or recognizable in England. To compete on equal terms in the colonial service Africans began to clamour for British qualifications. Whatever adaptations the British were willing to allow in the new university colleges were often resisted by Africans who remained suspicious that a second-rate curriculum was being foisted upon them. The position altered with the approach of independence when African nationalists began to launch brazen attacks on the British colonial heritage.

Meanwhile, from the 1950s the university colleges became serious burdens on the budgets of the various territories. Guided by British ideals, the pioneer staff, who were almost entirely British, embarked upon huge expansion and the erection of extravagant architectural structures. Although the Colonial Development and Welfare Act provided funds for capital development until independence, these were hardly enough. The increasing deficits and the recurrent expenditure were borne by the local governments. By 1954, for instance, the capital development at Ibadan was making huge financial demands on the Nigerian treasury. Worse still, the college could not, or perhaps was unwilling to, fulfil the expanding demand for university education in Nigeria. Increasingly, the new university colleges came under the attacks of African nationalists who had become disenchanted with their élitist, foreign and prodigal image.

During debates in the House of Representatives in Lagos in August 1954, Dr Nnamdi Azikiwe accused the Ibadan authorities of 'financial irresponsibility' and 'culpable negligence'. He insisted that: 'What this country sorely needs today is a first-class institution of learning and not a first-class exhibition of streamlined buildings'.[5] He did not see anything wrong with using prefabricated houses for junior and senior staff, and further suggested the admission of non-residential students.[6] Azikiwe was so furious that he dismissed the college as 'a million dollar baby'. Accordingly, 'every time the baby cried, he is given a kiss worth £1 million and so the baby has found out that it pays to cry and crying becomes his pastime'.[7]

The criticisms against the new university colleges, particularly Ibadan and Legon, were aggravated by the small number of students admitted and the few graduates turned out in their first seven years. By elevating the issue of high standards to a quasi-mystical concept, the number of students who actually gained admission could neither justify the huge local expenditure on them nor satisfy the hopes of the Colonial Office to expand considerably the class of educated Africans who would lead the process of colonial development. Contrary to the Elliot Minority Report view that there would be difficulty of getting qualified students for three universities, West African university colleges were actually unable to accommodate the large number of candidates who qualified for matriculation. Maxwell has noted that, in 1949, 700 qualified candidates applied for 120 places at Ibadan, and that at the end of the first year 77 of those ultimately admitted were withdrawn.[8] Ashby also reports that in 1954 only 300 candidates were admitted for degree work out of 1,100 who applied for placement at Ibadan, and that for its first seven years Ibadan had only 527 students; Makerere in its ninth year had only 448; and Legon in its seventh year had only 349.[9]

Certainly student admissions were not increasing at the rate the restive nationalists desired. It is also hard to believe that either Stanley or Creech Jones would have desired this extremely slow rate of growth. Public criticism mounted. The nationalists were quick to accuse the university college authorities of deliberately imposing high standards on Africans which could hardly be met even in London, in order to keep the number of graduates low. Ironically, many of those who were rejected by these colleges ultimately went to Britain and the USA to secure their qualifications, and later returned to teach at the same institutions which had rejected them.

None the less, as independence approached, African nationalists began to question intensely the rationale for the imposition of foreign standards on Africans. Anything indigenously African began to be lauded. British ideals became incompatible with nationalism. Returning to Blyden's views, the emergent 'statesmen' began to call for adaptation of university curricula to the basic needs of the African peoples. Having proved that they were intellectually equal to Europeans, as demonstrated by the high levels of their educational attainment, African élite leaders now began to relate the concept of independent status to economic, social and political development. The new university colleges began to be spurned as irrelevant 'temples of learning' and 'ivory towers' for the training of members of the élite class to the abject neglect of the productive stratum of society.

The nationalists had come to recognize that the emerging independent African states would need vocational expertise and high-level manpower as much as they would need the clerks. Colonial service had inculcated in Africans a deep preference for the clerkly office jobs. Clerks had, for so long, enjoyed an exaggerated prestige and it had become difficult to 'persuade Africans to accord an equally high status to jobs in technology'.[10] None of the new university colleges offered courses in rural economy, architecture, home economics, law, public or business administrations until the late 1950s. Kwame Nkrumah of the Gold Coast became very uncomfortable with the curriculum at Legon. As he insisted: 'While I fully subscribe to the vital principle of academic freedom, a University must relate its activities to the needs of the society in which it exists.'[11] Similarly, Azikiwe was appalled by these defects: 'We must frankly admit that we can no longer afford to flood only the white collar jobs at the expense of the basic occupations and productive vocations ... particularly in the fields of agriculture, engineering, business administration, education and domestic science.'[12] Adaptation was no longer feared as nationalists correlated the concept of development and basic societal needs to university education.

Africanization of academic curricula and syllabuses now became the war cry of the nationalists. To the nationalists, especially those trained in the United States, the university colleges were seen as grooming Africans for the 'second colonization', properly called 'neo-colonialism'. Azikiwe's attacks on Ibadan, and Nkrumah's denigration of the Legon curricula, although sometimes justified, were basically a revolt against the British system as opposed to the American pattern of education. The research conducted in the new university colleges between 1950 and 1960 resulted in the publication of a number of textbooks upon which Africanization of curricula subsequently depended. Some of these works include J. F. Ade Ajayi and Ian Espie (eds), *A Thousand Years of West African History*, Ibadan University Press, 1965; Joseph C. Anene and Godfrey N. Brown (eds), *Africa in the Nineteenth and Twentieth Centuries*, Ibadan University Press, 1966; Ezekiel Mphahlele and Ellis Ayiteh (eds), *Modern African Stories*, Faber & Faber, London, 1964; John Mbiti, *African Religions and Philosophy*, Praeger, New York, 1969; Bolaji Idowu, *Olodumare: God in Yoruba Belief,* Longman, London, 1962 and *African Traditional Religions*, Orbis Books, New York, 1973. Soon research began to concentrate upon the needs of Africa and Africans. In the History Department at Ibadan, for instance, the Africanist faculty led by Dr K. O. Dike began to demonstrate that Africa had a rich past worthy of inclusion in university curricula. Courses such as African literature, and African traditional religion were later introduced at Ibadan as degree programmes. Gradually, emphasis began to shift from what Europeans prescribed as ideal for Africans to what Africans considered best for themselves, and the University of London became less and less rigid over modifications to curricula under the special relationship scheme. Nationalism was in full swing as the new university colleges hastened to adjust to the ferment of the time.

By the late 1950s a combination of factors provoked agitations for the creation of more universities in Africa. These included the question of the small number of students admitted to the existing university colleges; the obsession with, and the imposition of too high standards; the irrelevance of foreign syllabuses and curricula to African needs; the neo-colonialist tendencies of graduates of the Asquith colleges; and, above all, the ethnic and regional tensions in African societies. The first moves were made in East Africa where Kenya and Tanganyika began to consider the University College at Makerere as an Ugandan institution. In 1954, the Kenyan Indian community collected £200,000 to finance the foundation of a degree-awarding institution in Nairobi.[13] The Baganda had lost their predominance in education to the Kenyan Kikuyu after the Second World War, and most Kenyans could not understand why they should continue to look towards Makerere for university work. Tanganyika also began to make demands for a separate university. These agitations resulted in the appointment of a Working Party under J. F. Lockwood to look into the future of higher education in East Africa.

The report of the Working Party[14] resulted in the institution of an independent federal university – the University of East Africa – established in 1963 with constituent colleges at Makerere, Nairobi and Dar es Salaam. Unlike West Africa, however, where by the late 1950s the number of qualified matriculation students exceeded the available places at both Ibadan and Legon, Makerere continually lacked qualified students to fill the available places. The university situation in East Africa, therefore, was clearly linked to territorial nationalism. As Bernard de Bunsen contended, it was only 'natural that new countries with growing political consciousness should desire their own institutions to match and serve their distinctive political aspirations'.[15]

In West Africa, the first move came from Nigeria where the government of the Eastern Region, under Nnamdi Azikiwe, passed a Bill in 1955 establishing the first independent Nigerian university at Nsukka along the lines of the American land grant college. Although this university was genuinely meant to focus on vocational studies, its establishment was ethnically motivated. The Igbo had begun to refer to the University College, Ibadan as a Yoruba institution by virtue of its location. Paradoxically, the Yoruba were also embittered that the

Igbo dominated the college staff and student body. In any case, Azikiwe's move startled the IUC and the Colonial Office because it was a deviation, in style and content, from the British pattern based on the Asquith scheme. It took another five years for the proposed University of Nigeria at Nsukka to be established. However, despite the widespread adoption of the American pattern at Nsukka at its foundation, over time the university came more and more to conform to the standards and practices of Ibadan University. It remained difficult to convince the Nigerian intelligentsia that the American standards were better than those of the British.

Nevertheless, the Nsukka scheme was remarkable because it inaugurated an Anglo-American and even broader international co-operation in higher educational matters in Africa. It also unleashed a series of demands for more universities from the other regions of Nigeria. In 1960 the Ashby Commission, composed of American, British and Nigerian educationists, was appointed by the Nigerian Government to report on the higher educational needs of the country over the next ten years. The Report of the Commission[16] led to the foundation of three new universities – in Zaria, Lagos, and Ife – by 1963. Thus, three years after independence Nigeria possessed five autonomous universities. Yet agitations for more institutions continued as the location of, and access to, universities became almost entirely politicized. Unfortunately, as Okwudiba Nnoli aptly asserted, the situation not only created competition but also increased personal alienation as well as inter-ethnic hostility.[17]

In the Gold Coast, Nkrumah was similarly dissatisfied with the small number of élitist graduates turned out by Legon. Since he was American-trained, the British pattern did not particularly appeal to him. Furthermore, the Ashanti were not pleased with the location of the University College in Fantiland. Both groups had been traditional rivals. In 1957, when the Gold Coast attained independence and changed its name to Ghana, the college was renamed the University College of Ghana. Constant feuding between the University and the College of Arts, Science and Technology at Kumasi (Ashanti) over the engineering degree led the Prime Minister, Dr Nkrumah, to appoint an international committee to advise on the future development of university education in Ghana. The inclusion of Americans, Russians and British on the committee demonstrated the new regime's belief in the principle of non-alignment in educational matters. By the time the committee reported the way was clear for the establishment of two more universities in 1961 – one at Kumasi and the other at Cape Coast. Clearly, Nkrumah created the University of Cape Coast primarily to gratify his region of birth.

In Sierra Leone, a Commission of enquiry on the educational needs of the territory, as required by the compromise agreement on the status of Fourah Bay College, was appointed under J. S. Fulton after the expiry of the interim period. It reported in 1954 in favour of the transformation of Fourah Bay College into a university college.[18] Though the number of students was small, and funds and physical facilities inadequate, the Commission reported that the university department was very 'viable in size and vitality'. As nationalist activities increased the Creoles vehemently pushed for a university. Nothing less was acceptable to them. In 1958, the teacher-training department was removed from Fourah Bay College. In May 1959 the College received the approval of the IUC, and in December it was granted a royal charter as Fourah Bay College – The University College of Sierra Leone. Although the College now had power to award its own degrees it retained its links with Durham while outside the University of London special relationship scheme.

With Sierra Leone's independence in 1961, however, the Durham links were severed even though the University continued to render solicited help to Fourah Bay. Since the Prime Minister, Milton Margai, and most of his ministers were non-Creoles, they heeded the demand for another university in the hinterland, outside Creoledom. Njala, an agricultural school in the interior, was quickly converted into an autonomous university. Fourah Bay College had no agriculture department and hence those who called for a new agriculture-intensive university in the hinterland had a genuine case. But in the face of a financial crisis in the country, coupled with a shortage of qualified matriculation students, it was political and ethnic considerations that dictated the establishment of another university at Njala.

In East Africa, the foremost nationalists of the 1950s and early 1960s were former graduates of Makerere, but almost all West African political leaders of the period were educated overseas. Milton Obote, Benedicto Kiwanuka and Kabaka Mutesa, all from Uganda, Julius Nyerere of Tanganyika and Ronald Ngala of Kenya all graduated from Makerere College before the institution gained university status in 1949. In West Africa, Nkrumah of Ghana and

Azikiwe of Nigeria were trained in the USA. Obafemi Awolowo and Tafawa Balewa, both of Nigeria, Dr J. B. Danquah of Ghana, and Milton Margai of Sierra Leone, were all educated in Britain. While those educated in Britain naturally admired the British system of education, American-educated nationalists showed little sympathy for Legon or Ibadan. For them, these colleges represented the imperial tradition, and since they were not products of that system it was only natural to view them with scorn. Conversely, East African nationalists, although few in number, did not look upon the University College of East Africa at Makerere with disdain. After all, East African nationalists owed their elevated status to their *alma mater*.

It was after independence, when links with the University of London had been broken, that the products of the university colleges began to make a visible impact on the social, economic and political sphere of their various countries. These graduates were the first to find employment in top government positions and as university lecturers in the independent universities which emerged from the 1960s. True to the foreign social and academic culture they had imbibed, the behaviour, taste and thought of the African 'Oxbridges' isolated them from their peoples. Flaunting British ideals, the new élite continued to wear English suits for business even when the African sun threatened to melt rocks! Furley and Watson have pointed out how Makerere produced an élite class of East Africans who 'developed notions of superiority, holding themselves aloof from the struggles of their own communities, for they were assured of jobs'.[19]

Finding themselves in positions of power in the post-colonial scheme, graduates of the Asquith colleges began to extol British standards. This signalled the triumph of the 'second colonization' as products of the university colleges extolled British academic tradition. Adaptation and Africanization of curriculum hitherto advocated by the nationalists once more became suspect. Although African universities were now independent degree-granting institutions, according to the new élite they should be guided strictly by British standards. Neo-colonial links could not be severed. As Nnoli puts it, the post-colonial leaders 'represent classes which have vested interests in maintaining the inherited colonial structures and therefore the nature and pattern of colonial education'.[20] Eventually all the universities retained the external examiner system with only a slight modification, almost along the lines which the University of London had pursued under the special relationship scheme, and which the nationalists had hitherto denigrated. The difference in the new system was that it was no longer the monopoly of the University of London Board of Examiners.

It should, however, be mentioned that by the early 1960s Africa's universities had achieved international reputations as first-class institutions. They had created a vast body of research conclusions which consolidated Africa-centred curriculum. They developed whole new fields of inquiry, such as specialized archaeology, pre-colonial historical research and research into the psychology of Africans. Furthermore, African universities were able to obtain substantial foreign financial assistance shortly after independence. Ibadan and Makerere, for instance, received millions of dollars from the Ford Foundation, the Carnegie Trust Fund, Nuffield and other bodies. Monies poured in, not only because this was the age of aid fundamentally driven by the cold war between the East and West, but also because aid was the prominent tool of the 'new imperialism' – neo-colonialism. However, international assistance soon fizzled out, and with the proliferation of universities African institutions of higher education began to face serious fiscal problems.

By and large, universities of the Western concept, style and content have proved just too expensive for most African states to maintain. The effects of weak economies have been shattering, and foreign exchange problems have worsened the situation in Africa's universities. The British legacy that a university must be an architectural masterpiece worthy of its name has continued to sap the meagre resources of most African states. Thus the available funds are spent on the erection of magnificent structures – laboratories, libraries, hostels and teaching hospitals – to the abject neglect of instructional supplies. In almost all of Africa's university libraries there are hardly any books published after 1980. Standard journal runs end about the same date. Laboratories have gone to ruin, or where maintained are poorly so.

Worse still, professors and lecturers, in the 1950s perhaps the most respected and prestigious African social group, are now poorly paid. They are often unable to do their jobs properly because they need to take on more lucrative outside work to feed their families.[21] Compared with the years from 1948–70 this is a sorry picture and a sad comparison. The volume of the 'African voice' in international scholarship has been reduced drastically since the 1970s. In a sense, we are back to the 1950s when most African research which received international notice and publication was conducted either by foreigners or by Africans working in European or American universities (part of a serious 'brain-drain'). As William Saint, a higher education expert with the World Bank in Washington, has warned: 'If African universities continue to be ignored, Africa will face a grim future with its greatest poverty being the lack of ideas.'[22]

NOTES

1. Ashby, *Universities and Western Tradition*, p. 20.
2. See John Flint, 'Mammon, Politics and Academe: The Foundation of the University of Nigeria, 1955–1963', Manuscript (undated), p. 3.
3. Pierre L. van den Berghe, *Power and Privilege at an African University*, Schenkman Publishing Company, Cambridge, Mass., 1973, pp. 18–19.
4. Ike, *University Development in Africa: The Nigerian Experience*, p. 1.
5. Nigerian Legislative Council Debates (House of Representatives), 28 August 1954, Government Printer, Lagos, 1954, p. 265
6. All the African university colleges founded under the Asquith and Elliot plans were residential.
7. Nigerian Legislative Council Debates (House of Representatives), 28 August 1954, p. 265.
8. Maxwell, *Universities in Partnership*, p. 96.
9. Ashby, *Universities: British, Indian, African*, pp. 258, 262. In 1957, the UCI could only admit 350 out of 1100 applicants. See *Hannah Papers*, Andrus to Hannah, 6 November, 1957, University of Michigan Papers as cited in Flint, 'Mammon, Politics and Academe', p. 4.
10. Ashby, *Universities: British, Indian, African*, p. 245.
11. *Daily Graphic* (Accra), 30 May 1953.
12. Nnamdi Azikiwe, 'Chancellor's Inaugural Address', as quoted in the University of Nigeria's *Prospectus*, 1962–1963, p. 7. See also as cited in Ashby, *Universities: British, Indian, African*, p. 245.
13. Ashby, *Universities: British, Indian, African*, p. 317.
14. ULAP, AC 11/2/4 Report of the Working Party on Higher Education in East Africa, July–August, 1955.
15. Bernard de Bunsen, 'University Notes from Makerere', *Universities Quarterly*, Vol. 10, No. 1, November 1955, p. 13. Bunsen was the Principal of the University College of East Africa at Makerere in 1955.
16. ULAP, AC 11/2/9 The Report of the Commission on Post-School Certificate and Higher Education in Nigeria, September 1960.
17. Okwudiba Nnoli, 'Education and Ethnic Politics in Nigeria' in Victor C. Uchendu (ed.), *Education and Politics in Tropical Africa*, Conch Publishers, New York, 1979, pp. 63–81.
18. SLC, RS 370.9664/SI17 Report of the Commission on Higher Education in Sierra Leone, 1954, p. 21.
19. Furley and Watson, *A History of Education in East Africa*, p. 309.
20. Nnoli, 'Education and Politics In Nigeria', p. 70.
21. Here one might be thankful to the external system which puts a real impediment in the way of possible corrupt grading. Otherwise the degrees of African universities might have long been designated 'for sale' in the face of poor pay.
22. John Stackhouse (Reporter), 'Grim Future at African Universities', *The Globe and Mail*, April 12, 1993. Starved of funds and desperate for staff, many of Africa's 97 universities are in 'suspended animation'.

Bibliography

A. PRIMARY SOURCES

1. Archival Manuscript

(i) Colonial Office Documents (CO): Public Record Office (PRO), Kew Gardens, London. Series:

    CO 554 – West Africa
    CO 822 – East Africa
    CO 847 – Africa (General)
    CO 958 – Asquith and Elliot Commissions (Papers and Reports)
    CO 987 – ACEC Files (Papers and Minutes of Meetings)
    CO 1004 – Colonial University Grants Advisory Committee (Minutes of Meetings and Papers)

(ii) Academic Council Files (AC): University of London Archives and Palaeography (ULAP), Senate Building, University of London, London.
AC 11 /1-15 – On Special Relationship Scheme between the University of London and Colonial Universities (Minutes of Senate Committee and Correspondence).

(iii) National Archives of Ghana, Accra (NAGA).
ADM 5/3/122 – Minutes and Papers of the Gold Coast Committee on Higher Education (contains Legislative Council Debates on higher education and documents on the Elliot Minority Report imbroglios).

(iv) National Archives of Nigeria, Ibadan (NAI), Colonial Secretary's Office (CSO) and Federal Ministry of Education Files.
CSO 26 and OX Series – University Education in Africa
MED (Fed) 1 Series – University College of Ibadan

(v) Sierra Leone Archives (SLC), Fourah Bay College, Freetown.
CSO – Miscellaneous and Confidential Files on Higher Education
CSO – Open File on Education (General)

2. Special Library Collections

(i) RS.379 Series, Fourah Bay College Library, Sierra Leone Collection (SLC) – Despatches, Papers and Pamphlets on Fourah Bay College and University Education in Africa.

(ii) DP and AF Series, Balme Library, University of Ghana, Legon (Africana Collection) – Bradley and other Reports on Higher Education in the Gold Coast.

(iii) A8 Series, Kenneth Dike Memorial Library, University of Ibadan (Special Collection) – Higher Education in Nigeria.

3. Parliamentary and Legislative Council Papers

House of Commons, Vol. 5, 26 June 1865, *Report of the Select Committee on the State of British Settlements in West Africa, 1865.*
Parliamentary Debates (House of Commons) Vol. 361, col. 42, 21 May 1940.
Parliamentary Debates (House of Commons) col. 725, 2 July 1940.
Parliamentary Debates, (House of Commons), Vol. 39, col. 47, 13 July 1943.
Nigerian Legislative Council Debates, 12th Session, March 1934.
Nigerian Legislative Council Debates, 28 August 1954.
Gold Coast Legislative Council Debates, 24 July 1946.

4. Published Official Sources

(i) *British Government Publications*
Command Paper (Cmd.) 2374 *Education Policy in British Tropical Africa*, HMSO, 1925.
Cmd.6647 *Report of the Commission on Higher Education in the Colonies*, HMSO, June 1945.
Cmd.6655 *Report of the Commission on Higher Education in West Africa*, HMSO, June 1945.
Cmd.7331 *Report of the Inter-University Council for Higher Education in the Colonies, 1946–47*, HMSO, February 1948.
Cmd.9515 *Report of the Inter-University Council for Higher Education Overseas*, HMSO, 1954.
Report of the Commission on Higher Education in East Africa, HMSO, 1937 (De La Warr Report) Non-Parliamentary.

(ii) *African Government Publications*
DP/LA 1151 *Report of the Committee Appointed to Inspect the Prince of Wales' College, Achimota, Accra, 1939.*
DP/LA 1161 *Report of the Committee on Higher Education in the Gold Coast* (Bradley's Report), Government Printer, Accra, 1946.
RS 378.9664 *Report of the Sierra Leone Education Commission* (Fulton Commission), Government Printers, Freetown, 1954.
ULAP, AC 11/2/9 *Report of the Commission on Post-School Certificate and Higher Education in Nigeria*, September 1960.

5. Contemporary Books, Memoirs, and Collections of Printed Documents

Azikiwe, Nnamdi, *Renascent Africa*, Zik Press, Lagos, 1937.
Blyden, Edward Wilmot, *Liberia's Offerings*, J. A. Gray, New York, 1862.
——, *The Aims and Methods of a Liberal Education*, Cambridge University Press, Cambridge, Massachusetts, 1882.
George, Claude, *The Rise of British West Africa* (first published in 1904), Frank Cass, London, 1968.
Guggisberg, Gordon, *The Keystone*, London, 1924.
Hailey, Lord, *An African Survey*, Oxford University Press, Oxford, 1938.
Hayford, Casely, *Ethiopia Unbound: Studies in Race Emancipation* (first published in 1911), Frank Cass, London, 1969.

Horton, James Africanus, *West African Countries and Peoples* (W. J. Johnson, London, 1868), reprinted by Kraus Reprint, Nendeln, Switzerland, 1970.
——, *Letters on the Political Condition of the Gold Coast*, first published in 1870, Second Edition, Frank Cass, London, 1970.
Jeffries, Charles, *Whitehall and the Colonial Service: An Administrative Memoir, 1939–1956*, The Athlone Press, London, 1972.
King, Kenneth James, *Pan-Africanism and Education*, Clarendon Press, Oxford, 1971.
Lynch, Hollis R. (ed.), *Black Spokesman: Selected Writings of Edward Wilmot Blyden*, Frank Cass, London, 1971.
——, *Selected Letters of Edward Wilmot Blyden*, KTO Press, New York, 1978.
Macmillan, W. M., *Warnings from the West Indies*, Faber and Faber, London, 1936.
Mayhew, Arthur, *Education in the Colonial Empire*, Longmans, London, 1938.
Nicol, Davidson (ed.), *Black Nationalism in Africa: Extracts from the Political, Educational, Scientific and Medical Writings of Africanus Horton*, Africana Publishing Corporation, New York, 1969.
Parkinson, Sir Cosmos, *The Colonial Office from Within, 1909–1945*, Faber and Faber, London, 1945.
Perham, Margery, *Colonial Sequence, 1930 to 1949*, Methuen and Co. Ltd., London, 1967.
Phelps-Stokes, (with an introduction by L. J. Lewis), *Report on Education in Africa*, Oxford University Press, London, 1962.
Shaw, Flora, *A Tropical Dependency*, London, 1906.
The West African University: Correspondence Between Edward W. Blyden and J. Pope Hennessy, Negro Printing Press, Freetown, 1872.

6. Newspapers

African Standard (Sierra Leone), August 1939
The Daily Comet, February 1940
West African Pilot, 1938, 1940, 1944–1950
Nigerian Daily Times, January–March 1934, March 1963
East African Standard, August 1939
The Gold Coast Observer, January–February 1944

The Daily Guardian (Sierra Leone), October–December 1945
The Daily Service, February 1944
The Daily Graphic (Accra), 1953

B. SECONDARY SOURCES

1. Books

Abernethy, David, *The Political Dilemma of Popular Education: An African Case*, Stanford University Press, Stanford, California, 1969.
Addison, Paul, *The Road to 1945: British Politics and the Second World War*, Jonathan Cape, London, 1975.
Afigbo, A. E., *The Warrant Chiefs: Indirect Rule in Southeastern Nigeria, 1891–1929*, Longman, London, 1972.
Ajayi, J. F. Ade, *Christian Missions in Nigeria, 1841–1891: The Making of a New Elite*, Longman, London, 1965.
——, and Tekena N. Tamuno (eds), *The University of Ibadan 1948–73: A History of the First Twenty-Five Years*, Ibadan University Press, Ibadan, 1973.
Apter, D. E., *The Political Kingdom in Buganda*, Princeton University Press, Princeton, 1961.
Ashby, Eric, *Universities: British, Indian, African*, Harvard University Press, Cambridge, Massachusetts, 1966.
——, *African Universities and Western Tradition*, Harvard University Press, Cambridge, Massachusetts, 1964.
——, *Adapting Universities to a Technological Society*, Jose-Brass, San Francisco, 1974.
Awolowo, Obafemi, *Awo: The Autobiography of Chief Obafemi Awolowo*, Cambridge University Press, London, 1960.
Ayandele, E. A., *Holy Johnson: Pioneer of African Nationalism, 1836–1917*, Frank Cass, London, 1970.
——, *The Missionary Impact on Modern Nigeria, 1842–1914*, Longman, London, 1966.
——, *African Historical Studies*, Frank Cass, London, 1979.
Azikiwe, Nnamdi, *My Odyssey*, C. Hurst and Company, London, 1970.
Burns, Donald G., *African Education*, Oxford University Press, London, 1965.
Busia, K. A., *Purposeful Education for Africa*, Mouton and Co., The Hague, 1968.

Cameron, John, *The Development of Education in East Africa*, Teachers College Press, New York, 1970.

Carr-Saunders, A. M., *New Universities Overseas*, George Allen & Unwin, London, 1961.

Cartey, Wilfred and Martin Kilson (eds), *The Africa Reader: Independent Africa*, Random House, New York, 1970.

Cassell, Abayomi C., *Liberia: History of the First African Republic*, Fountainhead Publishers, New York, 1970.

Chinweizu, *The West and the Rest of Us: White Predators, Black Slavers and the African Elite*, Random House, New York, 1975.

Coleman, James S., *Nigeria: Background to Nationalism*, University of California Press, Berkeley, 1958.

——, *Education and Political Development*, Princeton University Press, Princeton, 1965.

Constantine, Stephen, *The Making of British Colonial Development Policy, 1914–1940*, Frank Cass, London, 1984.

Couch, Margaret, *Education in Africa: A Select Bibliography*, Institute of Education, University of London, London, 1962.

Cowan, L. Gray, et al. (eds), *Education and Nation-Building in Africa*, Praeger, New York, 1965.

Crowder, Michael, *West Africa Under Colonial Rule*, Hutchinson, London, 1968.

Curle, Adam, *The Role of Education in Developing Societies*, Ghana University Press, Legon, 1961.

Curtin, Philip D., *Image of Africa*, Macmillan, London, 1965.

Davidson, Basil, *Old Africa Rediscovered*, Gollancz, London, 1961.

——, *Modern Africa* (Fourth Impression), Longman, New York, 1991.

Dike, K. Onwuka, *Trade and Politics in the Niger Delta, 1830–1885*, Clarendon Press, London, 1956.

Du Bois, W. E. B., *The World and Africa*, International Publishers, New York, 1946.

Fafunwa, A. Babs, *A History of Nigerian Higher Education*, Macmillan, Lagos, 1971.

——, *The Growth and Development of Nigerian Universities*, Washington, D.C. Overseas Liaison Committee, American Council on Education, 1974.

—— and J. U. Aisiku (eds), *Education in Africa: A Comparative Survey*, George Allen and Unwin, London, 1982.

BIBLIOGRAPHY

Fanon, Franz, *The Wretched of the Earth*, Grove Press, New York, 1968.
——, *A Dying Colonialism*, Grove Press, New York, 1967.
Flint, John E., *Nigeria and Ghana*, Prentice-Hall, New Jersey, 1966.
Foster, Philip, *Education and Social Change in Ghana*, University of Chicago Press, Chicago, 1965.
Freund, Bill, *The Making of Contemporary Africa*, Indiana University Press, Bloomington, 1984.
Furley, O. W. and T. Watson, *A History of Education in East Africa*, Nok Publishers, New York, 1978.
Fyfe, Christopher, *Africanus Horton: West African Scientist and Patriot*, Oxford University Press, New York, 1972.
——, *A History of Sierra Leone*, Oxford University Press, Oxford, 1962.
——, *Sierra Leone Inheritance*, Oxford University Press, London, 1964.
——, *A Short History of Sierra Leone*, Longman, London, 1962.
George, Betty Stein, *Education in Ghana*, US Government Printing Office, Washington, 1976.
Goldsworthy, David, *Colonial Issues in British Politics, 1945–1951*, Clarendon Press, Oxford, 1971.
Goldthorpe, J. E., *An African Elite: Makerere College Students 1922–1969*, Oxford University Press, Nairobi, 1965.
Graham, C. K., *The History of Education in Ghana*, Frank Cass, London, 1971.
Gukiina, P. M., *Uganda: A Case Study of Political Development*, London, 1972.
Harris, Joseph E., *Africans and Their History* (Revised Edition), Mentor Books, New York, 1987.
Hinchliffe, Keith, *Higher Education in Sub-Saharan Africa*, Croom Helm, London, 1987.
Hodder-Williams, Richard, *An Introduction to the Politics of Tropical Africa*, George Allen & Unwin, London, 1984.
Hopkins, A. G., *An Economic History of West Africa*, Columbia University Press, New York, 1973.
Ike, Chukwuemeka, *University Development in Africa: The Nigerian Experience*, Oxford University Press, Ibadan, 1976.
Isichei, Elizabeth, *A History of the Igbo Peoples*, Macmillan, London, 1976.

Jorgensen, J. J., *Uganda: A Modern History*, St. Martins Press, New York, 1981.
July, Robert, *The Origins of Modern African Thought*, Frederick A. Praeger, New York, 1967.
Karugire, S. R., *A Political History of Uganda*, Heinemann, Nairobi, 1980.
Katorobo, J., *Education for Public Service in Uganda*, Praeger, New York, 1972.
Keegan, John, *The Second World War*, Viking Penguin Press, New York, 1989.
Kerr, Clark, *The Uses of the University*, Harvard University Press, Cambridge, Massachusetts, 1963.
Kilson, Martin, *Political Change in a West African State*, Harvard University Press, Cambridge, Massachusetts, 1966.
Kirk-Greene, A. H. M., *A Biographical Dictionary of the British Colonial Service, 1939-1966*, Hans Zell Publishers, London, 1991.
Kitchen, Helen (ed.), *The Educated African: A Country-by-Country Survey of Educational Development in Africa*, Frederick A. Praeger, New York, 1962.
Kuper, L., *Race, Class and Power: Ideology and Revolutionary Change in Plural Societies*, Duckworth Press, London, 1974.
Lee, J. M., *Colonial Development and Good Government*, Clarendon Press, London, 1967.
——, and Martin Petter, *The Colonial Office, War and Development Policy*, Maurice Temple Smith, London, 1982.
Lewis, Julius (ed.), *The Struggle for Racial Equality*, Longman, London, 1967.
Livingstone, Richard, *Some Thoughts on University Education*, Cambridge University Press, London, 1948.
Lloyd, P. C. (ed.), *The New Elite in Tropical Africa*, Oxford University Press, London, 1966.
Louis, Wm. Roger, *Imperialism at Bay 1941-1945*, Clarendon Press, London, 1977.
Low, D. A., *Buganda in Modern History*, University of California Press, Berkeley, 1971.
——, and Alison Smith (eds.) *History of East Africa*, Vol. iii, Clarendon Press, London, 1976.
——, and R. Cranford Pratt, *Buganda and British Overrule, 1900-1955*, Oxford University Press, London, 1960.

Lugard, Lord, *The Dual Mandate in British Tropical Africa* (first published in 1922), Fifth Edition, Frank Cass, London, 1956.
Lyons, Charles H., *To Wash an Aethiop White: British Ideas About Black African Educability 1530–1960*, Teachers College Press, Columbia University, New York, 1975.
Macartney, William, *Dr Aggrey: A Biography*, SCM Press, London, 1949.
Macpherson, Margaret, *They Built for the Future: A Chronicle of Makerere University College, 1922–1962*, Cambridge University Press, Cambridge, 1964.
Madden, Frederick and D. K. Fieldhouse (eds), *Oxford and the Idea of Commonwealth*, Croom Helm, London, 1982.
Mason, R. J., *British Education in Africa*, Oxford University Press, London, 1959.
Maxwell, I. C. M., *Universities in Partnership: The Inter-University Council and the Growth of Higher Education in Developing Countries 1946–1970*, Scottish Academic Press, Edinburgh, 1980.
Mazrui, Ali A., *Political Values and the Educated Class in Africa*, Heinemann, London, 1978.
McWilliam, H. O. A., *The Development of Education in Ghana: An Outline*, Longman, London, 1964.
——, H. O. A., and M. A. Kwamena-Poh, *The Development of Education in Ghana*, Longman, London, 1978.
Mellanby, Kenneth, *The Birth of Nigeria's University*, Methuen and Co. Ltd., London, 1958.
Mitchell, Sir Philip, *African Afterthoughts*, Hutchinson and Co., London, 1954.
Morgan, D. J., *The Official History of Colonial Development*, Vol. 1, Macmillan, London, 1980.
Morgan, Kenneth O., *Labour in Power, 1945–1951*, Clarendon Press, London, 1984.
Moumouni, Abdou, *Education in Africa*, Frederick A. Praeger, New York, 1968.
Mudimbe, V. Y., *The Invention of Africa: Gnosis, Philosophy and the Order of Knowledge*, Indiana University Press, Indiana, 1988.
Nduka, Otonti, *Western Education and Nigerian Cultural Background*, Oxford University Press, Ibadan, 1965.

Nkrumah, Kwame, *Neo-Colonialism: The Last Stage of Imperialism*, Heinemann, London, 1968.
Northrup, David, *Trade Without Rulers*, Clarendon Press, London, 1978.
Obiechina, et al. (eds), *The University of Nigeria 1960–85: An Experiment in Higher Education*, University of Nigeria Press, Enugu, 1986.
Okafor, Nduka, *The Development of Universities in Nigeria*, Longman, London, 1971.
Oldham, J. H., *New Hope in Africa*, Longman, London, 1955.
Olubummo, A. and J. Ferguson, *The Emergent University*, Longman, London, 1960.
Padmore, G., *Africa: Britain's Third Empire*, Ennis Dobson Ltd., London, 1949.
Pearce, R. D., *The Turning Point in Africa: British Colonial Policy 1938–9*, Frank Cass, London, 1982.
Perkins, James A., *The University in Transition*, Princeton University Press, New Jersey, 1966.
Peterson, John, *Province of Freedom: A History of Sierra Leone, 1787–1870*, Faber and Faber, London, 1969.
Porter, A. N. and A. J. Stockwell (eds), *British Imperial Policy and Decolonization, 1938–1964*, Macmillan, London, 1987.
Prewitt, Kenneth (ed.), *Education and Political Values: An African Case Study*, East African Publishing House, Nairobi, Kenya, 1971.
Rodney, Walter, *How Europe Underdeveloped Africa*, Bogle-L'Ouverture Publications, London, 1972.
Saunders, J. T., *University College, Ibadan*, Cambridge University Press, London, 1960.
Scanlon, David (ed.), *Traditions of African Education*, Bureau of Publication, Columbia University, New York, 1964.
Shenton, Robert, *The Development of Capitalism in Northern Nigeria*, University of Toronto Press, Toronto, 1986.
Smith, Huston, *The Purposes of Higher Education*, Harper and Brothers, New York, 1955.
Spitzer, Leo, *The Creoles of Sierra Leone*, The University of Wisconsin Press, Madison, 1974.
Thompson, T. J., *The Jubilee and Centenary Volume of Fourah Bay College*, Freetown, 1930.

Trimingham, J. Spencer, *A History of Islam in West Africa*, Oxford University Press, London, 1962.
Ugboaja, Ohaegbulam F., *Nationalism in Colonial and Post-Colonial Africa*, University Press of America, New York, 1977.
Ukeje, B. O., *Education for Social Reconstruction*, Macmillan, Lagos, 1966.
van den Berghe, Pierre L., *Power and Privilege at an African University*, Schenkman Publishing Company, Cambridge, Massachusetts, 1973.
von Albertini, Rudolf, *European Colonial Rule, 1880–1940: The Impact of the West on India, Southeast Asia, and Africa*, Greenwood Press, Connecticut, 1982.
——, *Decolonization: The Administration and Future of the Colonies*, African Publishing Company, New York, 1982.
Wallerstein, Immanuel, *Africa: The Politics of Independence*, Vintage Books, New York, 1961.
Webster, James Bertin, *The African Churches Among the Yoruba, 1888–1922*, Clarendon Press, Oxford, 1964.
West African Intellectual Community, The, International Seminar on Inter-University Co-operation in West Africa, held in Freetown, Sierra Leone, 11–16 December 1961, Ibadan University Press, Ibadan, 1962,
Wilson, Henry S., *Origins of West African Nationalism*, Macmillan, London, 1969.
Wilson, John, *Education and Changing West African Culture*, Oxford University Press, London, 1966.
Wise, Colin G., *A History of Education in British West Africa*, Longman, London, 1956.
Wraith, R. E., *Guggisberg*, Oxford University Press, Oxford, 1967.
Wyse, Akintola, *The Krio of Sierra Leone: An Interpretive History*, C. Hurst & Co., London, 1989.
Yesufu, T.M. (ed.), *Creating the African University: Emerging Issues of the 1970s*, Oxford University Press, Ibadan, 1973.

2. Articles and Book Chapters

Adams, Bert N., 'Africanisation and Academic Imperialism', *East Africa Journal (EAJ)*, Vol. ix, No. 5, 1972.
Adewoye, O., 'The Antecedents' in J. F. Ade Ajayi and Tekena Tamuno (eds), *The University of Ibadan, 1948–73*, Ibadan University Press, Ibadan, 1973.

Adick, Christel, 'Africanization or Modernization? Historical Origins of Modern Academical Education in African Initiative', *Liberia Forum*, Vol. 5, No. 8, 1989.

Afigbo, A. E., 'The Eclipse of Aro Slaving Oligarchy of Southeastern Nigeria, 1901–21', *Journal of the Historical Society of Nigeria (JHSN)*, Vol. 6, No. 1, 1971.

——, 'The Warrant Chief System in Eastern Nigeria: Direct or Indirect Rule', *JHSN*, Vol. 3, No. 4, 1967.

——, 'Herbert Richmond Palmer and Indirect Rule in Eastern Nigeria: 1915–1928', *JHSN*, Vol. 3, No. 2, 1965.

Agbowuro, Joseph, 'Nigerianization and the Nigerian Universities', *Comparative Education*, Vol. 12, No. 3, 1976.

Ajayi, J. F. Ade, 'The American Factor in the Development of Higher Education in Africa', *James Smoot Coleman Memorial Paper Series*, African Studies Centre, University of California, Los Angeles, 1988.

——, 'The Development of Secondary Grammar School Education in Nigeria', *JHSN*, Vol. 2, No. 4, 1963.

——, 'Henry Venn and the Policy of Development', *JHSN*, Vol. 1, No. 4, 1959.

——, 'African Universities and African Traditions', *EAJ*, Vol. 8, No. 11, 1971.

Amare, Germa, 'Factors Affecting Standards in African Universities', *EAJ*, Vol. vii, No. xii, 1970.

Ashby, Eric, 'A Contribution to the Dialogue on African Universities', *Universities Quarterly*, Vol. 20, No. 1, 1965.

——, 'Some Problems of Universities in the new Countries of the British Commonwealth', *Universities Quarterly*, Vol. 22, No. 1, 1965.

Atieno-Odhiambo, E. S., 'Politics and Nationalism in East Africa, 1919–1935' in A. Adu Boahen (ed.), *Unesco General History of Africa*, Vol. vii, Heinemann, California, 1985.

Awori, A. S., 'Africanising the University of East Africa', *EAJ*, Vol. iv, No. 8, 1967.

Ayandele, E. A., 'An Assessment of James Johnson and his Place in Nigerian History, 1874–1890', Part 1, *JHSN*, Vol. 2, No. 4, 1963.

——, 'An Assessment of James Johnson and his Place in Nigerian History, 1874–1917', Part 2, *JHSN*, Vol. 3, No. 1, 1964.

Bakole, M. M., 'The African University, Today and Tomorrow', *Presence Africaine*, Vol. 25, No. 53, 1965.

Biobaku, S. O., 'Africa's Needs and Africa's Universities', *West African Journal of Education*, Vol. 7, 1963.

Bowden, Bertram Vivian, 'The Place of Universities in Modern Society', *Comparative Education*, Vol. 1, No. 2, 1965.

Carr-Saunders, A. M., 'Britain and Universities in Africa', *Universities Quarterly*, Vol. 19, No. 3, 1965.

Cooper, Frederick, 'From Free Labor to Family Allowances: Labor and African Society in Colonial Discourse', *American Ethnologist*, Vol. 16, No. 4, 1989.

——, and Ann L. Stoler, 'Tensions of Empire: Colonial Control and Visions of Rule', *American Ethnologist*, Vol. 16, No. 4, 1989.

Creech Jones, Arthur, 'British Colonial Policy with Particular Reference to Africa', *International Affairs*, Vol. 27, No. 2, 1951.

Crowder, Michael, 'The 1939–45 War and West Africa' in J. F. Ade Ajayi and Michael Crowder (eds), *History of West Africa*, Vol. 2, Longman, London, 1974.

Curtin, Philip D., 'The "Scientific" Roots: Nineteenth Century Racism' in Curtin (ed.), *Imperialism*, Walker and Company, New York, 1971.

——, '"Scientific" Racism and the British Theory of Empire', *JHSN*, Vol. 11, No. 1, 1960.

de Bunsen, Bernard, 'University Notes from Makerere', *Universities Quarterly*, Vol. 10, No. 1, 1955.

Deveneaux, Gustav Kashope, 'Public Opinion and Colonial Policy in Nineteenth-Century Sierra Leone', *JHSN*, Vol. ix, No. 1, 1976.

Dillon, Wilton S., 'Universities and Nation-Building in Africa', *Journal of Modern African Studies*, Vol. 1, 1963.

Ekejiuba, Ifeoma F., 'The Aro System of Trade in the Nineteenth Century', Parts 1 & 2, *Ikenga*, Vol. 1, No. 1 & 2, 1972.

Esedebe, P. O., 'Edward Wilmot Blyden (1832–1912) as a Pan-African Theorist', *Sierra Leone Studies*, New Series, No. 25, 1969.

Fajana, Ade, 'Colonial Control and Education: The Development of Higher Education in Nigeria, 1900–1950', *JHSN*, Vol. 6, No. 3, 1972.

Flint, J. E., 'Economic Change in West Africa in the Nineteenth Century' in J. F. Ade Ajayi and Michael Crowder (eds), *History of West Africa*, Vol. 2, Longman, London, 1974.

——, 'The Growth of European Influence in West Africa in the Nineteenth Century' in J. F. Ade Ajayi and Ian Espie (eds), *A Thousand Years of West African History*, Ibadan University Press, Ibadan, 1965.

——, 'Britain and the Partition of West Africa' in John E. Flint and Glyndir Williams (eds), *Perspectives of Empire*, Longman, London, 1973.

——, 'The Failure of Planned Decolonization in British Africa', *African Affairs*, Vol. 82, No. 328, 1983.

Fyfe, Christopher, 'Race, Empire and the Historian', *Race and Class*, Vol. 33, No. 4, 1992.

Gardiner, Robert, 'The University in Africa', *EAJ*, Vol. vi, No. 12, 1969.

Gyasi-Twum, K., 'Sierra Leone Students Leaving Fourah Bay College Between 1944 and 1956', *Sierra Leone Studies*, New Series, No. 10, 1958.

Hair, P. E., 'An Analysis of the Register of Fourah Bay College, 1827–1950', *Sierra Leone Studies*, New Series, No. 7, 1956.

Hodgkin, Thomas, 'African Universities and the State: Another View', *Comparative Education*, Vol. 3, No. 2, 1967.

Howard, Thomas C., 'West Africa and the American South: Notes on James E. K. Aggrey and the Idea of a University for West Africa', *JAS*, Vol. 2, No. 4, 1975/76.

Hyder, Mohammed, 'The University, the Government and National Development in Kenya', *EAJ*, Vol. vii, No. 4, 1970.

Igbafe, P., 'British Rule in Benin 1897–1920: Direct or Indirect', *JHSN*, Vol. 3, No. 4, 1967.

Ikejiani, Okechukwu, 'Nigerian Universities' in Okechukwu Ikejiani (ed.), *Nigerian Education*, Longman, Ikeja, 1964.

Ikime, Obaro, 'Reconsidering Indirect Rule: The Nigeria Example', *JHSN*, Vol. 4, No. 3, 1968.

——, 'Chief Dogho: The Lugardian System in Warri 1917–1932', *JHSN*, Vol. 3, No. 2, 1965.

Kiwanuka, M. Semakula, 'Colonial Policies and Administrations in Africa: The Myths of the Contrasts', *African Historical Studies* (now *International Journal of African Historical Studies*), Vol. iii, No. 2, 1970.

Lee, J. M., 'Forward Thinking and War: The Colonial Office during the 1940s', *Journal of Imperial and Commonwealth History*, Vol. 6, 1977.

Leys, Colin, 'The Role of the University in an Underdeveloped Country', *Journal of East African Research and Development*, Vol. 1, No. 1, 1971.

Lonsdale, J. M., 'Some Origins of Nationalism in East Africa', *Journal of African History*, Vol. ix, No. 1, 1968.

Low, D. A., 'Uganda: The Establishment of the Protectorate, 1894–1919' in Vincent Harlow and E. M. Chilver (eds), *History of East Africa*, Vol. 11, Clarendon Press, Oxford, 1965.
Lucas, Eric, 'Education in Africa: A Panoramic View', *EAJ*, Vol. vii, No. 2, 1970.
Lynch, Hollis R., 'The Attitude of Edward W. Blyden to European Imperialism in Africa', *JHSN*, Vol. 3, No. 2, 1965.
——, 'K. O. Mbadiwe, 1939–1947: The American Years of a Nigerian Political Leader', *JAS*, Vol. 7, No. 4, 1980–1981.
Machyo, Chango, 'The University: Its Role in Africa', *EAJ*, Vol. vi, No. 2, 1969.
Morris, Charles, 'The Idea of University Education', *Universities Quarterly*, Vol. 8, No. 4, 1954.
Mosha, Herme J., 'The Role of African Universities in National Development: A Critical Analysis', *Comparative Education*, Vol. 22, No. 2, 1986.
Munro, J. F., 'Colonial Doctrines and Practices' in Roland Oliver and Michael Crowder (eds), *The Cambridge Encyclopedia of Africa*, Cambridge University Press, Cambridge, 1981.
Nicol, Davidson, 'Politics, Nationalism and Universities in Africa', *African Affairs*, Vol. 62, 1963.
Nnoli, Okwudiba, 'Education and Ethnic Politics in Nigeria' in Vincent C. Uchendu (ed.), *Education and Politics in Tropical Africa*, Conch Publishers, New York, 1979.
Nyerere, Julius, 'The University in a Developing Society', *Presence Africaine*, No. 6, 1967.
Ogunlade, F. O., 'Education and Politics in Colonial Nigeria: The Case of Kings College, Lagos (1906–1911)', *JHSN*, Vol. 7, No. 2, 1974.
Okeke, P. Uduaroh, 'Background to the Problems of Nigerian Education' in Okechukwu Ikejiani (ed.), *Nigerian Education*, Longman, Ikeja, 1964.
Olusanya, G. O., 'Political Awakening in the North: A Re-Interpretation', *JHSN*, Vol. 5, No. 1, 1967.
Pearce, Robert D., 'The Colonial Office and Planned Decolonization in Africa', *African Affairs*, Vol. 83, No. 330, 1984.
Pickard-Cambridge, A. W., 'The Place of Achimota in West African Education', *African Affairs*, Vol. 39, 1940.
Porter, Arthur T., 'Crisis in African Education', *EAJ*, Vol. 5, No. 6, 1968.

Pratt, R. C., 'Administration and Politics in Uganda, 1919–1945' in Vincent Harlow and E. M. Chilver (eds), *History of East Africa*, Vol. 11, Clarendon Press, Oxford, 1965.

——, 'University and State in Independent Tropical Africa', *Universities Quarterly*, Vol. 21, No. 1, 1966.

Rimmington, Gerald T., 'The Development of Universities in Africa', *Comparative Education*, Vol. 1, No. 2, 1965.

Roberts, Andrew, 'East Africa' in A. D. Roberts (ed.), *The Cambridge History of Africa*, Vol. 7, Cambridge University Press, Cambridge, 1986.

——, 'The Sub-Imperialism of the Baganda', *JAH*, Vol. iii, No. 3, 1962.

Stackhouse, John, 'Grim Future at African Universities', *The Globe and Mail*, 12 April 1993.

Thomson, A. P., 'Higher Education in the Colonies', *Universities Quarterly*, Vol. 10, No. 4, 1956.

Uzoigwe, G. N., 'European Partition and Conquest of Africa: An Overview' in A. Adu Boahen (ed.), *Unesco General History of Africa*, Vol. vii, Heinemann, California, 1985.

Vanderploeg, Arie J., 'Africanus Horton and the Idea of a University for Western Africa', *JAH*, Vol. 5, No. 2, 1978.

Ward, Jennifer, 'The Expatriate Academic and the African University', *EAJ*, Vol. vii, No. x, 1970.

Willis, Justin, 'The Administration of Bonde 1920–1960: A Study of the Implementation of Indirect Rule in Tanganyika', *African Affairs*, Vol. 92, No. 366, 1993.

Wright, Marcia, 'East Africa, 1870–1905' in R. Oliver and G. N. Sanderson (eds), *The Cambridge History of Africa*, Vol. 6, Cambridge University Press, Cambridge, 1985.

3. Theses and Manuscripts

Emudong, Peter Charles, 'The Evolution of a New British Colonial Policy in the Gold Coast, 1938–1948: Origins of "Planned Decolonization" or of "Neo-Colonialism"', Ph.D. Thesis, Department of History, Dalhousie University, Halifax, 1981.

Flint, John E., 'British Colonial Policy and the Development of African Universities, 1872–1943', Seminar Paper presented at the Centre for African Studies, Dalhousie University, Halifax, February 15, 1979.

——, 'On the Defensive: Retreat from Reforms, 1940–1942', Manuscript, 1992.

——, 'Mammon, Politics and Academe: The Foundation of the University of Nigeria, 1955–1963', Manuscript (undated).

——, 'Critics of Empire and Colonial Reforms, 1919–38', Seminar Paper, History Department, Dalhousie University, Halifax, January 1985.

Kakembo, Patrick, 'Colonial Office Policy and the Origins of Decolonization in Uganda, 1940–1956', Ph.D. Thesis, Department of History, Dalhousie University, Halifax, 1990.

Mazrui, Ali A., 'The African University as a Multinational Corporation: Comparative Problems of Penetration and Dependency', Discussion paper at the University of Sussex, Brighton, England, 1975.

Naanen, B. Benedict, 'Economy and Society in Eastern Nigeria, 1900–1966: A Study of Problems of Development and Social Change', Ph.D. Thesis, Department of History, Dalhousie University, Halifax, 1988.

Ogunlade, F. O., 'Yaba Higher College and the Formation of an Intellectual Elite', MA Thesis, University of Ibadan, Ibadan, Nigeria, 1970.

Okeke, Uduaroh, 'Educational Reconstruction in an Independent Nigeria', Ph.D. Thesis, Department of Education, University of New York, New York, 1955 (on Microfilm).

Tenkorang, Sammy, 'The Gold Coast Aborigines Rights' Protection Society, 1897-1935', Bound Typescript, 1975.

Youé, Christopher, 'The African Career of Robert Coryndon: Personality and Policy in British Colonial Rule', Ph.D. Thesis, Department of History, Dalhousie University, Halifax, 1978.

Index

Abayomi, Kofo, 61
Aberdeen, University of, 156, 184
Abrahams, Fara, 161
'academic culture' 189; of University of London, 210–211
academic lobby, xvi, 68, 92, 100, 105–134, 156, 157, 205–208
Accra (Training College), 56, 175
Achimota (College), 38, 45, 56, 58, 62–63, 75, 79, 105, 183, 204; foundation, 49–50; as Prince of Wales College, 55–56; BSc. external (engineering) programme, 58, 108, 161–163, 176, 180; territorial college (Elliot Report) 164, 178; University College at (funding), 177, 179, 188, 205
Adams, Sir Walter, 156
adaptation, 18–20, 71–73; for indirect rule, 53–57; to local needs, 149–150, 218; for African intermediaries, 53–57; African suspicious of, 82–86; of curricula, 213–215; *see also* Blyden
Adesanya, S.A., 61
Advisory Committee on Colonial Colleges of Arts, Science and Technology (ACCCAST), 194
Advisory Committee on Education in the Colonies (ACEC): reconstitution, members, 56–57; on Currie's Report, 70–82; on De La Warr Report, 90–92; funding for Makerere, 92; three-year term membership, 109; Mouat Jones sub-committee Report, 111–117; on Channon sub-committee Report, 121, 125–129
Advisory Committee on Native Education in Tropical Africa (ACNETA), 38, 47–63, 71, 91, 204; appointment, 47–49; White Paper of 1925, 51–55, 71; response to 'Paragraph 19', 70–100

African educated élites, xi, 7–8; comparison, 45–47; antagonism against, 53–63, 176; triumph, 188, 208–209
African intelligentsia, pressures from, 134, 205
African medical officers (need for them), 3
African nationalism, xvi, xvii, 109, 120, 204; triumph of 'nationalists', 186, 188, 213–215
African predilection for British qualifications, 19–20, 82–86, 120, 149, 204, 211–212; *see also* overseas qualifications
African university colleges: British opposition, xiii–xiv, xvii; British support, xiv–xv; British model, xvi; agitations for more universities, 215–218
Africanisation, 64; civil (colonial) service, 46, 144; resistance to, 147, 202–203; curricula, 82–86, 205, 214–215, 218
Agbebi, Mojola, 61
Aggrey, J.E.K., 42, 50, 55, 64, 74
Agyeman, Sir Osei (Prempeh II), 168 (note 80)
Alakija, O., 61
Alamein (victory of),143
Alexander High School (Liberia), 14
America:
British fear of influence, xvi, 47–63, 74–77, 204, 216; racial discrimination, 13–14; Colonization Society, 13–14; Education Commission on Africa, 38; War of Independence (Revolution), 74
Anderson, G., 109
Anglican Bishop (Sierra Leone), 22
Anglo-American co-operation, 216–217
Anglo-Egyptian Condominium, xii
Anglo-Saxon, 96
Annexure II (response of African governments), 143–148; *see also* Asquith Commission

Anomabu (Gold Coast), 64 (note 26)
Anona Clan (Gold Coast), 38
anti-Catholic, 22
'anticipatory factor', 106, 206
anti-Protestant, 22
apartheid, xii
Archer, Governor of Uganda, 50
Aro middlemen, 28; slaving oligarchy, 31
Asantehene (Prempeh II, Otumfuo), 160, 168 (note 80)
Ashanti, 216
Ashanti–Fanti Wars, 6
Ashby Commission on Post-School Certificate and Higher Education in Nigeria: Report, 216, 220 (note 16)
Asians: artisans, 45; anti-Asian sentiments, 86
Asquith, Cyril (Commission), 134–135, 140, 166 (note 16), 150; appointment, 139–141, 147; Annexure II: modification of curricula/syllabuses, 143–148; inter-university organization, 152; Report, 154–156, 163, 165, 171, 190, 207
assimilation, policy of, 202–203, 205
Assine, 8
Atlantic Charter, 127
Atlantic Slave Trade, 20
Atta, Nana Ofori, 41, 82
Australia, 6
Awolowo, Obafemi, 218
Azikiwe, Nnamdi, 74, 160, 168 (note 78), 212, 214–215, 218

Baganda, 35, 45–46, 99; traditional and educated élite, 37, 46, 97, 100; sub-imperialists, 59, 215
Balewa, Sir Abubakar Tafawa, 218
Balme, David, 189–190
Barnes, Leonard, 95
Baskett, R.G., 156
Benin, 8
Bentwich, N., 156
Beresford-Stooke, Sir George, 192–194
Berkeley, George, 24
Belfast, University of, 156
Bevan, Aneurin, 95
Bidwell, M. (Bishop), 48
Birmingham, University of, 156
Blackall, Governor of Sierra Leone, 10
'Black Englishman', 28, 56, 202
blitzkrieg (German), 111
Blyden, Edward (Wilmot), xi, xvii, 13–28, 34, 48, 62; resettlement in Liberia, 13–14; training, 13–15; racial philosophy, 15; demand for a West African University, 16–28, 160, 201–202, 208; on miseducation of Africans, 16–21, 31; adaptation of education, 18–20, 53, 85, 202
Bombo (Uganda), 44

Bottomley, Sir Charles, 94
Bradley, Kenneth (Education Committee; Report), 183–184
'brain-drain', 220
Britain, Battle of, 116; war economy, fear of defeat, 111–113, 122–123
British colonial education in Africa: purpose, 44–63
British Empire: criticism of, xvi, 95, 112–113, 206; role of colonial universities for, 117–121; American prodding, 122–123; change of attitudes, 173–174
British Government: financial parsimony, 10, 35, 89, 96; Treasury funding for Makerere, 90–100, 103 (note 73); Lords Commissioners of Treasury, 95; Annexure II, 147; war-time changes, 140–141; Coalition Government, 170
British Parliament, 5; possible withdrawal from Africa, 6; and African élites, 6–8, 12–13, 303; Colonial Development and Welfare Bill, 110–113; Asquith and Elliot Commissions, 139–140, 163, 172
British qualifications (African preference for), 19–20, 82–86, 120, 149, 204, 211–212; *see also* overseas qualifications
Buganda, Kingdom of, 35, 37; Agreement of 1900, 37, 59, 87; interest in Western education, 46, 50, 59
Burns, Sir Allan, 176, 179, 183, 188; on Colonial Office centralization and control, 176–177
Burstall, Dr Sara, 56
Butler, C.R., 162

Cambridge, University of, 136–137, 139, 151, 156, 189, 211
Cameron, Sir Donald, 62, 141
Cape Coast, 38; University of, 217
Carnarvon, Earl of, 25
Carnegie Trust Fund, 219
Carr, Henry, 61
Carr-Saunders, A.M., xvi, 136, 141, 153, 156; IUC delegation, 184–185, 195
Carter, Governor of Nigeria, 34
Casablanca, 135
Catholic, 21–23
Ceylon, University of, 156
'civil disobedience', 35
'civilizing mission', 12, 202
Channon, Dr H.J., 109, 130 (note 14), 135; Channon's papers, xvii; memorandum, 117–121; sub-committee Report, 125–129, 141, 159, 165, 173
Christian Missions (West Africa), denationalizing methods of, 15–16
Christianity, xiii, 11
Church, A.J., 48, 70

INDEX

Churchill, Winston, 44
Church of England, 26
Church Missionary Society (CMS), monopoly of colonial education, 1–2, 9, 22–28, 181, 187, 189, 202
Clarke, Fred, 141, 148–150, 152
Claughton, Harold, 136, 148, 152
Clifford, Hugh, 41, 65
Codrington College (Barbados), 26
collaboration (transfer of), 197, 209
Colonial Development and Welfare Act (1940), xii, 96, 124, 155; Bill, 110–112, 130 (notes 18 and 19), 158, 160; funds, 164, 206–207
Colonial Development and Welfare Act (1945), 167 (note 69), 170, 176, 187; allocations for African university colleges, 189–192, 194, 212
colonial (imperial) 'partnership', 123, 155, 160
Colonial Office, xi; on Blyden's demand for a university, 20–28; response to American involvement, 47–63, 74–77; White Paper on Native Education, 51–55, 58, 71; on 'Paragraph 19', 70–92, 205–206; funding for Makerere, 70–100; Asquith Commission, 136–159; centralization and control of colonial policy, 147, 173–174, 176–177, 207; Asquith and Elliot Reports (African pressures), 170–197
colonial reform (reform process), xi, xvii, 165
colonial universities, role, 138–139
Colonial University Grant Advisory Committee (CUGAC), 155; appointment, 158
Command Paper, 154
comprehensive unitary university for West Africa, 170
Conservative Party, 140–141
Coryndon, Robert (Governor of Uganda), 44, 47, 50
Coupland, Reginald, 56, 112
Cox, Christopher, 109, 117, 156, 157
Cranborne, Lord, 116, 123–4
Creech Jones, Arthur, 129, 159, 165; on implementation of Elliot Report, 171, 173–174, 188–194, 213
Creoles, 2–3, 7, 17, 21, 28, 61, 177; anti-Creole, 179, 181, 182, 193–194, 196; Creoledom, 217
Crowther, Samuel (Bishop of Niger Mission), 9, 30, 202
Cunliffe-Lister, P., 70
Currie, James, 48, 109; sub-committee Report, 70–82, 92, 129, 100 (note 14), 119, 128, 148

Dahomey, 8
Danquah, Dr J.B., 175, 177, 183, 218
Dar es Salaam, 57, 215

Davey, T.H., 157
Davidson, R.A.M., 109
Dawe, A.J., 125
de Bunsen, Professor Bernard, 196
De La Warr, Earl of, 88, 160; Commission on Higher Education in East Africa, 69; appointment, 86–88; Report of, 90–100, 105, 112, 119, 128, 148
'democratic principles', 175–176
diaspora, 39
Dickinson, J.R., 159
Dike, Dr K.O., 214
Dual Mandate, 41, 52
Duff, Dr J.F., 135, 141, 156, 159
Dundas, Charles, 123–124
Durham, University of, 1, 25–26, 39, 62, 80, 91, 156, 161, 177, 187, 189, 193–194, 202, 217
Dutch Reformed Church, 13

East Africa: Directors of Education Conference, 69; 'Paragraph 19', 69–75, 205–206; inter-territorial conference, 97–99; IUC delegation, 184–185, 195; University College of, xvi, 91, 106, 195–196; Working Party on higher education, 215
Eastham, L.E.S., 156
Edinburgh, University of, 3, 4, 29 (note 11), 156
Egypt, xii
Elliot, Walter (Commission), 134–135; appointment, 139–140, 159; Report, 163–165, 171; Majority/Minority Reports' enigma, 171–197, 207
'employment discrimination' (African graduates), 107–108, 144–148
Esdaile, Dr Philippa, 70, 88
Evans, Geoffrey, 159
Evans, Ifor, 156

Fabian Colonial Bureau, 171
Fanti, 45
First World War, 36, 40, 48
Flood, J.E.W., 76, 81, 94, 100 (note 25), 103 (note 78)
Ford Foundation, 219
Foreign Office, xii
Fort Hare College (South Africa), 43
Fourah Bay College, xi, xvi, 80, 105, 108; founding of, 3, 8; inadequate funding of, 3, 27; affiliation to Durham, 1, 22–28, 62, 177; requisitioning of building, Elliot Report, 161, 162–164; territorial (regional) college, 164, 178, 187, 193; IUC delegation, 187–188; interim arrangement, 189–191; 'compromise solution' (composite college), 192–194; University College of Sierra

241

Leone, 179, 181, 187, 189–194; Fulton Commission, 217
Fourah Bay College Council, 178, 193–194
France, 7, 8; aggressive imperial activities, 7, 8, 12, 34–35; war disaster, 116
Frazer, A.G., 50, 55
'Freed Slave', 2
Freetown, 9, 161, 181
Friends of Fourah Bay, 192
Fulton, J.S. (Commission of Inquiry, Sierra Leone), 217
Fyfe, Sir W. Hamilton, 156; IUC delegation, 184–192

Ga, 45
Galea, R., 156
Gambia, xii, 13; response to Currie's Report, 79; Annexure II, 146; Elliot Report, 163, 177, 180–181; regional college, 193, 196–197
Garvey, Marcus, 74, 101 (note 18)
George V, King, 40
Germany, 51, 96
Ghana, xvii
Gladstone, W.E. 22
Glasgow, University of, 156
Gloucester, Duke of, 99
Glover Memorial Hall, 61
'Godless' University, 22–24, 26, 202
Gold Coast, xii, 3, 13; traditional élite, educated élites, 56, 174, 183; on Currie's Report, 80–83, 85; response to Annexure II, 144–145; on Elliot Report, 174–191; Bradley Report, 183–184; IUC delegation, 184–192, 199 (note 61); University College of: xvi, 188–189, (funding) 184, 186, 189, 191; criticism of curricula, 213–214
Gold Coast Central Advisory Committee, 174, 185
Gold Coast Cocoa Marketing Board, 191
Gold Coast Educationists' Committee, 44–45
Gold Coast Joint Provisional Council, 174
Gold Coast Legislative Council (on Elliot Report), 182–185; Budget Session, 188
Gold Coast Old Boys' Association, 175
Gold Coast Teachers' Union, 175
Gold Coast Youth Movement, 175
Gordon College (Khartoum), 70, 75
Grace, H.M., 109, 113
graduates of African colleges (employment), 107–108, 144–148
Grand Bassam, 8
Grant, William, 17, 20
GRAs, 36
Guggisberg, Sir Gordon, 44–50, 55–56, 176; biography, 65

Hailey, Lord, xiii, 122, 141; on the place of educated Africans, xiv

Hale, Sir E., 94
Hall, George H. (Viscount Hall), 154, 156, 158, 171; on Elliot Report, 172–176, 179–183, 188, 191, 194
Hayford, Casely J.E., 38–40, 48, 56, 62, 83, 106, 175, 183; demand for an African university, 38–42, 160, 170, 201; African identity and national consciousness, 38–40, 208
Hayford, Joseph de Graft, 38
Hennessy, Pope (Governor of Sierra Leone), 17–25, 27, 34, 201–202
Hindustan, 19
History Department (University College of Ibadan), 214
Horton, Frank (vice-chancellor, London), 139, 152
Horton, James (Africanus), xi, 1–13, 28, 34, 48; demand for African medical school, and University, 2–5, 7–12, 160, 201, 208; medical training, 3–4; adoption of 'Africanus', 4; assistant surgeon (British Army), 4; Africanization of medical profession, 5–7, 85; glorification of European civilization, 11
House of Commons 7, 8, 135, 139, 154; Select Committee, 7, 12, 21, 30; Colonial Development and Welfare Bill, 110–111, 171
Hudson Club, 175
humane studies, 155
Hussey, E.R.J., 50, 58, 62, 81, 88, 90
Huxley, Julian, 56, 57, 128, 159

Ibadan, xii, 168 (note 92), 183; University College of, xvi, 163, 180, 189; criticisms (admissions and deficit problems), 212–213; ethnic rivalries, 215–216
Ife, University of, 216
Igbo (ethnic group), 13, 28; acephalus, 63, 215
Ikoli, Ernest, 61
Imperial funds, 191
'imperial partnership', 155, 160; change of attitudes, 173–174
indigenous education, aim of, xiii
indirect rule, xi–xvii, 46–63, 75, 95; principle and practice, 35–37, 203–204; India and Malaya, 35; East Africa, 36–37; in West Africa, 38–42; disunity, 102 (note 65), 106
Inter-University Council for Higher Education in the Colonies (IUC), xvi, 154–155, 157; appointment, 156–159, 165; delegation, 184–192, 208; on Nsukka, 216
inter-university organization, 152–154
intra-regional jealousy, 163
Irvine, James, 141, 156, 158, 167(note 61)
Islamic science, xiii

INDEX

Ita, Eyo, 74
'ivory tower' (temples of learning), 213

Japan, 90; attack on Pearl Harbor, 122
Jennings, Ivor, 156
Jerusalem, University of, 156
Johnson, Reverend James, 15, 21, 24–25, 34, 62, 85, 201
Johnston, Sir Harry, 37, 64
Joint Provisional Council of the Gold Coast, 174; *see also* Gold Coast
Jones, B. Mouat, 109, 156; sub-committee Report; 111–117, 119, 128, 148, 159
Jones, Thomas Jesse, 42

Kabaka, King of Buganda, 37, 46, 59, 205
Kampala, 97, 98, 99
Kauntze, Dr W.H., 100
Keate, Governor of Sierra Leone, 21, 24
Kenya, 75, 92, 94, 98, 217; settlers, 98–99, 196, 215
Kikuyu, 42, 215
Kimberley, Earl of, 20–21, 24
King's College (Lagos), 57, 79
Kiwanuka, Benedicto, 217
Knox, Reverend, 13
Kololo, 97
Korsah, K.A., 159, 161
Kumasi, 38; College of Arts, Science and Technology, 216

Labour Party, 140–141, 143; victory, 154, 170
Lagos politics (British interference and annexation), 6
Lagos, University of, 216
Lamont, Dr W.D., 185
Law School (West African), 109
League of Nations, 40, 51–52; Mandate Commission, 52
Leeds, University of, 156
Legislative Council, 17, 41, 49, 61, 64, 82, 146, 147, 182–185, 188
legitimate trade, 7, 8
Legon, xii; Legon Hill, University College of Gold Coast at, 184, 189, 191, 214
Lewis, George, 5
liberal education, 155
'liberated Africans', 2, 19–20
Liberia, 14; College, 14, 27; mulattos, 15, 31 (note 61)
Libreville, 8
Liverpool, University of, 120, 156, 167 (note 64)
Livingstone College, Salisbury (North Carolina), 64 (note 26)
Livingstone, Richard, 141
Lloyd George, David, 95
Lloyd, Lord, 111–112
Lockwood, J.F., 215

Lokoja, 5
London, University of: external degree programme, 58, 91, 99, 119–121, 127, 136, 139, 143, 153, 208; special relationship scheme, xvii, xviii, 148, 154, 185, 190, 196, 210, 214, 217; Archives and Palaeography (ULAP), xvii; King's College, 3; Matriculation, 50; ambitions and apprehensions, 136–159, 166; School of Economics, 136; Institute of Education, 148; modification of curriculum and syllabuses, 149, 219; Senate, 151–153, 165, 189–190, 211; Board of Examiners, 219
Lords Commissioners of the Treasury, 95
Lucas, Jocelyn, 100
Lugard, Lord (Lugardian), 35, 41, 46, 48, 52, 54, 56, 75, 109

Mabang, 161
Macarthy, Charles, 3
MacDonald, Malcolm, xii, xvi, 92, 96, 99, 105–6, 109–113, 116, 122, 129, 206–207; centralization and control of colonial policy, 173–174
Maclean, Dr W.H., 56, 70, 88
Macmillan, W.M., 109
Macmurray, J.J., 156
Macpherson, Margaret, xvi
Majority Report (controversy), 163–197; *see also* Elliot Report
Makerere (College), xii, 38, 44, 46, 50, 55, 58, 63, 69; 'Paragraph 19', 69–75, 205–206; London Matriculation, 58, 195; curriculum, 103(note 93); Higher College of East Africa, 204–205, 217; funding/endowment for, 90–100, 154; Oxford University connection, 112, 131 (notes 28 and 29); 137, 165; IUC delegation, 184–185, 195–196; University College of East Africa, xvi, 91, 106, 195–196, 215
malaria, 3, 5–7
Malaya, 117
Mali, Kingdom of, xii
Malta, University of, 156
Manchester, University of, 156
Mandate Commission, 52
Mann, F.O., 70
Margai, Sir Milton, 217–218
Marrs, R., 141
Martin, Eveline, 159
Mate-Kole, Nene, 182–183
Mayhew, Arthur, 56, 70, 109
medical profession (prejudice against Africans), 5, 30
Mellanby, Dr Kenneth, 189–190
Mende, 179, 198 (note 17)
'mental colonization', 205

243

Minority Report (controversy), 163–197; see also Elliot Report
missionaries, 1, 21; opposition to university, 1–2, 7, 10; debasing of mission-educated, 7, 52; missionaries in Uganda, 37, 103 (note 93)
Mitchell, Philip, 86–88, 92, 97–98, 102 (note 58), 112, 126; on 'pyramidal imagery', 114
mongrelization, 15
Monroe, James (United States), 31
Monrovia, 14
Morris, N., 156
Mount Aureol, 187
Muganda, 37
Mulago, 44
Muslims, Muslim clerics, xiii, 22
Mutesa, Kabaka, 217

Nairobi, 215
National Congress of British West Africa (NCBWA), 38–41, 46; its frustrations, 40–42, 170, 175, 183, 204
Native Administration, 35–36, 41, 46, 54, 57, 81
Native Courts, 45, 85
Native Treasuries, 45
'natural divisions', 175–176
Negro mind (enslaved), 18–20
Negro, The (newspaper), 15, 17
Neo-colonial links (Neo-colonialism), 215, 218–219
New Zealand, 6
Ngala, Ronald, 217
Niger Expedition, 1841, 5; tragedy of, 5–6
Nigeria, xii, xiv; official opposition to higher education, 47, 85; educated élites, 60–62; on Currie's Report, 80–83; response to Annexure II, 145–147; site for West African University, 162–163; on Elliot Report, 179–180, 198; IUC delegation, 185, 190, 193; Ashby Commission, 216; see also Yaba Higher College
Nigerian complacency (Elliot Report), 179–180
Nigerian House of Representatives, Lagos, 212
Nigerian Union of Teachers (NUT), 179, 198 (note 24)
Nigerian Youth Movement (NYM), 162
Njala University (Sierra Leone), 217
Nkrumah, Kwame, 213–214, 216, 217
Nsukka, University of Nigeria, 215–216
Nuffield Foundation, 219
Nyerere, Julius, 217

Obote, Milton, 217
Old Boys' Association (Achimota), 175
Oldham, J.H., 48
Ormsby Gore, W.G.R., 48, 56, 92, 99, 206
overseas qualifications, African predilection for, 19–20, 82–86, 149, 204, 211–212; see also British qualifications
Owen, Dr H.B., 44
Oxford University (Makerere connection), 112, 120, 136–137, 139, 151, 156, 196; 'high table' culture, 211
Oxbridge, 211, 218

pan-African, 208
pan-West African, 40; British West Africa, 171, 183
'Paragraph 19', 69–75, 205–206
Pearl Harbor, 122
Penson, Lilian, 141, 156, 167 (note 64)
Perham, Margery, 109, 112, 122, 141, 167 (note 64)
Phelps–Stokes Commission on Africa, 38, 42, 45, 47, 49–50, 55, 74; Report: criticism of British education of Africans, 42–44
Pickard-Cambridge, Dr A.W., 108
Pine, Governor of the Gold Coast, 5–6
Popos, the, 8
Porto Novo, 8
Prempeh II (Otumfuo), 168 (note 80)
Priestley, R.E., 141, 156
Princeton Theological College (Liberia), 14
Principal-Designate, University College of Gold Coast (UCGC), 189; see also Balme
Principal-Designate, University College of Ibadan (UCI), 189; see also Mellanby
Privy Council, 91
Public Record Office (PRO), xvii
Pugh, W.J., 156
'pyramidal educational growth', 109, 114

Quebec, 135
quinine, 6–7

racism, racialist ideas, xv, 9–17, 81–82, 84–85, 96, 107, 113, 202–203, 211; paternal racism, 94; 'scientific' racism, 28, 106
Ransome Kuti, I.O., 159
Read, Margaret, 159
Reading, University of, 156
'Regional Colleges', 186–187, 191
reparation, provision of universities as, 19–20
Richards, Sir Arthur, 179
Rodger Club, 175
Rome, 11
Roosevelt, Franklin D., 122
Roye, Edward, 14–15
Russians, 216
Ryle, J.A., 141

Sadler, Michael, 48, 109
Sankore, University of, curriculum, xii, xiii
Saville, H.O., 44
'scramble and partition', 34, 202
'second colonization', 159, 218

INDEX

Second World War, xi, xvi, 109, 129; British post-war changes, 105, 155–156; Allied forces, 122, 124; impact on colonial peoples, 138–143, 170, 195, 207–208
self-government, self-governing, 1, 8, 28, 95, 103 (note 84), 122, 126, 129, 135, 138–143, 145, 154, 155, 158, 172, 183, 201, 207; self-determination, 122–123, 175–176
Senate Committee on Higher Education (University of London), 153
Senegal, French activities, 7
Sheffield, University of, 156
Sibly, Dr Franklin, 56, 129
Sierra Leone, xi, xii, 146; response to Currie's Report, 79–80; Annexure II, 146–147; Elliot Report, 177–179, 181–182, 187–188, 189–194; Legislative Council, 181–182, 194; IUC delegation, 187–188; territorial (regional) college, 164, 178, 187, 191, 192; University College of, 179, 181, 187; Fulton Commission, 217
Sierra Leone Ordinance of 1950 (Fourah Bay College), 194
Singapore, 122
slave trade, 7, 19–20, 28
South Africa, xii; University of, 91
Southwell, R.V., 141
'special relationship scheme' (University of London), xvii, xviii, 148, 154, 185, 190, 196, 208, 210, 214, 217
Stallysbrass, W.T.S., 156
St. Andrews, University of, 167 (note 61)
Stanley, Oliver, 124–125, 129; Asquith and Elliot Commissions, 134–141, 154, 158, 159, 163, 171–172, 207, 213
Stevenson, Sir Hubert, 181, 192
Stopford, Mr (Principal, Achimota College), 125
Stopford, John, 129
St. Paul's River (Liberia), 14
Strachey, C., 48
Stroughton, R.H., 156
St. Thomas (Danish West Indian island), 13
Sudan, xii
Sunter, Metcalfe, 22–23, 26

Tachie-Menson, C.W., 182–183
Tanganyika, 92, 94, 98, 215, 217
Taylor-Cummings, E.H., 159
Temne, 179
territorial colleges (Elliot Report), 164, 178; funding of, 186–187
territorial nationalism (patriotism), 88, 163, 165, 173–174, 180–181, 183, 188, 208
territorial parochialism (jealousy), 163, 183
Thorp, W.A., 145
Timbuctu, xii
Tomblings, Douglas, 50

Trueman, A.E., 159
trusteeship, principle of, 49, 93–94, 117, 160
Turner, Charles, 3
Turner, George, 100, 125

Uganda, 45, 94, 196; National Archives, xviii; Education Committee, 44; Advisory Committee on Education, 51; Empire Cotton Growing Corporation, 98; IUC delegation, 184–185, 195–196; University College of East Africa (Makerere), xvi, 91, 106, 195–196
Umuahia (Government College), 162
universities, ideal role, xv
University College of West Africa (site), 160–163, 180
'university imperialism', 150–152, 165, 208
University of Nigeria, 185, 199 (note 45)
Vaughan, Dr W.W., 56, 70
Venn, J.A., 141, 156, 202
Vischer, Hans, 48, 56, 70, 77, 88, 109; visit to West Africa, 89, 130 (note 12)

Wales, Prince of, 55, 115; University of, 156
Washington, 135
Wesleyan Training College, 21
West Africa: official opposition to universities, 79–83, 89–90; education conference, 106–109; élite conflicts, 106; governors' conference views, 106–109
West African University (for cultural identity), 39
Western education/influences, aim of, xiii, xvii, 52; for 'self-government', 8, 18; negative impact of, 17, 38–40, 45–46, 52–55
Western technologies, 18
West Indian crisis (riots), xv, xvi, 68, 95–97, 106, 110, 129, 206–207
West Indies, 28
War Office (British), 3–6
'White Man's burden', 203
'White Man's grave', 5, 6
'White superiority', 203
Wilson, Reverend, 14
women and higher education, 72–73
Wright, J.G., 156

Yaba Higher College, Nigeria, 38, 75, 79, 98, 105; establishment, 57–63; medical diploma, 109, 211; public criticisms, 60–62, 145, 162–163, 204; credibility/discrimination, 84, 130(note 11), 211; engineering programme, 108; requisitioning of, 162, 183
Yoruba Mission (CMS), 162
Yoruba states, 8

Zanzibar, 69
Zaria, Ahmadu Bello University, 216

245